New Haven Publishing Ltd

Email: newhavenpublishing@gmail.com
director:
teddie@newhavenpublishingltd.com
rights:
jan@newhavenpublishingltd.com

Website:
newhavenpublishingltd.com

First Edition
Bookazine 2021
All Rights Reserved

....

The rights of Ian Snowball, as the author of this work, have been asserted in accordance with the Copyrights, Designs and Patents Act 1988.

All rights reserved. No part of this book may be re-printed or reproduced or utilized in any form or by any electronic, mechanical or other means, now unknown or hereafter invented, including photocopying, and recording, or in any information storage or retrieval system, without the written permission of the Author and Publisher.

....

Cover and interior design © Pete Cunliffe
pcunliffe@blueyonder.co.uk

Photographs (unless credited otherwise)
© Jason E Abrams

Copyright ©2021 Ian Snowball

ISBN 978-1-949515-10-7

....

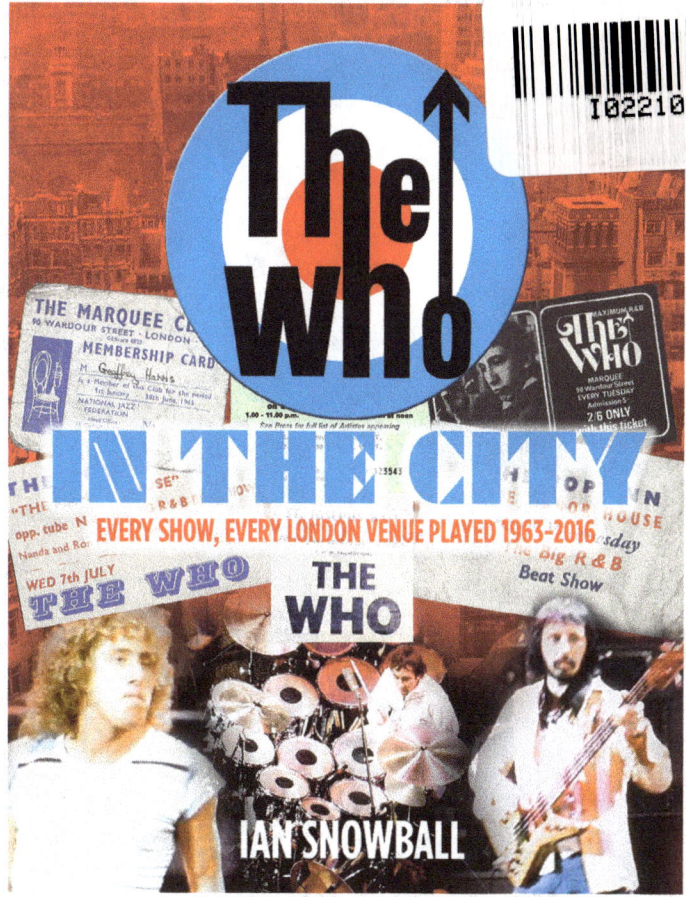

THE WHO: IN THE CITY is an exciting new book that has never been attempted before.
The book tells the unique story of one of rock and roll's greatest bands and their personal history with the city of London.

All four original members of The Who were born and grew up in London and this book documents the facts and figures of this time and then adds to the story further by taking the reader on an amazing journey through all of the band's London concerts and gigs across a fifty year period.

The story is further brought to life with contributions from friends and fans of the band, including **Kenney Jones** (Small Faces and The Who), **Jim McCarty** (The Yardbirds), **Steve White** (The Style Council/Paul Weller) and **Peter 'Dougal' Butler** (Keith Moon's PA).

The book also includes other London places of Who related interest, such as their hang-outs, homes and places where they got their hangovers. Additionally there are features that serve as a walking tour for any serious Who fan visiting London. These include venues relating to the band like the Goldhawk Club, locations from Quadrophenia (the movie) and many more from around the city.

Ian Snowball is the author of the best-selling *Keith Moon: There Is No Substitute*, *That's Entertainment: My Life In The Jam* (Rick Buckler of The Jam's autobiography) and *Thick As Thieves* (Personal Situations With The Jam).

INTRODUCTION

THE WHO: IN THE CITY is about taking the reader through an amazing journey of the venues in which The Who performed at in London and reaching out into the towns that fell within what was known as Greater London, such as Romford, Richmond, Farnborough and Croydon.

The book also delves into some of the most significant Who-related locations in London such as the Speakeasy Club, Trident Studios, Ramport Studios and Chesham House (where Kit Lambert and Pete Townshend lived).

The book dives straight in at the band's first gig at the Paradise Club in South London, rather than digging too deeply into their appearances as the Confederates at the Congo Club, or the Jewish Club or the Acton Congregational Church Hall Youth Club. Even though these are important events and of historical interest to any Who fan, they have been well documented in other wonderfully written books on the band. I have also tried my utmost to record each live appearance that The Detours/High Numbers/Who performed in London and have also provided some biography about what was happening for the band as they navigated their way through the ups and downs of their career.

To bring The Who's story of their connection to London to life, the book also includes contributions from people who witnessed what was going on with the band and these come from Kenney Jones, Mick Avory, Jim McCarty, along with friends and fans and people that helped to forge the legacy of The Who and put them on the map...the City of London map!

I have also included a map that plots the various venues and significant locations, should the reader be interested enough to take the time to go seeking these places out, and get a feel for how these places in London contributed to The Who's own unique story. An enjoyable feature includes some of the Quadrophenia locations, such as Jimmy's house in Wells Road and the pie and mash shop in which Jimmy meets his Rocker friend (Ray Winston) called A. Cooke's in the Goldhawk Road.

Just in 1963 alone, The Detours played over 150 times in London (and many more than that in 1964). They would go on to be one of the most hard-working bands in rock music and certainly one of the bands that played the most in their beloved home town of London.

Ian Snowball

CONTENTS

Who Are You 7
1964 - Maximum R&B 17
1965 - My Generation 31
1966 - One Quick One, While He's Away 43
1967 - I Can See for Miles 49
1968 - You're All Forgiven.....................................51
1969 - I'm Free 53
1970 - See Me, Feel Me 57
1971 - Who's Next 58
1972 - Join Together 58
1973 - I Woke Up in a Soho Doorway 59
1974 - Long Live Rock...63
1975 - Dreaming From the Waist 65
1976 - The Punk and the Godfather....................66
1977 - The Kids are Allright..................................67
1978 - Not to be Taken Away 68
1979 - Who's Next..69
1980 - The Whooligans 71
1981 - You Better, You Bet....................................71
1982, 1983 and 1984 - It's Hard...........................72
1985 - Who's Last 72
1988 - Who's Better, Who's Best 73
1989 73
1990, 1991, 1992, 1993 and 1994 - No London Gigs 74
1995 74
1996 75
1997 77
1999 77
2000 78
2002 78
2004 79
2005 - Live8 Concert 79
2006 80
8th February 2007 - The Hospital London 81
2008 81
2009 82
2010 82
2011 82
2012 83
2013 83
2014 84
2015 85
The Who London Concerts 1962-2015 89
Going Mobile - Locations for The Who 93
Walking Tour Maps 103

CHAPTER ONE
WHO ARE YOU

Following soon after some low-key performances at the Jewish Club in Ealing (and Pete Townshend's first performance with the band at the Chiswick Swimming Baths), The Detours, consisting of Roger Daltrey, John Entwistle, Pete Townshend, Dougie Sandom and Colin Dawson up front on vocals, managed to secure themselves their first proper gig at the Paradise Club.

While Pete spent his days studying at the Ealing Art School, Roger as a sheet metal worker, Dougie a bricklayer and Colin a sales rep, in between attending his day job at the tax office, John also furthered his education going to day school in Holborn once a week. It was through someone John had met at the day school that the Paradise Club opportunity presented itself.

On Sunday 1st July 1962 The Detours unloaded their equipment into the Paradise Club, which was located at number 3 Consort Road, Peckham, South East London. In the early 1960s the area of Peckham was undergoing a great deal of redevelopment. Much of the area, which had once boasted well-kept terrace houses, was being demolished and high-rise flats being built to replace them. The area of Peckham hadn't appeared the same, at least to an outsider, for many generations. The area of Peckham had been populated for hundreds of years; the Saxons knew it as the village near the River Peck, the Romans settled there and it even got a mention in the infamous Doomsday Book of 1086.

> 'WHAT WE DIDN'T KNOW IS THAT THE OTHER CLUB WOULD COME BY THE FOLLOWING WEEK, AND IT WOULD BE OUR TURN TO GET OUR GEAR TRASHED'

But coming from the 'other' side of town, it's unlikely that the members of The Detours had ventured much into the streets near the Paradise Club. However, it's quite possible that once they had set up their equipment, they may have taken a stroll in the direction of Peckham High Street and stumbled across Manze's Eel and Pie House, and perhaps even sampled a plate of pie and mash drenched in liquor.

When recalling his own memories of The Detours' first performance, John Entwistle said 'The first time we turned up to play, there was hardly anybody there, just some girls. Around 10 o'clock, their boyfriends all turned up with bloody noses and black eyes. It turns out they'd been at another club and started a brawl. What we didn't know is that the other club would come by the following week, and it would be our turn to get our gear trashed'

So this was The Detours' first proper public performance. They went down well enough to be asked to return for at least two more gigs. They got paid the grand sum of six pounds for each night that they played.

The Detours continued to rehearse up their set, and add extra songs as they approached their next live performance, booked for Saturday 1st September at the Town Hall in Acton (They returned to play again on 26th November). John Schollar, former Beachcombers band member and friend of Keith Moon, recalls 'I don't think Acton Town Hall was one of Commercial Entertainments' venues but it was a place that bands like The Detours, The Beachcombers and Bobby King and The Sabres all still got bookings at. Bands like ours would get extra work via Bob Druce, because they acted as our agents and had connections all over the place. I don't think the Acton Town Hall held regular dances; it was more of an occasional thing. Acton Town Hall was a big place, and I especially remember playing one superb gig with Tony Sheridan and The Shirelles, who were part of the Rik Gunnell organisation. Gunnell had been a boxer since he was fifteen years old; he then worked in Smithfield Market before finding work as a bouncer at the Studio 51 Jazz Club. His work at the jazz club gave him a taste for a new direction, and he decided to turn his hand towards promoting his own Modernist Jazz club nights. He opened the 2 Way Jazz Club; then the Blue Room, then he ran nights at the Mapleton Hotel before eventually starting up the club he became most famous for - The Flamingo in Wardour Street, and many a night, Gunnell would be found loitering around the Flamingo's entrance, a triple whisky and coke in hand trying to drum up custom from passers-by. The Beachcombers got a fair bit of work from Rik Gunnell as well as from Bob Druce. I actually bumped into Chris Farlowe a few years back, he also got work from Gunnell and he informed me that Gunnell had only recently died. All those promoters and agents in those days were pulling scams. They used to book us bands at American military bases and command a lot of money, but the bands only saw a small percentage of it.'

The area of Acton, the ancient Anglo-Saxon village once known as 'Farm by Oak Trees' was already a familiar stomping ground for Townshend, Entwistle and Daltrey, who had all attended the Acton County Grammar School. Countless times they would have passed the various examples of Victorian architecture down the High Street, such as the Library, swimming pool and Town Hall. They possibly learnt, during their school lessons, about some of the history of Acton and how, for over three hundred years, the area had the nickname 'soap sud city', which was a result of the laundry industry that grew up around the numerous springs in the area. But they may have known this because some of these historic laundries were still operating during the sixties.

But on that Saturday night in September, going under the name The Detours Jazz Group, they supported the Ron Cavendish Orchestra at the grand re-opening of the town hall. The band's future promoter Bob Druce was in the audience that night, and although not completely 'blown away' by what he witnessed, he must have seen enough to arrange for them to audition for him a short while after at the Oldfield Hotel in Greenford. Thankfully, Pete's mum, Betty, provided a much needed helping hand in steering the band towards their ultimate destiny.

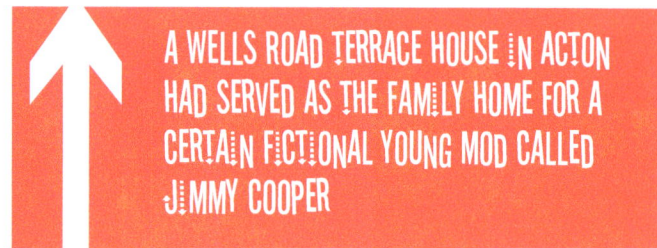

A WELLS ROAD TERRACE HOUSE IN ACTON HAD SERVED AS THE FAMILY HOME FOR A CERTAIN FICTIONAL YOUNG MOD CALLED JIMMY COOPER

John Schollar remembers his time with Bob Druce and Commercial Entertainments fondly: 'I got to know Bob Druce well over the years and we'd go out for meals and what have you. I remember he told me the story of how he got into the business. Bob was an apprentice at Hoovers and Lou Hunt was an inspector in the tool room, and they pulled in Barry Foran too. They came up with the idea of putting on dances for the employees and, because the dances went down well, they realised that they could make some money from doing it. That's when they started booking bands to play at places like the Oldfield Hotel. Bob was of a similar age to us lot. I'm not convinced he genuinely liked the music that we were playing, but he did like making the money-he was a business man. I remember he bought a brand new TR5 a few weeks before I got mine and we would chat about cars. As time went by, we saw less of him because he started to mix in different circles and started up other business ventures, but Bob was liked by all of us.

Lou Hunt helped Bob Druce and Barry Foran run Commercial Entertainments, and when I stopped working with The Beachcombers I worked on the doors of the various Commercial Entertainments venues with him. My duties mainly included just taking the door money; but occasionally I had to throw someone out if the bouncers couldn't be found. I didn't like that side of it though.'

A few months on from the Acton Town Hall event, The Detours would return to Acton to play again and the venue, the White Hart, would become one of the band's most important launch pads to take their careers further. Acton's neighbours, Shepherds Bush and Ealing, would also figure heavily in the history of the Who.

Two decades on from Townshend's first public appearance in Acton he would include a song called Stardom in Acton on his solo album All the Best Cowboys Have Chinese Eyes; and a couple of years before the album was released, a Wells Road terrace house in Acton had served as the family home for a certain fictional young Mod called Jimmy Cooper. It seems that the members of The Who would never really cut their ties with Acton.

On the 11th January, The Detours played their second gig of the New Year. Their first had been the previous week in the Kentish seaside resort Broadstairs. It was a lengthy journey into one of Kent's finest and more impressive coastal towns. The Fox and Goose Hotel, Hanger Lane, Ealing advertised The Detours' arrival on their poster with 'Jiving and Twisting Fridays, Featuring The Dynamic Detours'. Surely the young musicians, so new to the 'biz' must have been thrilled with such a welcoming advert-and all for the admission price of 4/-.

The Detours played their set in the modest licensed Fox and Goose Hotel's ballroom to an appreciative crowd. John Schollar played at the Fox and Goose with The Beachcombers when Keith was still drumming for them - the Fox and Goose Hotel was in Ealing Road, heading out towards Alperton, and an area very familiar to Keith Moon, as his home was less than a mile away. I think the pub is still there. Although a lot of these venues were called hotels, really they were just pubs. Some may have had rooms above them where people could stay. Most had function rooms, so the local people would hire them for weddings and parties and so on. I remember that The Fox and Goose had a big long bar and back in those days licensed bars could only stay open until about 10.30. The barman would ring the bell announcing that it was last orders, everyone would rush up and get their drinks, and soon after everyone had to leave and the pubs closed. Once The Beachcombers had finished playing for the night we'd pack away our gear, maybe have a quick drink and then often go and have a Chinese meal.'

Eight days later, on 19th, The Detours ventured into Middlesex to perform a set at the C.A.V Sports ground, Northolt, for what was advertised as a 'New Year's Rave'. They returned for a second gig on 6th April.

Then the band took to the stage at Douglas House, Clanricarde Gardens in Bayswater, which was a club frequented by American servicemen. They got the gig via Betty Townshend and got paid £75. At the time Gabby O'Connolly, one of the members from the Bel-Airs was on vocals, but he would sometimes play bass when John switched to play the trumpet during one of The Detours' trad jazz slots.

The Detours' first appearance at Douglas House was on the afternoon of 17th February 1963 and then they returned for many more dates starting on18th Feb, 24th Feb, 10th March, 17th March, 24th March, 31st March, 7th April, 14th April, 21st April, 28th April, 5th May, 12th May, 19th May, 26th May. And it was on the 26th May that O'Connolly played with The Detours for the last time.

It was after The Detours' first Douglas House first performance that they went on to play again at another new venue (they would repeat this act several more times). It was at the White Hart Hotel in Acton's High Street and this was where The Detours' first manager Helmut Gorden would see and hear the band.

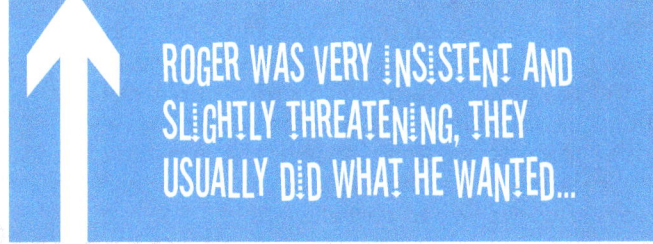

ROGER WAS VERY INSISTENT AND SLIGHTLY THREATENING, THEY USUALLY DID WHAT HE WANTED...

17th February 1963. White Hart Hotel, Acton.
(and 24th Feb, 25th Feb, 3rd March, 4th March, 11th March, 18th March, 25th March, 1st April, 8th April, 15th April, 22nd April, 29th April, 5th May, 9th May, 26th May, 6th June, 9th June, 23rd June, 30th June, 7th July, 14th July, 21st July, 11th Aug, 15th Aug, 18th Aug, 25th Aug, 1st Sept, 8th Sept, 15th Sept, 22nd Sept, 29th Sept, 24th Nov, 29th Dec).

In 1964 dates included 12th Jan, 19th Jan, 15th March, 5th April, 12th April, 26th April, 31st May, 26th July.

Richard Barnes: 'The first Detours gig I ever went to was at the White Hart, Acton. It always represented the typical Commercial Entertainments venue from then on to me. The Detours' second most-played location after the Oldfield Hotel in Greenford. Quite a big pub with a long room next to it for dancing.

That first day, Roger arrived in the group van to pick Pete and I up from our flat by Ealing Art School and they gave me the passenger seat instead of sitting on the floor with the equipment in the back as I was a guest.

The Detours' Austin 15cwt van was a bit scruffy. It had several dents in the bodywork and the passenger door was permanently closed because it got damaged and dented when Roger hit a bridge, and never opened after that. This meant that everyone had to get in through the driver's sliding door and clamber over the driver's seat to get to the back. So Roger had to keep getting out and standing in the road while any passenger climbed in or out.

Welded to the roof at the back of the van was a metal chimney, made up from a section of six inch black steel pipe with a sort of steel witch's hat affair fixed to the open end to keep the rain out. I think it had the words THE DETOURS in tape alongside an arrow symbol like the medical symbol for a male (an idea later updated and used for the famous The Who Maximum R&B Marquee posters).

I hadn't met the other band members before. When we arrived outside the White Hart in Acton High Street I thought I should help them unload the gear, but to my surprise Pete said to Doug, "Get the gear out, I'm gonna take Barney for a drink." It was about ten minutes past six and the bar had just opened. Pubs had very strict and heavily enforced opening hours back then in 1963. I think they opened from 12 am - 2:30 pm, closed in the afternoons until 5:30 or 6:00, then re-opened until 10:30 pm. These hours were bought into law in the First World War in order to get the nation's farm and factory workers out of the pubs after lunch and back to work relatively sober. Much to the annoyance of the drinking classes these perplexing archaic rules were still in force fifty years after the war to end all wars.

Pete's action seemed very high-handed, but despite a dirty look from Doug and the others they didn't say anything and unloaded the gear, including his guitar, as Pete and I went to the bar. I had never met the rest of the band and was apprehensive. I didn't think this was the wisest move from Pete. I later realised that it wasn't typical behaviour from him as The Detours appeared to be Roger's band. It had been Roger who'd started a group and, after several incarnations, styles and personnel changes had settled on these three. Their four-piece line-up was based on another nationally famous but local group, the pre-Beatles British pop group, Johnny Kidd and The Pirates, who'd had two big charts hits. The five-piece Detours changed to a four-piece like the Pirates after playing warm up at a Johnny Kidd gig in late 1962.

Roger, as well as driving the van, generally called the shots and the others, including Pete, automatically and unconsciously deferred to him. It wasn't exactly spelt out. I think they were supposed to be equal members of a group but as Roger was very insistent and slightly threatening, they usually did what he wanted. They could almost have been called Roger Daltrey and The Detours - Roger Daltrey as the vocalist, the centre of attention onstage and the Detours being the backing band.

In John Entwistle's words, *"Roger would punctuate his arguments with his fists"*. But I didn't see a lot of that in those very early days. In fact, he was always quite civil to me and I actually found Roger could be very funny with lots of corny jokes. Another factor in the band hierarchy might have been that, although they were all eager and willing, Roger seemed to be ten times as keen and ambitious for the band as the others. He definitely appeared the main driving force in those early days.

ROGER SEEMED TO BE TEN TIMES AS KEEN AND AMBITIOUS FOR THE BAND AS THE OTHERS. HE DEFINITELY APPEARED THE MAIN DRIVING FORCE IN THOSE EARLY DAYS.

However, this particular hierarchical structure lasted another six to eight months, but I then watched the inter-band relationships and power struggles gradually break down and evolve as the personalities altered and circumstances drastically changed.

At art school, despite Pete and I hanging out together and spending time on the same course and social scene, for a long time I wasn't aware that Pete could play guitar or was in a band. He kept his two worlds separated for a long time. Even when Pete and I had started renting a flat together near the art school, I'm sure that attending art school was the most important, glamorous and exciting thing in his life over playing in The Detours. When I knew he played guitar in a local band, as interesting as it was, it seemed small beer by comparison to the buzz of the art school. It was, of course, quite exciting, but, in a way, seemed slightly local and semi-amateurish. Like a hobby. Or an extra-curricular evening activity. Looking back I suspect that, at that stage, Pete was not as dependent on The Detours for creative satisfaction and fulfilment as the others in the band.

In fact, dare I say it, the early Detours didn't seem all that great. Not that I was in a position to judge. I wasn't used to live electric amplified bands in echoey smoke-filled pubs and The Detours were, like most bands at the time, 'learning on the job'. Although they rehearsed regularly it seemed to me that mostly they got to know, improved on and adapted numbers while playing them at the gigs.

They'd moved on a long way from just doing occasional weddings, birthdays and bar mitzvahs and from playing simple beginners' material like Hava Negela, and were doing covers of current British chart bands like Cliff Richard and The Shadows and The Beatles, plus other recent top ten hits with some Country & Western thrown in. I assume they had a big repertoire of top ten covers as I noticed they were getting lots of requests from the audience, mostly for Beatles numbers, which they usually managed to meet.

They had regular well-paid gigs and already built up a small following. It was great to experience the actual live group in front of a real live appreciative yet critical audience, but The Detours seemed to be several months behind the sort of stuff we were listening to on record both at the Art school and on our jukebox in the café over the road.

As interesting and exciting as I found it, looking back I'm sure I thought it a bit behind the times, seeing as the Beatles and Stones were filling the charts and newspapers around that time.

Basically the girls danced with each other whilst the boys stood at the bar or sat at tables drinking and watching the girls. The pub had to shut at 10:30 and 'Closing Time' had to be announced ten or 15 minutes before to enable people to get in their last drink. When closing time "Time Gentlemen Please" was called it usually meant a queue at the bar, as the staff had to cater with all the final orders. There was a 15-minute 'drinking-up' time after the bar stopped serving. Often this was extended up to 30 minutes as the manager and staff would try to coax the punters to drink up and leave, and the punters tried several ways to drag out the drinking-up period for as long as possible while the staff cleared up.

Towards the end of the evening, just before or around 'Time' being called, several of the boys who'd been talking and drinking at the tables and bar would go up and dance with a girl for the last dance or last few dances. They'd probably been exchanging flirtatious glances at each other for some time. This seemed to be the rather dated mating ritual operating at the time. Often the boy would then leave with the girl he'd picked to dance with, and it was traditional that the last dance would be a smooch or slow romantic number so the couple could dance closely or hold each other.

Even to an outsider like me it looked quite dated and old-fashioned in the days of Beatlemania. The audience was quite mixed, some working class apprentices out with their girlfriends, some young smartly dressed office workers, young blue collar workers, some students from the then Acton-based Brunel College, lots of shop girls and typists, plus a sprinkling of leftover or married 'Teds' in their late twenties and early thirties.

Usually while The Detours were on stage I'd just sit at a table on my own with a drink watching it all. Sometimes I'd be with someone else connected to the band, usually this was John's girlfriend, Alison Wise, later to become Mrs E.

Half-way through the set there would be a break where Roger would leave the stage to rest his voice, and Pete could play a Shadows guitar instrumental or Duane Eddy number. This also meant Roger could slope off out the back in the alleyway by the empty barrels and the rubbish bins for a quick fumble with whichever girl he'd picked out of the audience that evening. This was the accepted vocalist's perk, and Roger was very good at it.

The two most regular Commercial Entertainments' fixtures were the Oldfield Hotel, Greenford and the White Hart, Acton. A bit later the Goldhawk Club, St Mary's Hall Putney, the Glenlyn Ballroom in Forest Hill and another White Hart, the White Hart Southall were added to the list.

The Oldfield Hotel gigs were every Thursday plus a lot of Saturdays. These Thursday nights were the most consistent and permanent fixture for the band.

Next most frequent gig was the White Hart, Acton. For a time the Detours played this venue every Sunday and Monday. On Sundays they played two regular gigs. The Sunday evening gigs at the White Hart were after Sunday afternoon gigs for the American Services Institute at Douglas House in Bayswater - a very lucrative gig which Pete's mum Betty and his dad Cliff arranged for the band.'

John Schollar points out 'the White Hart in Acton was one of Commercial Entertainments' venues. It was a rough place and one night that we played, a fight broke out and the Police arrived with their dogs to sort it all out. That particular night was horrendous though and people were grabbing stuff off the bar like bottles and using them to smash over people's heads. The barman leaped over the bar in attempt to stop them but he got stabbed. I knew him well because he also worked as a barman down the Oldfield. It wasn't uncommon for brawls to kick off on the dance floors. We'd just watch and continue to play. Like many of the pubs back in them days the bands played in the function rooms attached to the pubs. The White Hart was like this. There was an entrance where you had to pay your admission fee, it wouldn't be much, just a couple of bob. People that didn't want to see the bands just stayed in the other areas of the pub and were left alone.'

The Detours managed to get an audition for local promoter Bob Druce of Commercial Entertainment Ltd. Druce and his business partner Barry Foran booked bands to play the circuit that The Detours were desperate to get on to, to get noticed and make some regular money. The audition took place at the Oldfield Hotel, Greenford. The Detours acted as a sort of support in the interval, playing just a handful of songs, for one of Bob Druce's top bands The Bel-Airs. The audience cheered and that was enough for Bob Druce to offer them a contract, which they gratefully accepted. Once Gorden became The Detours manager an agreement was struck with Bob Druce where he would continue working for the band in the role as their booking agent. Things were certainly heading in the right direction now that The Detours had both a manager and a promoter on board.

The Detours played their usual mix of Shadows and Country and Western songs at their first proper performance at the Oldfield Hotel on 21st February 1963and then returned for many more dates throughout the remainder of the year, these included:

22nd Feb, 23rd Feb, 28th Feb, 7th March, 9th March, 14th March, 21st March, 28th March, 4th April, 11th April, 13th April, 18th April, 25th April, 27th April, 30th April, 11th May, 18th May, 23rd May, 28th May, 1st June, 8th June, 15th June, 20th June, 27th June, 29th June, 4th July, 6th July, 11th July, 18th July, 20th July, 23rd July, 25th July, 10th Aug, 17th Aug, 20th Aug, 22nd Aug, 27th Aug, 29th Aug, 5th Sept, 7th Sept, 19th Sept, 26th Sept, 28th Sept, 3rd Oct, 10th Oct, 12th Oct, 17th Oct, 24th Oct, 26th Oct, 7th Nov, 9th Nov, 14th Nov, 21st Nov, 28th Nov, 5th Dec, 12th Dec, 14th Dec.

And then one night at the Oldfield, a young man wearing a ginger suit joined them on stage for a few numbers; his name was Keith Moon. The first song that Keith, Pete, Roger and John played together was Roadrunner, a song which Bo Diddley had a mild hit with. Dougie Sandom had recently left the group. In his absence The Detours, now calling themselves The Who (Richard Barnes had suggested the new name and it had stuck) had auditioned several drummers, Mitch Mitchell amongst them, but none had fitted in. Keith Moon was something different and almost cut from the same cloth as Townshend, Daltrey and Entwistle, and as is often the case with the unique way a band 'comes together', The Who came together.

The next Saturday, The Who picked Keith up and they went off to play a full gig together. Over the next few weeks Keith juggled his drumming duties with The Who and the band that he had been playing in for some time, The Beachcombers. But in the end there was only going to be one band for Keith. He joined The Who as their permanent drummer, a position he would hold down until his death in 1978.

John Schollar recalls his visits to the pub 'The Oldfield was one of the bigger venues. The bands played in the pub's function room,which held a capacity of about three hundred people. I worked the door there for Commercial Entertainments. You got into the function room through a side-entrance which was near a small car park. There was a tiny area where I took the door money. This area was only about twenty foot square and it's also where the ladies and gents cloakrooms were. Then you passed through two big double doors and then you'd be in the main room. The Oldfield had a really nice wooden floor, almost ballroom like.

Passing through the big doors you'd see the stage at the far end of the hall on the right. It was only a small stage of about eighteen inches high. It was far too small to get all the band's gear on it. The bands used to have to stack their amps on some cabinets that were positioned on either side of the stage. There was no flash lighting, no spot lights; it wasn't a sophisticated set up. In fact most of the venues back then were very primitive.

There were council restrictions on how many people were supposed to be in the venue and Lou Hunt's son Ray would count the heads as they arrived-only I wasn't allowed to know the actual figure. So Lou and I ran the door and then there'd be two bouncers.

Often, when The Beachcombers played these venues like the Oldfield or St Mary's Hall, we didn't have any support acts. In the early days we were actually doing better than The Detours. We got better gigs and we got paid more.

I had a joke with Roger Daltrey over this matter a couple of years back. I remember he was telling me about a string of concerts he had just been doing with The Who at the same venue and I joked saying 'bloody hell Roger it's like playing back down the Oldfield again', he laughed and replied 'yeah, but we're getting more money now.' I then returned 'we used to get fifteen quid for playing the Oldfield.' 'Fifteen quid' cried Roger 'fifteen quid, hang on a minute, we only used to get twelve.' 'Yeah but we were better than you' I replied, 'but there were five of you and we only had four, plus we were better looking than your lot' Roger shot back, to which I casually chuckled 'I don't know about that Roger-look at your guitarist.

During the intervals at all these pubs, there would be no music, there weren't any deejays or anything like that. The bands would normally just go and have a drink at the bar and people would come and have a chat. Keith Moon and John Entwistle were great for this but Roger and Pete would often disappear to their dressing room.'

The 1964 dates kicked off at the Oldfield on 2nd January and were followed by:

11th Jan, 14th Jan, 16th Jan, 18th Jan, 21st Jan, 23rd Jan, 25th Jan, 30th Jan, 6th Feb, 13th Feb, 20th Feb, 22nd Feb, 27th Feb, 5th March, 17th March, 19th March, 26th March, 2nd April, 16th April, 23rd April, 30th April, 7th May, 14th May, 28th May and then the band simply outgrew the venue.

Saint Eugene de Mazenod, from which the church hall

took its name, was a French Catholic priest who became the patron saint of dysfunctional families; which could be attributed to some of the events that contribute to The Who's history as they progressed to becoming one of the world's greatest rock acts.

The Detours played at the Mazenod Church Hall, on Mazenod Road, Kilburn, on 13th March 1963. Kilburn was an area North of where the band members were living. What developed into the populate area of Kilburn had its roots going further back than when the Romans set up camp. The first settlers built their communities along the banks of the Kilburn Brooks and over the next few hundred years their numbers swelled. By the time The Detours played at the Mazenod Church Hall, the Gaumont State Cinema had been a firm attraction for cinema goers since the late 30's and throughout the 60's would host many popular bands.

There were also two tube stations, the Kilburn and the Kilburn Park, and that helped to pull in visitors. However, as modest and as low-key as The Detours' appearance at the church hall was to be, their visit to Kilburn was a success and they wouldn't return until much later in the next decade.

::

John Schollar describes the area during this period: 'The Beachcombers played in some small halls in the area, it was a really rough place, horrendous. I remember we parked the van up outside one of them and a bunch of young teenagers gathered around us. They demanded that we give them half a crown or said they'd let the tyres down on the van. Especially in the skiffle days us bands would play anywhere, places like youth clubs, working men's clubs, social clubs, church halls, people's parties - and places such as Mead Hall were commonplace. They weren't proper music venues.'

On 29th March 1963 The Detours played two sets at The College of Distributive Trade in the Charing Cross Road and got paid £25 for their work. They returned again on the 31st to play again before heading over to Douglas House to perform again. The College of Distributive Trade was founded in 1921 but by the 90's had merged with the London College of Printing (where the Who returned to play on19th December 1964 and 3rd April 1965 (Elephant and Castle)) to become the London College of Printing and Distributive Trade.

It was in a Victorian hotel called the Park Hotel in Greenford Avenue, Hanwell, where the classic tune from World War One 'Keep the Home Fires Burning' took place. Hanwell itself is an area surrounded by many of the other Detours' stomping grounds. There was Perivale to the north, Ealing to the east, Brentford to the south and,to the west, Southall. The hotel has since been demolished and flats have been built. But on17th May 1963 in Park Hotel, Carnival Ballroom, The Detours played a one off gig.

Townshend describes including some 'funkier R&B' tunes in the set at this performance.

The first time that the band played at the Goldhawk Social Club, Shepherds Bush was on 7th June 1963. They returned the following month on 5th July and then 12th July, 16th Aug, 6th Sept, 25th Oct, 8th Nov, 22nd Nov, and 29th Nov. By the end of 1963, one of the Mods' anthems,Green Onions by Booker T and the MGs, was being included in the set.

The Detours returned to the Goldhawk Social Club many more times in 1964 just as Mod was really picking up momentum. It was from the loyal fan base that gathered in the Goldhawk that the '100 faces', a group of hard core Mods, originated. The first date of the year was on 7th February 1964 and the remainder on 28th Feb, 6th March, 27th March, 11th April, 17thApril, 8th May, 31st July). On the first February date The Detours supported The Kinks. The Kinks had their noses in front of the Who and already had a growing fan base. They also had You Really Got Me to excite their audiences with. Townshend became a great admirer of Kinks'frontman Ray Davies and in the years to follow would openly cite Davies as a source of inspiration for his own songwriting. On Saint Valentine's Day, the week after supporting the Kinks, the Detours had dropped their name for good and became the Who.

On Friday 12th March 1965, Townshend recalled playing I Can't Explain over and over again and being joined back stage by local Mod Irish Jack Lyons and some of his friends. Irish Jack would become one of The Who's most loyal fans and champion. There were fewer performances in 1965 that only included 20th March, 16th April, and 3rd Dec. The Who didn't return after 1965.On that last December night that The Who played at the Goldhawk, a massive fight broke out on the dance floor. It was a reflective tribute of the rough, ready and sometimes violent environments that the band and their Mod fans had been finding themselves pulled into since their pebbled beach battle days of 64. Also observing the events that night was film make Michelangelo Antonioni. Soon after, he made Blow Up; a film that included The Yardbirds smashing their equipment up on stage- just like he had witnessed The Who do.

::

John Schollar on the Goldhawk: 'The Beachcombers played at the Goldhawk a few times, in fact I nearly got killed there because of an electric shock. I didn't know what had happened until I woke up the next morning in a bed in Hammersmith hospital. Apparently one of the bouncers threw me in the back of his car and took me up to the hospital. We had played the first set and had come back for the second, we launched into Poison Ivy by The Coasters and as I stepped up to sing the backing vocals and grabbed the mic stand, I got the electric shock. I was out cold.

THE WHO IN THE CITY

However my fondest memory of the Goldhawk concerns Keith Moon. The stage was quite high in the venue, about six-foot high. Positioned directly in front of the stage was a great big old sofa. Keith used to love jumping onto the sofa and, because it hadn't been cleaned for years, each time he jumped up and down on it he would fill the Goldhawk with clouds of dust.

Most of the bands that came out of West London played at the Goldhawk, it was one of our most popular venues. Arriving at the venue you'd carry your gear up a handful of stone steps and walk into a reception area and then, passing through that, you'd enter another room where the bands played. It was an unusual place, it looked like it could have been an old Masonic type building.'

On 16th November 2014 a blue plaque was erected at the site of the Goldhawk Club, the club that owed much to The Who's early career. Melissa Hurley was one of the driving forces behind the campaign: 'My husband Gary and I arranged for the blue plaque to be placed at the Goldhawk Club to commemorate The Who's fifty year service to the music industry. The Goldhawk was an important stepping stone for The Who in their career. Over the years lots of Who fans visiting from around the world would go to the Goldhawk just to have a look at it, it represents an important Who starting point for them. That's why we chose that location to have the blue plaque placed. Thankfully it was a lot easier and a lot quicker to arrange compared to what it was like for the 'Keith Moon' blue plaque at the site of the Marquee Club in Wardour Street. We didn't have to seek council permission because the site of the Goldhawk is privately owned. We had help with the funding for the plaque too, because Pete Townshend graciously signed some copies of his autobiography and they were auctioned off for £350 each. On the day that the blue plaque was unveiled, sadly neither Roger nor Pete could make it. Thankfully Bill Curbishley came down for the unveiling event and he made a fantastical wonderful speech, and he had tears in his eyes.'

The G.E.C Pavilion, just off the Preston Road in Wembley, was the venue where The Detours performed on 14th June 1963. The General Electrical Company building was a large white stone building that in the 1980s was sold off to be used as a carpet and rug warehouse. The Beachcombers also played at the same venue and John Schollar remembers one of the perks 'We played at their do's a couple of times, they were great to do, we got paid well and we always got 'posh nosh'. John also adds 'There were a lot of big companies located around the Wembley area, and every Christmas they would hire a venue like the Wembley Town hall to put a dance on for their employees. When The Beachcombers played those sort of occasions, we played to some of the biggest crowds we ever did, often there would be five hundred or more people present. The Beachcombers played at the Wembley Town hall twice and the second time we supported Paul Dean and the Dreamers. Paul Dean was actually Paul Nicholas, who went on to become a famous actor.'

A few days later, on Saturday the 22nd June, The Detours played at a wedding in the Mylett Arms, Western Avenue in Perivale, Greenford. Then they were back at the White Hart Hotel and then, following this, they returned to Greenford to play a one-off gig at the Railway Hotel later in the year on 30th November (63).

Advertised as the 'Notre Dame De Danse' The Detours' first appearance at the Club Durane (which took its name from DRU (ce) and (For) AN of Bob Druce and Barry Foran), Notre Dame Church Hall, 5 Leicester Place, Leicester Square was on Friday 26th July 1963 (they returned on 30th Aug, 27th Sept). The original building had been bombed in World War Two but a new building was erected and opened as a club in 1953.

In 1965 the Cavern in the Town opened on the Notre Dame premises. The Who returned to play again on 10th April and 19th June and in 1966 on 11th March.

It didn't last long, but it was the place where another young mod band caught the attention of their London Mod peers, and they were called The Small Faces. They made their debut at the venue on 29th May 1965 performing just five songs. Throughout the remainder of the sixties and the seventies, the premises continued to serve as a popular music venue, and was especially prominent during the first Punk wave of 1977. Nowadays the building is the home of the Leicester Square Theatre.

Exactly next door was another important 1960s club which was called the Ad lib. To access the club the punter would have to enter an elevator via some double glass doors and be transported skywards. The Ad lib was owned by Bob and Al Burnett, but run by Bob Morris, and became a haunt for many of the 'faces' of the day. The club was especially favoured by The Beatles. From the venue's large windows those 'faces' could look out across London whilst they freely smoked a joint away from the interfering eyes of the local Police or journalists. Due to a fire incident in 1966 the club was forced to close down.

It was on 9th September 1963 that The Detours first played in St Mary's Hall (ballroom), Putney. They returned several more times and supported the Rolling Stones on the 22nd December gig. That particular night would be the first time that Townshend would meet Mick Jagger and Brian Jones. It was also the occasion where Townshend observed Keith Richards swinging his arm, in a windmill fashion, as he warmed up for his own performance.

By the time The Detours were next supporting the Stones (at the Glenlyn Ballroom), Townshend had adopted that windmill movement as his own, and had incorporated it as part of his stage act, something he would still be doing on stage fifty years on. Johnny Kidd and the Pirates was another act who The Detours supported at this venue. John Schollar 'I don't know if Commercial Entertainments ran St Mary's Hall, but both The Beachcombers and The Who played there a few times. In fact lots of good bands played there whilst it was running. And it really had been a church hall before being turned into a music venue. I don't recall there being a licensed bar at St Mary's. At that time not all venues did and, because only soft drinks were available some people started using the pills like the purple hearts and French blues. The wooden floor in St Mary's was quite large and there was a big stage that was a good four foot high. Big curtains hung over the windows and the ceiling was high up. It was a good venue to play at.'

The other dates played at this venue in 1963 were:
6th Oct, 17th Nov, 1st Dec, 8th Dec, 15th Dec, 22nd Dec. The 1964 dates were 5th Jan, 26th Jan, 31st Jan, 2nd Feb, 9th Feb, 23rd Feb, 1st March and 8th March.

The Detours first played at the Glenlyn Ballroom, 15 Perry Vale, Forest Hill on 13th September 1963 (and again on 4th Oct, 11th Oct, 1st Nov, 6th Dec, 20th Dec). By the end of 1963, the Glenlyn Ballroom was recognised as one of London's most serious Mod strongholds. At the time, South London didn't provide many live music venues that met the Mods' tastes and needs. On their doorstep they did however have several Jamaican Reggae and Ska clubs to spend a night at, and soak up the sounds and atmosphere that those unique clubs had to offer.

John Schollar: 'The Glenlyn Ballroom was one of the few venues had had lights installed. There were some ultraviolet lights beaming down onto the stage and we would have to be constantly brushing the dandruff off of our mohair suits. The suits we wore were lovely but they looked like they had been covered in soap powder. Because the Glenlyn was a decent size, and a well-run venue, it attracted some fairly big names. The Beachcombers played there one time with Cliff Bennett and the Rebel Rousers. I think the venue had once been an old dance hall and it had one of the highest stages that I ever played on. The stage also stuck out, which meant that the audience would gather around the sides as well out at the front. Lots of venues around that period were either upstairs above shops or in the basements below them but the Glenlyn was street level. You simply carried your gear straight in without having to struggle up or down stairs.'

Richard Barnes: 'We always had to leave early on in the afternoon for the Glenlyn ballroom. The Glenlyn and St Mary's and, to a lesser extent, the Goldhawk were much more important venues than the bread and butter regulars like the Oldfield and the White Hart. These venues could book big-named charted bands, for which The Detours would provide the support act. These were very influential shows. This was a way the band got to see successful named acts live, and be inspired and influenced. These gigs were totally different to the usual Detours only gigs. We had to leave earlier to set up, as the first half band. Especially for the Glenlyn Ballroom, as it involved this lengthy complicated journey.

I only ever went to the Glenlyn when the band were supporting some big name act - The Big Three, The Undertakers and The Merseybeats. All big named bands from Liverpool. All had been top acts on the bill at the famous Cavern Club.

The Undertakers and the Big Three had also followed the Beatles to play in Hamburg, and it was inspiring to hear the loud, edgy raw Merseybeat sound from hard, experienced no-nonsense bands like these. Also at the Glenlyn, we supported the Hollies. A Manchester-based pop band who were promoting and just about to release their version of Doris Troy's 'Just One Look' in the charts at the time.

> ON ANY NIGHT IT WASN'T UNUSUAL TO SPOT UP-AND-COMING MUSICIANS WITH A TASTE FOR THE BLUES. SUCH WERE MEMBERS FROM THEN UNFORMED BANDS LIKE THE YARDBIRDS, MANFRED MANN, THE ANIMALS AND OF COURSE THE ROLLING STONES.

Apart from benefitting from seeing these tried-and-tested, hard-bitten experienced bands, I'm sure the four members of the Detours were, like me, also watching the way they were promoted. Their gimmicks. For instance, the Liverpudlian band the Undertakers were great musicians but also took their image seriously. They arrived in a big hearse and wore black undertakers' clothes with long overcoats and black top hats. They used coffins to pack their equipment in. Dougie was particularly impressed, as their music was more to his liking.

And when the band opened for Brian Poole and the Tremeloes at the St Mary's Hall in Putney, they were plugging their current hit single Candy Man, and gave out sticks of pink seaside rock to every member of the audience. Inside, instead of the word 'Blackpool' or 'Brighton' running through it, they had the words 'Candy Man'.

I took my stick of rock back to our flat and Pete and I discussed this promotional stunt afterwards. In a way it was very Art School and clever, but the record was a little bit naff so it didn't really work for us.'

The 1964 dates at the Glenlyn Ballroom began on 3rd January (supporting The Rolling Stones) and were followed by: the 24th Jan (supporting The Hollies), 14th Feb (supporting Carter Lewis and the Southerners), 16th March, 23rd March, 3rd April, 6th April, 10th April, 20th April, 24th April, 4thMay, 11th May, 15th May, 18th May, 21st May, 25th May, 1st June, 8th June, 15th June, 22nd June, 29th June. On 21st January 1966, The Who performed at the venue for one last time. Once the Glenlyn ceased serving itself up as a music venue it became Crystals Snooker Club.

On the 15th November 1963 the Detours played at Feather's Hotel, Ealing Broadway, Ealing. They returned the next month, on 13th December, to perform at the Evershed and Bignoles Apprentice Association Social Club Dance. The 'Feathers' had a large basement area where bands played. Several years after The Detours played there, the Pink Floyd and Jeff Beck also played there.

> THERE WAS A HIPPY DIPPY LIQUID LIGHT SHOW WITH AN OLD BILL BUS FLASHING BETWEEN THE RUNNING IMAGES. ROD STEWART AND LONG JOHN BALDRY WERE IN FRONT OF US.

Ealing, and what was bubbling away in the area, would have been familiar to the various members of The Detours and, unknown to them at the time, other key figures that would shape the direction in which popular music was destined to head also lived in the area. These included Dusty Springfield (she also worked in Squires Record Shop on Ealing Broadway), Mitch Mitchell (who would go on to play alongside Jimi Hendrix in the Experience) and Alexis Korner who in 1962 co-founded the Ealing Blues Club with Cyril Davies.

The Ealing Blues Club, which opened on 17th March 1962, had previously been the Ealing Jazz Club, established in early 1959. The club became the birthplace of what evolved into the British R&B scene, and was the epicentre of everything that a select group of young people desired. It was in the club that Mick Jagger and Keith Richards first met their future bandmate Brian Jones. \The club was also the meeting place where the cream of the British R&B scene gathered and learnt to 'cut their teeth'. On any night it wasn't unusual to spot up-and-coming musicians with a taste for the blues. Such were members from then unformed bands like The Yardbirds, Manfred Mann, The Animals and of course The Rolling Stones.

The club was situated at 42a The Broadway, below the Aerated Bread Company and accessed by carefully navigating one's steps down a narrow alleyway that led towards Haven Place. The basement area wasn't massive and at the very most only held 200 people. But those that were fortunate to attend the club, and perhaps even contribute to it, went on to help develop a scene and pave the way for other R&B clubs such as the Crawdaddy and Eel Pie Island. David Dry saw The Who at Eel Pie Island: 'I saw The Who at Eel Pie Island for 7/6d, Magic Bus was in the charts at the time. There was a Hippy dippy liquid light show with an Old Bill bus flashing between the running images. Rod Stewart and Long John Baldry were in front of us. I hadn't a clue who Rodders was at that time and the Baldry man was blocking the view. My mate asked, "Who's that big cunt in the way?" a little loudly, as it happened, but he didn't give a toss.'

Peter 'Dougal' Butler, Keith Moon's friend and driver/minder for several years, remembers: 'The Ealing Club was a great night out. It was located in a small room below a shop. It was opposite Ealing Broadway Station and to get to it you had to walk down some steps. It's still there now, which is something that can't be said about many of the venues that The Who played at. There was always a great atmosphere in the club, and that may have had something to do with the intimacy of the venue. I would go as far as to say the atmosphere had a Parisian feel to it. It was very nice to be around.'

On the 17th March 2012, fifty years to the date after the Ealing Blues Club first opened, a blue plaque was unveiled. It read 'The Ealing Club, 17th March 1962, Alexis Korner and Cyril Davies Began British Rhythm and Blues on This Site'. To mark the location of the club and have the blue plaque installed is without doubt a most fitting and deserved tribute because, without what occurred there, one has to wonder if such bands like The Rolling Stones and The Yardbirds would have ever existed.

The Who played at the Ealing Club on 21st November and 27th December in 1964
(and in 1965 on 2nd Jan, 9th Jan, 30th Jan, 11th Feb, 18th Feb, 25th Feb, 4th March, 10th March, 17th March, 24th March, 26th March).

CHAPTER TWO
1964 - MAXIMUM R&B

Playing at the Oldfield Hotel, Greenford on 2nd January kicked off 1964 for the band and at the same venue on 20th February they went out, for the first time, with their new name The Who. The change of band name had been forced upon them, after John Entwistle had seen another band on the television programme Thank Your Lucky Stars called Johnny Devlin and the Detours.

The days and weeks that followed playing at the Oldfield also took The Who back to the Glenlyn Ballroom, St Mary's Hall, White Hart Hotel and the Goldhawk Social Club before they played at a new venue, the Evershed Sports Pavilion in Brentford, on 29th February. They then played at two more new venues, a wedding reception at the Old Oak Institute, Shepherds Bush on 7th March and at the Mead Hall in Ealing, also on the 7th March. The wedding reception had been for Joan Wilson, the sister of Harry, who at one time had been drumming for The Detours. Three weeks later, on 28thMarch (nestled between a gig at the Goldhawk Social Club and the Florida Rooms, Brighton), Roger Daltrey married Jaqueline Rickman at the Wandsworth Registry Office.

The band's first appearance at the legendary 100 Club was on 13th April 1964 (they returned on 27th April). It was also to be the last time that their drummer Dougie Sandom was to play with them. On this particular night they provided support for the Mike Cotton Sound. Cotton was a jazzman and his band had formerly been known as the Mike Cotton Jazzmen. They had been a familiar outfit from the London jazz scene since the mid-50s.

Before the 100 Club was called the 100 Club, it was a restaurant called Mack's. This was in 1942, in the middle of WW2, and was on occasion used as an air raid shelter due to the club being deep under Oxford Street. Jazz drummer Victor Feldman's father hired the venue on Sundays to give jazz bands the opportunity to play. The opening night was on 24th October 1942. The club quickly gained the attraction of American servicemen and local jazz fans. The club was advertised using the slogan 'Forget the doodlebug- come and jitterbug at the Feldman Club'. In 1948 the club had a name change and was called the London Jazz Club. By now Bebop was swinging. The ownership of the club transferred to the Wilcox Brothers and then onto Lyn Dutton.

Dutton was an agent, and one of his main clients was Humphrey Lyttelton. In 1956 the club became known as the Humphrey Lyttelton Club. Throughout these jazz years Billie Holiday, Acker Bilk, Louis Armstrong and Glenn Miller graced the stage. Yet another name change in 1964 to The Jazz Shows, and a new owner called Roger Horton, introduced new styles of music and then a further name change eventually settled on the 100 Club. Throughout the sixties the 100 club boasted performances from Muddy Waters, Bo Diddley, BB King, Julie Driscoll, The Who, The Kinks, The Pretty Things (who were the house band during 1964), The Moments (Steve Marriot's band prior to the Small Faces) Spencer Davis Group and Steam Packet amongst an incredibly impressive, very long list.

Peter 'Dougal' Butler frequented the legendary club:
'The 100 Club was a good venue. Once you walked through the entrance you went down some stairs and they took you to the basement, which is where the club was. I don't think the venue has changed much at all over the years. It's the stage they have moved around I think. I saw The Who a couple of times, but I don't remember them playing there much. Just opposite the 100 Club was the Tiles Club. I only ever went there once but that wasn't to see The Who.'

Generally accepted as the venue 'unknown', but playing this venue on 2nd May 1964 was Keith Moon's first gig with The Who. The event was either a wedding or a twenty-first birthday party, the facts remain uncertain (although John Entwistle remembered it as being a girl's 21st birthday party). The following Tuesday, the group gathered in the same basement at the Zanzibar Club-come-restaurant on the Edgeware Road, where they had auditioned for Fontana A&R man Chris Parmenter back in April, to audition again in front of Parmenter (he had previously considered Dougie Sandom to have been unsuitable for the group) and Fontana's chief A&R man Jack Baverstock. Keith Moon was now sat on the drum throne due to Sandoms' recent departure from the band. Brian Redman, who had been the drummer with the Fourmost, was also present and both drummers took turns to play during the audition. The band (and both drummers) bashed through the song 'I'm the Face'.

The White Hart, Southall became a regular Thursday night appearance throughout June, starting on the 4th June and then the 11th June, 18th June, 25th June and 6th August. Each gig earned the band £12.

John Schollar recalls 'the White Hart in Southall was run by a guy called Peter Lindsey, and Commercial Entertainments got its bands into it. The first time that I saw Keith Moon play with The Who was in the White Hart. Keith had only recently left The Beachcombers; which at the time we were a bit upset with, I mean he was great fun to be around and he was a great drummer. But we all kept friendly, and that night The Beachcombers weren't playing, so me and my band mate Tony went to see them. The White Hart was just a typical small pub. The bands would set up in one of the corners of the pub and about 150 people would cram together in front of the band as they played. Everyone would be smoking and dropping ash everywhere and spilling their drinks on the floor. I remember The Who went out and bought some long leather jackets that were all the same, and Tony and me thought it was really funny.

> THE WHO WENT OUT AND BOUGHT SOME LONG LEATHER JACKETS THAT WERE ALL THE SAME, AND TONY AND ME THOUGHT IT WAS REALLY FUNNY.

It was in the White Hart that I saw my first ever band, and that was the Chris Barber Band which included a certain Lonnie Donegan. Soon after that I saw Lonnie playing again, that time he was with his own band at the Granada in Harrow. That would have been 1956. It's so disappointing nowadays when I drive through London because most of the old pubs and clubs that us bands used to play in are now long gone: they're either car parks, convenience stores or have been turned into flats. As a thriving music city, London is a far cry from what it once was.'

The Refectory, Golders Green was a pub on the Finchley Road, Golders Green, where The Who played on 26th June 1964. Bands would have to drag their equipment down into the basement area and then set up. Jimi Hendrix played at the Refectory in January 1967. However, The Who only performed at the venue once, because their preference for turning up their amplifiers, and Keith's loud drumming dissuaded the owners to invite them back.

Golders Green also has a very poignant place in the history of The Who. On 6th September 1978, Keith Moon and his girlfriend at the time, Annette Walter-Lax, attended the preview of the film The Buddy Holly Story. They had been invited by Paul McCartney to the Peppermint Park in Covenant Garden. The event was to be the last time anyone would see Keith in public.

Kenney Jones was another of McCartney's guests on the night and recalls 'I was with Keith at the Buddy Holly film after party, which was held before the film was shown. He was in good spirits and we had time to talk. I have a couple of photographs somewhere of Keith and me from that night. He seemed to be genuinely on his way to something else and sorting some personal things out. He had even told me about some medication that he was on that made him violently sick if he had a drink. But he looked alright and he looked in great shape.'

Keith Moon died at his flat in Curzon Place on 7th September 1978 and was buried at the Golders Green Crematorium. Interestingly, the practice of cremation wasn't made legal in Britain until 1885 and the Golders Green Crematorium in Hoop Lane was the first of its kind to be built in London. It opened in 1902. The crematorium was built by Ernest George and Alfred Yeates, and the famous Victorian gardener and journalist William Robinson designed the gardens that surround the main building and mausoleums. The Golders Green Crematorium is only a few minutes' walk from Golders Green Tube Station and faces the Golders Green Jewish Cemetery. Keith Moon shares the crematorium with fellow friends and musicians like Phil Seamen, Ronnie Scott, Tubby Hayes and Marc Bolan, and one of his old managers, Kit Lambert, isn't far away either.

John Schollar attended Moon's cremation: 'the funeral was held at Golders Green Crematorium and was an actually brilliant, but sad day out. Every major rock star was there, and after the service they were all sitting around telling stories about Keith, it was amazing. In fact the table that I was sitting on was getting louder and louder and Kitty (Moon's mother) came over. I looked at her and said 'oh sorry Kit' but she said 'no John, you're telling stories aren't you, you carry on, that's what Keith would have wanted.'

Keith Moon (23.08.1946 – 07.09.1978) 'There is no substitute' are the words on Keith's plaque at the Golders Green Crematorium; and it was a no-brainer for the author of this book to use the title Keith Moon: There Is No Substitute (Omnibus Press 2016) for his tribute book to Keith. His ashes were scattered in the garden of remembrance. Shortly after Moon's death, The Jam recorded a version of The Who song So Sad About Us and this was included as the B-side to their single Down in the Tube Station at Midnight. It was a fitting tribute to Keith Moon that was embraced by the second generation of Mods.

It's fitting that, at this point, some thoughts from fans about Keith are included, beginning with the late and wonderful Megadeath drummer **Nick Menza**: 'One time when I was at the Hard Rock Café in Israel I climbed up onto a shelf and played on one of Keith Moon's drum sets. The guy below was yelling at me 'get down; the shelf won't support your weight.' But I had to do it. I couldn't miss an opportunity to play one of Keith's drum sets. I had to check it out. It was one of Keith's white sparkle kits; real old-school looking.

I liked the fact that Keith was a pretty wild player and really busy. He had such an unorthodox style too that is really cool to listen to. I sometimes hear people say that he couldn't play drums that well; but he was really innovative and imaginative. He hardly ever kept a straight beat and that made his drumming exciting.

When Keith was starting out, there was no one like him. I think another player like Mitch Mitchell had similarities in that he was a busy player too, but they had different styles. Keith was more of a wild thrashing drummer, who didn't seem to know how to play a straight beat. It was crazy but it was great.

I didn't model my own playing on Keith Moon, but I certainly took some notes and I totally respect the Who and their songs. I think they influenced a lot of guys. And they came from a different time. I mean, back then there were a lot of personality players. It's not like that anymore; it's not allowed to be like that anymore. There are so many great drummers out there today, but they don't really have any identity. If Keith was around today he probably wouldn't get the recognition either. He would probably be told what to play, he would be held back, and whatever he recorded in the studio, the producers would chop his drumming parts up and process them through pro-tools and so on. This is one of the problems with music today, it's all being done through a computer, it's all perfect and there's no mojo anymore left in the music. Bands hardly ever play together in the same room anymore. Thankfully Keith Moon and the Who were from a different time.'

Dermot Bassett: 'Keith Moon was the first thing I noticed about The Who. One evening in early 1965, on a long forgotten TV programme, I saw The Who for the first time. Saw? Fell in love with more like. I didn't know it at the time, but it was the start of a lifelong obsession. I'd never seen or heard anything like it before - and who was that drummer? At school the next day the big discussion seemed to be "Did you see that drummer on TV last night?"

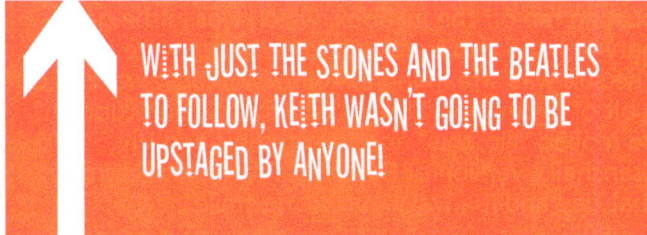

It was just over a year later that I got to experience him and them live, at Rochester Odeon, both houses of course, and a further 8 days before I'd see them again, this time at the Empire Pool Wembley for the NME Poll Winners Concert, where Keith was on a very high drum riser and finished their two song set by kicking his drums off the front of the riser. With just The Stones and The Beatles to follow, Keith wasn't going to be upstaged by anyone!

Other highlights came and went. Seeing what people call the Pictures Of Lily drum kit, but what I remember Keith calling "the engine", live for the first time, shining in the lights as the curtains came back at Maidstone ABC. Especially as Keith had beaten The Tremeloes' drum kit into submission in the first house!

Seeing Keith up close for the first time at The Marquee in 1968 was special as well, but it wasn't until the latter end of 1968 during the run in towards Tommy and beyond, that he really came into his own. The Who managing to bring Tommy to the live stage with just three instruments was a staggering achievement and couldn't have been done without Keith. Taking nothing away from Pete & John, Keith was a phenomenon, filling out the sound in a way no other drummer could have done. Also, the on-stage rapport between him and Pete was worth the entry admission alone. Listen to Live At Leeds for proof of both.

Eventually, though, we came to the long decline. Keith was always as famed for his excesses and antics as he was for his playing, which is a great shame. Of course, I used to laugh as much as anyone else, but there came a point where I stopped. I started seeing him as a tragic figure and it made me sad to see his powers gradually leaving him.

One afternoon I received a phone call from a friend, "Have you heard about Keith?" She didn't really need to say anything else, I knew what was coming. I felt the tears in my eyes. I think for the first time in my life, certainly outside of family, I was crying over someone dying.

I only met him a couple of times. In Le Chasse in Wardour Street, a club (well, a room above a bookies') frequented by musicians and roadies. As I walked in Keith, who was standing by the bar, spun round and started shouting at me "Get out, go on get out! We don't want your sort coming in here causing trouble." We then had a laugh and a drink. Of course, his outburst wasn't aimed at me, just at who walked through the door next. On another occasion he pushed me off the jukebox, which was in the gap between the two front windows, which were open. The sun was streaming in. Keith said "Just want to do a bit of promotion." I said "Not that Seeker rubbish" he replied "No, this" and selected his and Viv Stanshall's version of Suspicion. I always remember that day and it always makes me smile.'

> KEITH SAID "JUST WANT TO DO A BIT OF PROMOTION." I SAID "NOT THAT SEEKER RUBBISH"

Brett 'Buddy' Ascot (The Chords): 'Everyone who has an opinion or view on Keith Moon has their own version of him. Who fans of course see him as a vital component of the unique and combustible mix that was the sound of the 'orrible 'Oo. Moon the incorrigible showman, doing his level best to be the centre of attention, both onstage and off. Tabloid readers think of "Moon the Loon", the sensational and entertaining loose cannon - always guaranteeing a good time and an even better story for their lurid headlines. But musicians, and especially drummers, think of a different side to Moon: the craft and genius of the most inventive, visceral and original drummer to ever play rock 'n' roll music. Personally, I love all aspects of the great man, but the one that I return to again and again is the Keith Moon that first drew me into The Who fold - one that I chanced upon over forty years ago.

As a young teenager I bought Join Together, the 1972 single that featured a somewhat atypical performance by The Who - sonically it was worlds apart from most of the material I would later hear and come to love. And it was the B-side, a live rendition of the Motown classic Baby Don't You Do It, that tipped my casual interest in the sunny pop of the A-side into a full blown obsession with both Moon and The Who. The singer sounded as if his very life depended on him getting his heartfelt plea across to his estranged girl. The guitar and bass were trading blows in a battle to be the dominant musical force, both competitive and complementary at the same time. But it was the thrashing, crashing, exhausting cacophony beneath it all that held me in rapture - what the hell was this force of nature that sounded like 10 drummers on speed? How could one man make such a racket and yet also still enhance, punctuate and emphasise the song's wanton misery?

Ladies and gentlemen, on lead drums, Mr Keith Moon!

I had never even thought of picking up a drumstick until that moment of epiphany - and all was changed within five minutes - I now knew what I wanted to do with my life! Initially there were a few obstacles in the way - nobody in my house was at all musical, we had no instruments (or money!), and only a handful of records. But pencils became knitting needles, biscuit tins and cushions became drums, and I built up drumming muscles playing along to a newly-acquired Meaty Beaty Who compilation and my education was underway. I next bought a pair of sticks - Premier, naturally! And continued playing along with my hero every day - I was a disciple. I managed to purloin a snare drum from Dad's second-hand shop up in Camden, and then coupled them with an old bass drum that I found at the back of the garage at home. All this time I was feeding my Who addiction - I was working my way back through their hitherto unknown (to me!) history until I knew every single, every album, every catalogue number and UK chart position. My Frankenstein's monster of a kit continued to grow as I added odd-shaped Triton tom-toms and discoloured cymbals. Some of the other kids at school had started drum lessons, but I wasn't interested - I was only interested in playing like Moon, and to do that I thought all I had to do was copy him - or at least try to.

And here is the very essence of my fascination with Moon - I DON'T know what he's playing a lot of the time! Other drummers do things I can only dream of, but at least I sort of understand - and can visualise - what they're doing. With Moon, there are times when he virtually explodes with energy - think of the staggering Young Man Blues from Live At Leeds - and all you can do is wonder at the sheer complexity, speed and inventiveness of the fills and the timing. In retrospect I sometimes wish I had taken a more scholarly approach to my drumming education - I still find it hard to keep the bass drum going during rolls -

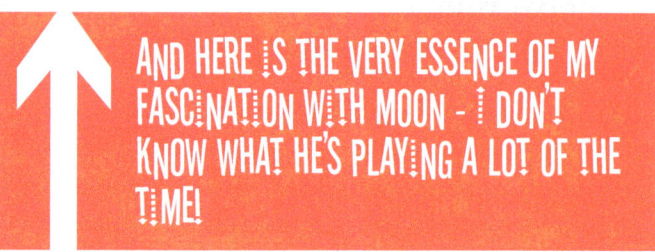

> AND HERE IS THE VERY ESSENCE OF MY FASCINATION WITH MOON - I DON'T KNOW WHAT HE'S PLAYING A LOT OF THE TIME!

and learned some of the basic stuff before I became so gung-ho in trying to emulate the master. The opening drum break into Who's Next's Bargain still takes my breath away - and baffles me, and I fear it always will.

> ALONG COMES A MOMENT WHEN I NEED A MOMENT OF INSPIRATION, AND SUBCONSCIOUSLY I THINK, "WHAT WOULD KEITH DO HERE?"

Almost inevitably I ended up replying to an advert for a "Keith Moon-type drummer" in the pages of the NME in early 1979, and in The Chords, I would find the perfect vehicle for my Moon obsession. As a four-piece, with a charismatic blond singer, a laconic but gifted bassist and a talented, Gibson-wielding songsmith I was soon in my element. The Who's template was a great one to follow, but in our case, the rivalry between the four egos comprising the group were not tempered by wise management, and within three years the whole thing had fallen apart. And since 1982 I've sometimes struggled to again find a combo that would offer such freedom to express myself musically. Modern music - and recording techniques - have necessitated a stricter approach to drumming, but Moon still informs virtually every track played since, both in the studio and more especially live. And then along comes a moment when I need a moment of inspiration, and subconsciously I think, "What would Keith do here?" and I have the answer. In idle moments I sometimes contemplate how Moon would have coped with click-tracks, Pro Tools, digitalisation and all the other restraints his style would have encountered - I think the caged animal in him would have hated it all.

One aspect of Moon's playing I have tried to follow is his ability as a great interpreter of songs - he doesn't just keep a backbeat as a foundation on which others will build, he takes the song by the scruff of the neck, accentuates the highs, anticipates the lows and amplifies the emotion of the words. Substitute, I Can See For Miles, Baba O'Riley and a hundred other Who songs owe their impact to Moon's drive and subtle translation. Crucially, Moon would follow the guitar (as opposed to the more traditional amalgam of drums and bass guitar), and it is due to the deft abilities of John Entwistle that The Who were able to operate as a musical three-piece. A more prosaic bass player would have left too many gaps, but John was the fluid cement that held together the often shambolic duo of Keith and Pete. Almost impossibly, at other times Moon would follow the vocals as a means to underscore a song's delivery. In the TV documentary series of "Classic Albums", the Who's Next album is dissected song-by-song. Moon's tendency to go off-piste is highlighted when Roger Daltrey draws the mixing faders down to leave just his singing and Moon's drums - it is clearly evident that Moon is "drumming the words"! To the chagrin of many a bass player I have also employed this technique, albeit subconsciously most of the time - if a song is so damned exciting I don't want to just sit and keep the beat.

The songs that really inspired me - and taught me - were some that are so drum-led as to be positively orchestral in their manner - think of the rolls at the end of The Song Is Over, or the glorious looseness of Pure And Easy. On a different note, I think it's a shame that the production and mix of the original Tommy album left the drums sounding somewhat flat in tone - the true dynamics of songs such as Sparks only coming to the fore when played live. Indeed I think it's really only Moon's live work that bears true testimony to his genius - I was lucky enough to see him play twice before his tragic demise – and, happily, there are now many DVDs available to showcase this side of his craft. Mercurial, powerful, exciting - and so inspiring.

There are a thousand great drummers in the pantheon of rock, but I believe none more influential than Moon. It's not just the musicianship of course, though that alone would be enough to elevate him to God-like status. In my opening paragraph I wrote of Moon's off-stage shenanigans, but they were merely a continuation of his quest to make the drummer be noticed. There is a theory that up until Moon's wild appearances on "Ready Steady Go" in 1965, drummers were rarely - if ever - shown in close-up on TV. After Moon had destroyed that pre-conception, the gloves were truly off as drummers came to be seen as musicians and personalities in their own right. His influence pervaded an entire generation of drummers, particularly coming to fruition during the punk and mod-revival years of 1976-1982. If you see a picture of a drummer from that time with Premier drums, horizontal tom toms and a forest of cymbals, chances are he was a Moon aficionado. Martin Chambers (The Pretenders), John Maher (Buzzcocks), Blondie''s Clem Burke and Generation X's Mark Laff were all obviously indebted to Moon. That style of drumming fell out of fashion as drum machines and dance music began to dominate, but Moon's influence would continue to surface in drummers as diverse as the peerless Chris Sharrock (Icicle Works/Robbie Williams), The Killers' Ronnie Vannucci, Jr. and of course the great Zak Starkey, now doing his own interpretation of teacher Moon's drum heroics.

If you were asked to explain the power, the humour, the poetic art, the beauty of rock 'n' roll music, to an alien just landed on Earth, I would sit their little green arse down, show them the live performance of A Quick One from the film The Kids Are Alright... and freeze-frame Moon's smiling, beatific face at the song's conclusion as the refrain, "You are forgiven" ring out... Keith Moon - there will never be another.'

Since the May bank holidays of 1964, the national media had become very much 'up to speed' with the growing Mod movement. Many of these Mods were also very much 'up to speed', but this was due to their consumption of French blues and Purple Hearts.

The media had brought the Mods to the attention of the nation's public by reporting their presence, and sometimes violent clashes with their rivals the Rockers, at various seaside resorts such as Margate, Briton and Hastings. The British summer of 1964 would provide a keen hacker with numerous opportunities to record and document (and at times fabricate) the activities, attitudes and seemingly strange and untraditional behaviours of the Mods, who one judge termed the 'Sawdust Caesars' (a phrase later used in the court scene in Quadrophenia).

The momentum of the Mods' surge into mainstream youth culture didn't go unnoticed, and therefore various promoters across London set up club nights to attract Mod customers, and in many cases move the trend forward supporting the Modernist ideals and ways of thinking that the movement had originally been propelled by, back in 1958.

One such club night was held at the Railway Hotel in Harrow and Wealdstone, by Richard Barnes and Lionel Gibbins. The first night was on the 30th June. And then throughout the remainder of the year on:
4th July, 7th July, 14th July, 21st July, 28th July, 4th Aug, 11th Aug, 18th Aug, 25th Aug, 8th Sept, 15th Sept, 22nd Sept, 29th Sept, 6th Oct, 20th Oct, 2nd Nov.

The Bluesday R&B club nights were held each Tuesday and The Who/High Numbers would play two sets during the night. Their performances earned them £20 at first, which was still a few pounds more than what they got working under Bob Druce. And because of the type of music being played, groups of Mods made the club night a popular hang-out. They were also witnessing the evolvement of someone who really was quite unique.

Richard Barnes: 'I remember one night down the Railway Hotel. I was stood beside two Mod guys. One of them was a drummer and he said 'fuckin' Moon, he is useless. He hasn't got a clue what he's doing. He is all over the place.' And yet these two guys continued to come back every week and they would stand in front of the band and just watch Moon. They never took their eyes off of him. They stopped slagging him off. But they had been right-when he played he was all over the place. But when he played he did it in such a tight-knit, controlled way it worked. Drummers said he wasn't obeying the rules, but he was-it's just that he created his own rules.'

John Schollar was another who frequented the Railway: 'We all used to get gigs at the Railway, in fact the Beachcombers used to rehearse in there on Sunday mornings. It was while we were rehearing one morning when some fella heard us and then got us a gig in the place. Over its time, people like Graham Bond and Long John Baldry all played at the Railway.'

It was during one of the band's Tuesday night appearances that Pete Townshend jammed the head of his Rickenbacker into the venue's ceiling. It had been an accident but one that didn't go unnoticed by some members of the audience. Feeling somewhat embarrassed by the way the guitar incident was being received, he attempted to turn the event to his favour. Maybe the image of Gustav Metzger, a familiar figure from his art student days flashed through his mind, and the thoughts of auto-destructive art inspired him further as he set about smashing up his guitar. Whether those in the audience took it as a deliberate part of Townshend's act or saw it for it was, an impulsive, yet inspired moment, never been seen before, some definitely wanted more of it.

A certain degree of hope and expectation hovered in the smoky atmosphere at the Railway the following week, but Townshend had no intention of destroying another guitar - instead Keith Moon kicked over his drum set. Little did Townshend and Moon know that both their acts of auto-destructive art would become a regular feature in the band's live performances and would remain so for several 'very' expensive years.

The Railway Hotel had stood derelict and abandoned for several years, before it burnt down in 2002. Flats were built on its site, and whilst one of the blocks was named Daltrey House, another was named Moon House. In 2009 a blue plaque was pinned to one of the walls at Daltrey House, the words on it saying 'Where The Who made rock history by smashing a guitar in 1964'.

It was on one of the Tuesday nights at the Railway (14th July) that Kit Lambert visited the club and saw

Railway Tavern © Shaun 'Duke' Cassidy

The Who/High Numbers. Lambert couldn't wait to tell his partner Chris Stamp all about the band, and the ideas that he had bubbling away inside of him. Lambert considered The Who to be the perfect band for a certain film project that he and Stamp were working towards.

Lambert described the time he saw the band with Stamp by saying: 'I shall always remember that night we first saw them together. I had never seen anything like it. The Who/High Numbers have a hypnotic effect on an audience. I realized that the first time I saw them. It was like a black mass. Even then, Pete Townshend was doing all that electronic feedback stuff. Keith Moon was going wild on the drums. The effect on the audience was tremendous. It was as if they were in a trance. They just sat there watching or shuffled around the dance floor, awestruck'.

A few days after Lambert had seen The Who/High Numbers down at the Railway, Stamp saw them at the Trade Union Hall in Watford. Stamp immediately understood his partner's enthusiasm and set the wheels for the film project in motion. On 11th August, using a 16mm camera, Kit Lambert, with the assistance of Mike Shaw (who would also take on the band's light show responsibilities) filmed The Who/High Numbers on the stage at the Railway Hotel. A film about Lambert and Stamp was released in 2015.

> KEITH MOON WAS GOING WILD ON THE DRUMS. THE EFFECT ON THE AUDIENCE WAS TREMENDOUS. IT WAS AS IF THEY WERE IN A TRANCE.

Kit Lambert grew up in the wealthy Knightsbridge area of London, his father was the notable composer Constant Lambert. Lambert and Stamp's relationship began after they had met one another whilst doing some filming at Shepperton Studios.

Lambert and Stamp lived together at 113 Ivor Court in Gloucester Place, near Baker Street. The premises became the early headquarters for the High Numbers/Who. Andrew LoogOldman had offices in the building also, at numbers 138 and 147. The premises served as a good shop-front from where they could run their ventures. To have a postal address from this part of London was quite an eyebrow raiser in the 1960s.

Chris Stamp was a Londoner, born in the East End, his brother Terence became a famous actor. Stamp took an interest in the production side of The Who's recording affairs, and was credited with helping to co-produce many of their albums including Magic Bus, Tommy and Quadrophenia. Stamp died in New York on 24th November 2012, having spent the latter years of his life as a psychodrama therapist.

Kit Lambert died on 7th April 1981. When Lambert died, Pete Townshend arranged for a private memorial service at St Pauls Church in Soho. Members of the London Symphony Orchestra performed some music for the small amount of guests that had been invited.

In the early days of taking on The Who's management, Lambert and Stamp also set up the company called New Action and the record label called Track Records. The label also signed and co-managed the Jimi Hendrix Experience and The Crazy World of Arthur Brown. During the many years that Lambert and Stamp managed The Who, it wasn't always the most harmonious of affairs, but they were all friends and between them they did create something brilliant, and something that has gone on to stand the test of time.

Alongside the Railway Hotel, another Mod stronghold and without doubt one of the most important Mod clubs running in the centre of London throughout the 'peak' Mod years was the Scene Club in Ham Yard, 41 Great Windmill Street, Soho. Like so many clubs in London and indeed Britain at the time, the Scene also operated out from a dingy basement.

By the time The High Numbers were playing at the Scene Club, they had their first single Zoot Suit/I'm the Face to promote. The band's Mod manager Pete Meaden had had 1000 copies of the record pressed and was busily running around London trying to boost sales and generate interest in 'his' Mod creation. Peter 'Dougal' Butler knew Meaden: 'In terms of fashion and clothes, Pete Meaden handled The Who really well.

Pete was a great guy, whenever The Who played live, he would be there, standing right up near the front of the stage. In The Who's early days Pete Meaden was very important for them. He steered them in a direction that really helped to set them on a course that would give them a career. Pete tapped into that Mod market very early on, and songs like Zoot Suit were produced and it all worked. I think the members of The Who were grateful to Pete for that.' In 2015 a biography about Meaden, called I'm The Face, written by John Hellier and Pete Wilky, was published.

The Scene Club had originally been the site of a jazz club called the Piccadilly. The Piccadilly was run by Giorgio Gomelsky. Gomelsky left in early 1962 to open a new club in Richmond called The Crawdaddy. The Crawdaddy would become one of the most influential hot spots in the British R&B scene.

The Scene Club's atmosphere and opening times, running through to 5am on a Sunday, suited the

Mods' nocturnal lifestyles, and it had an affordable admission price of just 5 shillings. It was a Soho club that offered value for money. One Mod girl, Shelagh Laslett O'Brian, remembers her frequent visits to the Scene, 'I would go to the Scene on a Tuesday and Thursday night and of course the Saturday all-nighters, and we would flit between the Scene and the Flamingo. The all-nighters would finish and we would all get thrown out and go and sit over in St James' Park, waiting for the Scene morning session to start.'

The owner of the club, Ronan O'Reilly, was connected to the hip radio station Radio Caroline and he pulled in one of the most respected and knowledgeable Deejays around, Guy Stevens. Guy Stevens became the resident deejay and served up all the sounds that the Mods wanted to hear. He was also responsible for 'breaking' and introducing many new acts and artists that would become mainstay features in the Mods' world. In 2013, a compilation CD called The Scene Club, Ham Yard, London 1963-1966 got released, it included Scene Club monsters like Just For You by Jerry Butler, Mathilda by Cookie and the Cupcakes, and Let The Good Times Roll by Alvin Robinson.

The club was, however, bound to attract the attention of the Metropolitan Police Force and had to endure several raids where Police officers would burst into the club, flick on the lights and search the scene clubbers for Purple Hearts and French blues. 'If you weren't dancing with a guy at the time, you would grab one and then the Police would leave you alone.' recalled Shelagh Laslett O'Brian, remembering those raids and the clubbers' avoidance tactics.

The Scene Club was only short lived, and by late 1966 had closed, making way for a new club night with a different name and a different crowd. The closure of the Scene around that period was also reflective of where Mod was in its evolvement. The whole scene was moving in a different direction. Swinging psychedelic London was being quickly ushered in, which in turn meant that many of the original Mods were being ushered out.

The Who/High Numbers first played at the Scene Club on 22nd July 1964 (and then on 29th July, 5th Aug, 12th Aug, 19th Aug, 26th Aug and 2nd Sept). But as Scene Club regular Yvonne Otzen comments: 'I remember the High Numbers coming to the Scene and some of the 'faces' stood at the back moaning and grumbling about them. The thing was - the standard of music was so high in the Scene and, the scene goers were very particular about their music and the High Numbers just didn't cut it at that time. They did however, come back a few weeks later dressed like us.' And by the end of the year Pete Townshend, Roger Daltrey, Keith Moon and John Entwistle were very much a part of the Mod scene, anyway, anyhow and anywhere.

On 15th August the High Numbers joined the Thomas Riverboat Shuffle. This was an event organised by the Hoover LTD company. Joining the High Numbers on the boat trip was another band called the South Beats.

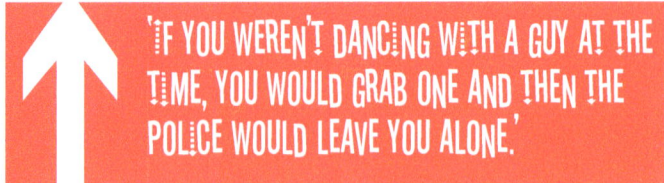

'IF YOU WEREN'T DANCING WITH A GUY AT THE TIME, YOU WOULD GRAB ONE AND THEN THE POLICE WOULD LEAVE YOU ALONE.'

At the end of September the High Numbers accepted another new booking to play at the Town Hall in Greenwich. London Mod and 'face about town' Jeff Dexter had been promoting nights at the town hall with his friend Ian 'Sammy' Samwell. Dexter would feature in The Who's history further down the timeline. The bands first gig was on 23rd September and then on the 30th Sept and then back again on 14th and 28th October and again on 24th June 1965. The Boys, later to change their name to The Action, supported The Who at this venue. The Action, led by their enigmatic frontman Reg King, were from Kentish Town, North London. They were another authentic Mod band and during their career recorded and released some wonderful versions of Stateside soul tunes, such as I'll Keep Holding On, Harlem Shuffle and Land of One Thousand Dances.

One Who fan wasn't that impressed with the venue, **Geoff Harris:** 'Of all the venues that I saw The Who in, the Greenwich Town Hall was the one that I didn't like. There was a room in which The Who played and some people sat in balconies above your heads. I don't exactly know why I didn't like the venue; maybe I was just used to seeing them in home places like the Marquee.'

Another act to play alongside The High Numbers was the Spectres, and their drummer **Steve Coghlan** remembers an interesting conversation with Roger Daltrey: 'The Who's songs were 'out there' and charged with so much energy I don't think any other drummer but Keith Moon could have done that job. Keith was so right for The Who. Before we became Status Quo we were the Spectres, and we actually played with The High Numbers in Greenwich Town Hall. I remember Roger Daltrey telling me that he just got his girlfriend up the spout. They were great though but I've always thought it would have been great to have seen Keith play with someone else. I mean you listen to some of the drumming on the albums and the way he would shuffle along on his ride cymbal was amazing. Some of it he did really fast, like on My Generation. Yeah, Keith Moon was in front of everyone else.'

'Keith Moon (1946-1978) Legendary Rock Drummer With The Who Performed Here At The Site Of The Marquee Club In The 1960s', are the words written on the Heritage Foundation blue plaque that Roger Daltrey helped to unveil at number 90 Wardour Street on Sunday 8th March 2009.

We have Melissa and Gary Hurley's driving force to thank for making the plaque happen: 'My history with The Who started in the sixties. I grew up in America with a brother who was into The Who, so I had no choice. I had a cousin who worked for MCA who represented The Who and in the 70s I also worked for the band. I handled the fan mail and some ticketing. I also worked briefly for Pete Townshend in his New York office. In the 70s and 80s I also helped run a Who magazine called Who's News, and during that time hung out with the band a lot. I met my husband Gary because of The Who. At the time he also worked for The Who. We got together and the rest is history. We now have a son whose name is Joshua John Alec Entwistle; and now I'm involved in arranging a blue plaque for John Entwistle and that will be unveiled in 2015.

I got the motivation for a blue plaque for Keith after I saw the blue plaque for Jimi Hendrix and said to Gary that this needs to happen, because Keith Moon was the best and most zaniest drummers that ever lived and he played in the ultimate rock band.

I initially contacted the English Heritage, but they were a bunch of snobs and said no. They said they couldn't support something that happened as a result of a drug overdose. I fought with them for years over this matter. And then a woman I got to know, Shona Watts, put me in touch with Gary Bushell and he helped by putting me in touch with the Heritage Foundation and things started to happen. In the end it took us fourteen years to get the blue plaque for Keith unveiled on the wall above the entrance to the Marquee Club in Wardour Street.

Pete Townshend was due to unveil the blue plaque but had to cancel at the last minute so Roger, ever so graciously, stepped up and did the honours. Roger helped us a lot on the day of the unveiling. He did a lovely speech and Keith's mum Kit and two sisters were also present. We had to have Wardour Street closed off for the unveiling and hundreds of Mods on their scooters showed up.

Following the unveiling of the blue plaque, we had a wonderful after-party where people like Kenney Jones, Doug Sandom and Zak Starkey all turned up. There's a lovely photograph of those other Who drummers all together.

Both Gary and I are literally over the moon to have been instrumental in having the blue plaque put up for Keith. We just felt that Keith needed to be seen forever and the blue plaque had to be placed at the site of the Marquee Club; which has such an historical Who connection. Originally we wanted the blue plaque to be placed at Keith's home at the time of his death but it was blocked and we couldn't get the permission required.'

Also present at the unveiling was Keith's mother Kit, who, like Daltrey, also said a few words thanking people for the gesture and remembering her son. The Who, Keith Moon and the Marquee Club represent an almost rock and roll holy trinity.

Perhaps the London haunt most associated with The Who is the Marquee Club. The Who started their Tuesday night residency here soon after their residency at the Railway Hotel had ceased.

The Club was opened in March 1964 by Harold Pendleton, following the closure of the Oxford Street venue (which was also called the Marquee). The Yardbirds, Long John Baldry and Sonny Boy Williamson performed on the opening night. A week later The Yardbirds returned to record their Five Live Yardbirds album.

The Who played their first gig at the Marquee to approximately only thirty paying customers. The iconic slogan Maximum Rhythm and Blues, with the image of Pete Townshend demonstrating his windmill arm motion, while clutching his Rickenbacker only came later. Anyway, Anyhow, Anywhere was written in the Marquee. The song was used as one of the Ready Steady Go theme tunes.

John Schollar frequented the Marquee: 'For me, the Marquee was the best venue to go and see The Who. The Marquee was like The Who's crowd, in football terms it was like playing a home game for them. I remember there'd always be a crowd of Chelsea supporters turning up, that was the football team from the West side of London. The Who's Marquee crowd were mainly Londoners and mostly London Mods. You'd always recognise faces from the other venues like the Oldfield or the Goldhawk.

The original Marquee was very dark inside, with black walls and it had thick stripy drapes that represented a marquee I suppose. I saw lots of other bands in the

THE WHO IN THE CITY

Marquee too. I went to see loads of modern jazz bands. Because of the club's location we would also drop into the 100 Club and watch another band on the same night. I got to see people like Dave Brubeck sitting in with a band at the Marquee before the club was moved down to Wardour Street. And many a night I would end up giving Keith or John a lift back home after the gig because we all lived closed to each other.

Playing venues like the Marquee really helped launched The Who, it helped get them onto shows like Ready Steady Go and Top of the Pops. Top of the Pops used to be filmed live in studios down in Wembley and I remember Keith would phone me up about half hour after doing it, asking me if I saw it and was it any good. Keith would often ask my opinion about some Who performance or a Who gig, that's how he was with me during all the years that I knew him.'

Other bands to play at the club during the mid-60s included The Small Faces, The Action, John Lee Hooker, The Animals and Manfred Mann. The Move played their debut gig at the club in 1966, and then the likes of Cream, Hendrix, Pink Floyd and the new Yardbirds (soon to become Led Zeppelin) also sweated on the stage, whilst peering out into the dark club with its large mirrors positioned around the room. At the rear of the club on Richmond Mews was a rehearsal and recording studio, where The Who and The Spencer Davis Group recorded and rehearsed up new material. The club continued through the seventies until its closure in 1988.

Jim McCarty of The Yardbirds recalls that: 'The Yardbirds played all the same clubs that The Who did, although we were going before and playing at places like the Crawdaddy Club. They were great days and very full-on, and the popularity for bands like us and The Who built very quickly because of the scene. Both bands had a residency at the Marquee when it was in Wardour Street, and there were always long queues of people waiting to get in to see us.

Before we played with The Who I had already come across them. I had actually noticed The Who "Maximum R&B at the Marquee" poster, and thought the arrow looked interesting but weird. But it was enough for me to go inside and check them out and I thought they were great. While I watched them I stood beside Ronnie Wood, who was playing with The Birds at the time. We both dug The Who, and thought they had the most amazing sound for a four piece band.'

The Marquee was also the place where the 'Hundred Faces' expanded. The Hundred Faces swelled the numbers of The Who's 'unofficial' fan club. It was also in the Marquee that The Who were joined on stage by Sonny Boy Williamson, who played his harmonica.

Geoff Harris was one of The Who's early Marquee regulars 'I was from Camberwell in South London, and would travel into the West End to see The Who, on average three times a week at one stage. The first time that I saw The Who I actually got to the gig travelling on the back of my mate's scooter. After that sometimes I would drive, but it was difficult to park around the West End, even back then it was terrible. But the majority of times I would get a taxi or catch a bus; it depended on what the weather was like.' Geoff continues: 'I started seeing the girl that ran the cloakroom, so, often after the gig and everyone had left the club, I would hang about with her. Sometimes the members of The Who would still be around. They got to know me by sight and would always say hello. I do remember being out by the rear entrance during one of the half time breaks. I used to go and stand there and talk to the doorman. Often Keith would come and join us so that he could get some air and cool down. Now one time Keith came out and was sweating like hell. He stooped down and picked up one of the milk bottles that was near the door and wrung out his tee shirt into it; and it almost filled up with the sweat from it.

Another time I spoke to Pete Townshend and standing with him was Jimi Hendrix. Out of all the members of the band the only one I never got to speak to was John Entwistle. At any Who gig I saw, as soon as the band had finished playing, John would just pack all his gear away into a holdall and walk out. The other three however would usually hang about and have a drink and a chat.

On another occasion, when I was sitting by the cloakroom, Kit Lambert came over to me. He asked me if I would be interested in going into one of the magazines that was around at the time, wearing my pop art jumper because there was going to be an article on those style of jumpers. I used to make my own pop art jumpers. I would get a jumper and then stick pieces of felt or whatever onto them. The idea was to be different and original. I was a bit shy in those days so thanked him but declined his offer. I think he got Keith Moon to do it in the end.'

Janice Beckett was a young Mod girl who frequented the Marquee: 'The first time I saw The Who was at the Marquee, and they were brilliant - so much better than all the other groups around at that time. This was in '65 and I was already into the Mod thing. I used to go with my mate Mo. Playing the Marquee must have felt to The Who like they were playing to their home crowd. It definitely felt like that to us.

For us The Who were the ultimate London Mod band. Liverpool had The Beatles but we had The Who and they were our band. The thing was it just wasn't about their music- it was about the four individuals too.'

And, being a regular at Who gigs at the Marquee, Janice was part of the thriving Mod scene and describes how it was being in the crowd on the fashion front 'Around that time the look for us girls was Levi jeans and nice smart jumpers under longish leather coats, and I had a college boy haircut. I usually only wore outfits in red, brown or black and I also liked to wear mohair dresses. A lot of us used to go to a tailor's in Wood Green and get dresses and suits made there. The guys wore Levis, crisp button-down shirts (plain or check) under nice V-neck jumpers and loafers or brogues. They never wore anything chunky or baggy; it was more streamline and sharper. It was all about the cut and the sharp creases. I remember some guys also used a tailor's on the Holloway Road; right next to the Wimpy Bar, or they'd go to Aubrey Morris in Highbury. The guys seemed to have a new suit virtually every week, but then they used to pay for their suits 'on the book'. At first the guys impressed me with their new suits; I thought they had a few quid, but then I twigged they were paying off their suits in instalments. There was more money floating around in them days. I mean I used to spend five pounds on bottles of green or blue nail varnish from Italy.'

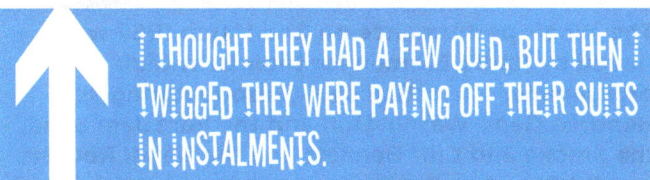

I THOUGHT THEY HAD A FEW QUID, BUT THEN I TWIGGED THEY WERE PAYING OFF THEIR SUITS IN INSTALMENTS.

Being young and having time and some money in her pockets, Janice describes a typical day in her life at that time, 'Going to see The Who would start during the day. We would often head off into Soho at lunch time; then we would just walk around going in and out of shops. Even at fourteen or fifteen years old, we had so much more freedom compared to what kids have today. My parents would ask me where I was off to and I would tell them the West End and the Marquee and they would say 'OK mind how you go, have you got enough money' and that was that. We would try to get to the Marquee early to avoid the queue; there was usually a big queue that stretched down Wardour Street.' Janice continues: 'The Marquee wasn't a big club, it was dark, but not dingy, and it had pillars positioned around the venue. There were a few spot lights aimed at the small stage and above the stage hung the red and white stripes that made it look like the roof of a marquee. People would gather about and wait for the bands. Then someone would walk onto the stage and announce that the band was coming on. The band would start to play and everyone would start to dance. And you'd dance where you were standing; there was none of this rushing to the front like you see nowadays. Janice also recalls an especially memorable moment that occurred one night - 'Mo and I walked into the Marquee one time and just past the desk in the reception we noticed a door that was partially opened. I dared Mo to go and push the door open so we could see what was inside. She pushed the door wide open and standing there was Roger Daltrey wearing just his jeans and behind him we could see the other members of The Who. Neither of us knew how to react or what to do but I blurted out 'cor aint he skinny'. And with that we quickly shut the door and disappeared into the club.'

Janice also describes what it was like inside the club, and how dancing was an important factor to her: 'There was always a brilliant atmosphere in the Marquee and I never once saw any fighting or trouble. I got offered drugs a couple of times but I turned them down and that was that. Dancing was really important to us. I think it's funny too when you see footage on the TV of Mods dancing in the clubs and they are doing all sorts of strange movements, like swinging your arms about like a monkey; it just wasn't like that for the majority of us, but people see that stuff and think that's how we all danced, but we really didn't. I was at the Marquee one time when some radio station did a showcase night. The Who and Stevie Wonder were there. It was one of Stevie Wonder's earliest trips to the UK, he was really young, just a boy. When we were at the Marquee, or any of the Mod clubs like the Flamingo, that we also went to, we would dance all night. That night when the film crew was in, one of the crew asked us if it was okay for them to film us dancing. Of course we said yeah.'

Geoff Harris has his own memories regarding audience participation and dancing at the Marquee: 'I only remember a small group who would dance at the Marquee, there was only about a half a dozen of them and I got the impression that they were art students. They may have had something to do with Pete Townshend, maybe friends from his art college, but I don't know for sure. They used to stand right in front of the stage and dance once The Who started playing. Everyone else just stood around watching the band. There was no screaming or pulling hair like you see in films on bands like The Beatles. There was absolutely no rubbish like that at the Marquee gigs. But I do remember one occasion when this girl standing right in front of Townshend started screaming. Townshend kicked his microphone stand at her and said 'shut up or fuck off'.

It wasn't just The Who that Janice would visit the Marquee to watch on a regular basis. Another young London band were also firm favourites, but in her opinion there were some differences, as she explains: 'I used to go and see The Small Faces a lot too. For me, The Who was about the music but The Small

Faces were as much about the music and the fashion. That's how me and my mates felt about it. We started going to see The Who at the Marquee first when we were only young Mods and The Small Faces came after. Pete Townshend would wear things like Union Jack jackets and that was unusual for most Mods, he was very original in that sense. The majority of Mod guys wore nothing like the clothes Townshend did.'

But as important as Townshend and his band mates were, one in particular stood out for Janice the most: 'I loved Keith Moon. For me he was the best drummer around. Back then most of the drummers in the bands that we would go and see just held down a beat, played at the back and played small drum kits, but Moon would play all sorts of things, hit the drums loudly and he two bass drums. He just wasn't your normal drummer. When he played his drums you couldn't help but watch him; everyone's attention would be drawn towards him. Keith Moon was a one off.' Janice also adds 'The Who never slipped up on stage. Daltrey for example, never forgot any words to a song. They were already seasoned professionals by the time they were playing regularly at the Marquee.'

Janice saw The Who many times at the Marquee and has plenty of fond memories to choose from, she continues: 'Boris The Spider was always my favourite Who song that I liked to hear them play live. I always enjoyed watching Entwistle sing that. My Generation was always great too and it always went down well with the audience. The Who would also sing a song where they'd include some reference to the various gangs around London, so they would mention the Highbury Mob or the Archway gang. They didn't do this often but I heard them do it on a few occasions.' Janice also shares her thoughts on an aspect of The Who's legendary stage act: 'I saw them smash up their equipment a few times. Townshend would bash his guitar on the speakers and Keith would kick his drums over. I remember the first time I saw them do that. I thought 'what the bloody hell are they doing?' I didn't know that The Who had a reputation for doing it so I wasn't expecting to see anything like it. At first us and the audience didn't understand and then everyone started to cheer. The next few times they did it, the Marquee crowd expected it and almost willed them on to do it. But, after I saw the smashing up routine a few times I found it boring to watch. It became predictable and sometimes you could even read when Townshend was going to do it. It lost its originality and the edge had gone.'

Geoff Harris frequented the Marquee at an earlier point and has different memories: 'In the days when I was going to see The Who at the Marquee they weren't really into smashing up their equipment. Townshend would occasionally give one of the speakers a wack with the head of his guitar and find ways to get the feedback. Their speakers had loads of

tears in them from where Pete had poked his guitar through on other nights. He would get that by rubbing the guitar neck along the side of the microphone stand. Heatwave was always the song that The Who started off their set with. Daltrey used to shake a tambourine and by the end of that song it would be smashed to smithereens and he would scrape his microphone across Moons cymbals and that made a hell of a noise. I never saw Moon smash his drums up or Townshend smash up his Rickenbacker. I think that sort of stuff came a bit later. They just wouldn't have been able to afford doing it every gig back then.'

The Who's performance on 2nd March 1967 was filmed by Radio Bremen for their Beat Club programme. The actual show, also featuring Jimi Hendrix, Geno Washington and the Ram Jam Band, the Smoke and Cliff Bennett and the Rebel Rousers and DJ Dave Lee Travis was broadcast on 11th March.

The Who's first appearance at the Marquee was on 24th November 1964 and then again on:
1st Dec, 8th Dec, 15th Dec, 22nd Dec and 29th Dec. And then in 1965 starting on 5th January and 12th Jan, 19th Jan, 26th Jan, 2nd Feb, 9th Feb, 16th Feb, 23rd Feb, 2nd March, 9th March, 16th March, 23rd March, 30th March, 6th April, 13th April, 20th April, 27th April, 25th May, 7th June, 13th July, 2nd Nov and 21st Dec. And in 1967 the only date was 2nd March but in 1968 they played on 15th April and 23rd April and 17th Dec.

The Who played a one off performance for the students' Christmas dance at the Northwick Park site of the Harrow Technical College on 12th December 1964. The hall in the Northwick Park area of the college complex had only been opened for three years. In the surrounding buildings the subjects of Engineering, Science, Photography, Commerce and Domestic studies were taught. The older part of the college that still catered for the School of Art continued to be located at the college's Station Road premises. On the night The Who played, Cathy McGowan, one of the Ready Steady Go presenters, was in the audience. Harrow Technical College would have already been familiar with at least one member of The Who. When Keith Moon was fourteen he left Alperton Secondary Modern to join Harrow Technical College and it was then that he met Gerry Evans, who would be responsible for introducing Keith Moon to the drums.

The Red Lion, 640 High Road, Leytonstone on Mondays 14th, 21st and 28th December, was Kit Lambert and Chris Stamp's attempt to gain some additional support from the East End Mod scene that was thriving. These local Mods would have been familiar with the songs that The Who included in their sets around this time, such numbers as Young Man's Blues by Mose Allison and Here Tis by Bo Diddley would have already been in many of the East End Mods' record collections. The Who would have also been pushing their single Bald Headed Woman with its B-side I Can't Explain, which was still several weeks away from its UK release.

But The Who still had a way to go to truly reach a wider audience and venues in Greater London offered more opportunities like Small Faces/Pete Meaden biographer John Hellier remembers: 'I first saw The High Numbers in 1964 on a Sunday night at a place called the Shandon Irish Club in Romford, which was part of Greater London by then(The High Numbers played their gig at the Shandon Hall on 2ndOctober).

I hadn't long left school, so I was about fifteen and also into the Mod scene. The Shandon was a venue above a parade of shops in the Quadrant Arcade. There was an entrance-waybetween two shops in the parade, and then some stairs that led up to the club. The actual venue ran along the length of probably three shops. It was a similar set up to the Lotus Club in Forest Gate. And, similarly to the Lotus Club, I don't recall the Shandon having a stage. This meant the groups just set up their gear on the floor and the audience would stand in front of them, everyone on the same level. Although it was called the Shandon Irish Club, there wasn't many Irish that frequented the club.

The thing is, when I saw the group (we didn't call them bands back then), I had no idea that they would go on to become one of the greatest rock bands. At the time they were just another group playing around London, so I didn't really take that much notice. But I do remember noticing that they were very Mod.

Mostly the Shandon just hosted local groups and most of those didn't dress like Mods. The High Numbers also played songs that other groups weren't playing, for example like Heatwave. They were supported that night by a local group called the Kinsmen, they were a really good Hammond-led outfit. It wasn't until I heard I Can't Explain by a group called The Who that I realised it was same group I had seen in the Shandon a year or so earlier. And by that time they were playing a residency at the Marquee Club.

In October 1968 I went to see The Who again at Bubbles in Brentwood, which was an old disused cinema and was also due to be demolished. Some promoter got the use of the venue for six weeks to put on groups. Across those six weeks The Who, Small Faces, the Move and Hendrix all played. All the groups played at the same level as the audience, with just a metal crash barrier separating them from the audience. Keith Moon was amazing doing what he did and my girlfriend Gill (who became my wife) caught a piece of one of his broken drumsticks that had flung into the air. For years and years we kept it, but sadly I have since lost it in various house moves and so on, otherwise it would be framed and on my wall.'

Geoff Harris' Marquee Club Membership card

The Who completed their run of shows for 1964 on New Year's Eve at a dance in Pinner, Middlesex. Things were now starting to hot up. The band had their own songs to promote, were establishing themselves on the UK Mod scene, and even had their official fan club up and running from premises at 74 Kensington Park Road under the enthusiastic eye of Jane Fearnley-Whittingstall.

1965 was going to be the year that would introduce to the world what would become The Who's most cherished anthem, My Generation, and Paul McCartney would be quoted to say of The Who that they were 'the best thing to happen on the 1965 scene'. Surely Townshend, Moon, Daltrey and Entwistle couldn't have asked for any higher recognition?

CHAPTER THREE
1965 – MY GENERATION

The Who launched into 1965, the year that would properly elevate their career, with a gig at the Ealing Club on the 2nd January. Two days later they revisited the Red Lion in Leytonstone and then they were back at the Marquee playing to even more impressive crowds.

They then ventured into north London on 9th January to play their songs to the crowd at the Club Noreik in Tottenham. In 1965 they also played the Ealing Club again on 23rd Jan (playing alongside the Muleskinner, whose organ player Ian McLagan would go on to join the Small Faces) 13th March, 24th April and 26th June.

John Walters, original Mod, provides an insight into the tone of 1965 and describes a backdrop that The Who and their fans would have been all too familiar with: 'I went to Brighton twice in the sixties. I cannot remember dates but I know for certain that one was on Bank Holiday Monday in June 1965. The reason I know is because that weekend was one of the most memorable in my life.

It started at La Discotheque on Wardour St. This was our favoured club (we being a little firm from Archway in North London). Following the previous Bank Holiday 'events' at various seaside destinations, this weekend was being discussed in some length by many clubgoers. Not that there was any chance of discussing anything in the club over the sounds of Stax and Motown blasting out of the speakers!

We had met up earlier in the Coffee An Cellar coffee bar down Whitcomb Street and had arranged with some girls from Borehamwood to meet up on the Monday morning at Victoria station. There was going to be around 20 or so of us in total, which was a nice number (safety in numbers!)

The Saturday night was like most other nights in Soho – lots of great music, dancing and a few 'mothers little helpers' to keep pace! Sunday was normally a 'day of rest' but this, being a bank holiday, was different. The sun was shining as I remember and we spent most of the morning just mooching around our local coffee bar – DeMarco's at Archway. I got some kip Sunday afternoon in the local Odeon (this was par for the course!).

Sunday evening was a big event – The Who were playing at St Joseph's Hall on Highgate Hill. The hall had started putting on concerts a short while ago and this was the big one. The band had a following within the Mod community, featuring regularly at some of the West End clubs. They had hit the big time with I Can't Explain and were currently riding high with Anyway, Anyhow, Anywhere. Although both songs were very popular with Mods we found the 'B' side of their first single more interesting, being a version of Bald Headed Woman.

Early evening found us ensconced in the lounge bar of 'The Cat' on Highgate Hill. Not one of our regular drinking spots it was however, next to the venue and was soon full of punters. Most of the talk was of the following day and our 'trip to the seaside'. We were building up in preparation for the event. We had a few 'sherbets' and had been joined by a couple of the top local 'faces' – 'Haggis' and 'Birdy'. Obviously Haggis was of Scottish origin and Birdy? – no idea! All of a sudden we found that we had been joined by Keith Moon and Pete Townshend, who knew Birdy, and the trip down to Brighton was mentioned several times. Moon said he was going down but we took that with a pinch of salt. By now the place was heaving and it was time to make a move.

The hall was sold out and the band was – well, as you would pretty much expect-Loud, brash and full of energy. Lots of young girls squealing and shouting seemed to be the order of the day. We were mob-handed, as the event was on our manor and there were probably fifty or sixty of us in the hall. We danced and looned about and tried showing out to a few birds as we normally did. Then someone spotted a small contingent of faces from another local firm. The sheer effrontery of them - on our turf as well. Of course words were exchanged and before long there was a fight. I was across the other side of the dancehall, and seeing the melee dashed across with all guns blazing, so to speak, only to be met by a right hook smack on my jaw which sent me flying down the highly polished dancefloor to end up in a heap under a table full of girls by the front of the stage! Talk about embarrassed - I was livid. The fight was broken up by the bouncers (all good local chaps) and the invaders were put to flight very quickly. The night continued and the skirmish had whetted our appetite for the Bank Holiday. The Who were giving it large with the guitar smashing bit which livened up the crowd (although it seemed a bit pointless to me).

My mate 'Mac' and I had scored with a young lady who had come in with the other firm but decided to stay on after they 'left'. My family had moved from the area recently but I still had the keys to the old place and there were a couple of old beds left behind so along with another lad, John (who had his girlfriend with him) we decided to camp for the night. I won't go into detail but suffice to say that we didn't get a lot of sleep and John in the next room got even less! The reason for which became apparent the next morning when he discovered countless bites inflicted by bed bugs.

The following morning found us meeting up at Victoria station. There were around a dozen of us in all (not sure where the remainder were). A few paid for tickets, some even bought returns! I didn't believe in paying for anything if I could avoid it so I just bundled my way through with the crowd (no turnstiles in those days!). The train was packed with Mods heading off to the seaside (minus buckets and spades!). We settled into a compartment to ourselves – not difficult, as the few other members of the public around were not really partial to sharing the journey with a bunch of herberts!

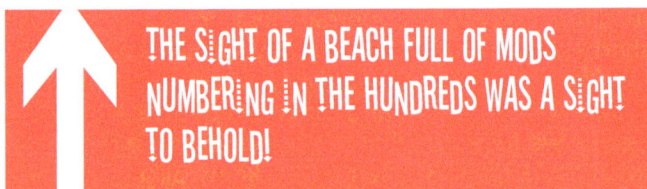

THE SIGHT OF A BEACH FULL OF MODS NUMBERING IN THE HUNDREDS WAS A SIGHT TO BEHOLD!

All the talk was of what we were or weren't going to do when we got to the coast (most of it just waffle). Word came that Keith Moon was on the train but I am not sure if that was true? At one stage a ticket collector tried to make his way down the corridor checking tickets. I hid in the overhead luggage rack (just a basket-like arrangement in those days) covered with coats etc. I am sure he was perfectly well aware of what was going on but did not fancy getting involved!

We hit Brighton like a plague. There were dozens of erstwhile hooligans disgorging onto Queens Road and heading down to the beach. The sight of a beach full of Mods numbering in the hundreds was a sight to behold! All along the promenade were police, shepherding and cajoling Mods onto the beach where they could be kept under some kind of control I suppose – at least that was the theory!

It was like Soho on a Saturday night. Groups from various clubs and different manors in London mixed side by side, oblivious to the fact that under normal circumstances they might have been at each other's throats.

All around the beach many girls had transistor radios which were tuned into pirate stations which were blasting out a heady mix of Motown, Soul and chart hits. There were familiar faces everywhere and most of the day was spent wandering up and down the beach/front, catching up with others or trying to chat up the ladies.

Rockers were few and far between to be honest. Every now and again a convoy of bikes would make its way along the front, but going fast enough to avoid direct confrontation and keeping within sight of the accumulated police forces. The pebble beach made for some very handy missiles, ideal for pelting at the passing enemy.

The previous year (1964) had seen a much larger Rocker representation and there had been more skirmishes but they were massively outnumbered in 1965. The Rockers tended to keep to the outskirts of town where they could ambush Mods as they came in on scooters.

Whenever boredom set in some bright spark (Birdy a couple of times) would stand up and shout 'Grease' or some such war cry! Immediately a large mob would rise as one and head off at speed chasing the 'invisible' enemy. To be fair there were a few instances when Rockers were really being chased, but on most occasions it was simply an excuse to rampage through the town creating havoc.

The damage caused was mainly superficial and consisted of knocking over signs, litter bins and so on with the odd shop window being put through. There were a few minor cases of theft from shops but again this was minimal. Most of the fighting consisted of scuffles with the police. I was grabbed on a couple of occasions but managed to get away without having my collar felt (leaving one member of the constabulary with a sore shin!). I saw at least one of our number dragged into the back of a paddy-wagon though.

There were several coffee bars around the town, some of which were equipped with juke boxes and a few with pinball machines. These were popular spots but tended to be packed out. My abiding memory of walking about the town is Sonny and Cher's I Got You Babe, which seemed to be playing on every jukebox or radio. The song still evokes memories of Brighton today.

We had decided to stay overnight and make our way back to London by train the following day. The year before we had spent up and attempted to hitch a lift back to town. There were four of us and we walked for a full day and into the evening eating scrumped apples for sustenance without one lift. Eventually we had to hide behind a hedge and let one of our number hitch a ride. A mini eventually stopped and we all jumped out and piled in! To be fair the driver was a real diamond - he was a French student of some kind, and not only dropped us in Sloane Square but bought us all tea and toast on the way. No, this year it was going to be the train.

We were hanging around the town centre trying to 'get lucky' with some local girls with the view to finding somewhere to crash out for the night but without much success. There were very few venues in Brighton in those days and to be honest I think a lot of places just shut up shop in case of trouble. The area around the Aquarium was very busy and the Florida was open if I remember, but packed out so no chance of getting in there.

We decided to find somewhere to 'kip' once the pubs had closed. Of course, there were plenty of others with the same idea! We eventually picked a spot in the grounds of the Pavilion and made ourselves as comfortable as possible. I drifted off to sleep only to be awoken by a copper's size 10s in my ribs. We were told in no uncertain terms to 'move on' although the terminology was a little more blue in content.

After a while wandering around we settled under the pier with a dozen or so other sorry looking Mods and spent a sleepless night, to put it mildly, what with the breeze off the sea and the sound of the waves.

I remember I was wearing a pair of bottle green desert boots. We had taken to dyeing desert boots in various colours (seemed a good idea) and at one stage I removed my shoes to find that my feet were a lovely shade of deep green where my boots had got wet whilst messing about on the beach.

By morning we were damp and miserable. Whatever cash we had brought was just about gone and we decided to head back to London. There were three of us by this time and my two mates both had return tickets. Not to worry, I thought – a quick check revealed enough cash to get a ticket to Redhill which was just outside Brighton – once on the train I would be away.

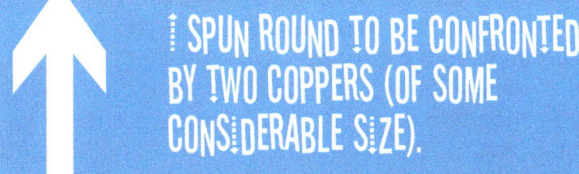
I SPUN ROUND TO BE CONFRONTED BY TWO COPPERS (OF SOME CONSIDERABLE SIZE).

We duly made our way up to the station where I purchased my ticket and we headed toward the platform where the London train was waiting. We showed our tickets and walked past the ticket inspector toward the train when I felt two hands grab me by the shoulders! I spun round to be confronted by two coppers (of some considerable size).

'Going to Redhill, are we? There's a special train just for you'

They dragged me across to the other side of the platform where a sorry looking bunch of similar Mods were waiting 'under guard' to be put on a slow local train that was only going a few stops.

Now I was sweating! I watched my mates get on the train and then the whistle sounded and she began to pull away. My mates were at the door and I made a decision - as the train began to build up a little speed I broke away and made a dash along the platform.

The lads had the door hanging open (no locks in those days) and I ran alongside until I made a grab and jumped aboard. James Bond would have been proud of me.

The journey back was uneventful as almost everybody was asleep and we exited Victoria without any trouble. That was the last trip to the coast as Mods. The following year was the World Cup so our minds were on other things and by 1967 things had begun to change. We were a little older and wiser perhaps or simply a little less energetic.

Brighton 1964 and 1965 will always hold a special place in my memories. It was all a part of coming of age I believe. The camaraderie, the sense of belonging, the excitement, the sheer bloody-mindedness and being part of that wonderful revolution will stay with me forever.

I still visit Brighton and I love the place. Outside of Soho there is no better place for a sixties Mod to relive those heady moments.'

....

South Londoner **Geoff Harris** explains how it was for him: 'I was sort of into the Mod thing but had also owned motor bikes. I only started dressing like a Mod because I found you got more girls that way. But there's also a lot of nonsense written about Mods and Rockers not liking or mixing with each other - it's rubbish. We used to take trips down to the coasts on bank holidays and in our group we would have both scooters and motorbikes, there'd be Vespas and Triumphs all mixed together. I even used to wear Mod clothes when I rode a motorbike. I think the media and even the film Quadrophenia exaggerated certain aspects.

The kids were more against the Police really than against each other and we would sleep together on the beaches and under the piers and in shelters and the Police would come along in the morning, give you a kick and tell you to move along. I certainly woke up in the mornings, several times with the sound of the sea crashing against the pebbles, that bit was right in Quadrophenia.'

On the very same day that The Who played at the Technical College in Chelsea on 15th January 1965, I Can't Explain with its B-side Bald Headed Woman got its official UK release. The college (the Chelsea School of Art) on Manresa Road was in the district more familiar to The Who's R&B peers The Rolling Stones.

The Stones had been living and hanging around the area of Chelsea for a couple of years. The Kings Road was also gaining momentum as more and more 'hip' young people were discovering the fashions being made available in the boutiques of Mary Quant and Tuffin and Foale.

However, while some of the dedicated followers of fashion flocked to see what the boutiques on the Kings Road had to offer, the members of the Who had found their own preferred street to shop in. Naturally Carnaby Street would play its part in the history of The Who's story in London.

The origins of the street date back to when Karnaby House was built in 1683, the actually street wasn't built until a few years after and only then, two hundred years later, did the first shops and market place appear. The first club that opened in Carnaby Street was the Florence Mills Social Club. This was in 1934 and catered for the early lovers of jazz. It would be a further twenty years before the Roaring Twenties opened its doors and the sounds of Jamaican Ska and calypso burst out. Pete Townshend visited the club on several occasions.

But it's not the clubs that have made Carnaby Street famous, it's the fashions - and spearheading this was a certain John Stephen (who said 'Carnaby is my creation' in 1967) who opened his boutique 'His Clothes' in the street in 1957, after his other shop in Beak Street was burnt down. Stephens was from Glasgow but had moved to London in 1952. He found employment working in Vince Mans shop in Newburgh Street. It was with his partner and boyfriend Bill Franks that the Carnaby Street venture was initially shared. Other shops were created, with names like Mod Male and Domino Male-they catered for the London mod scene.

John Stephens (the king of Carnaby Street) paved the way, and several other colourfully fronted boutiques soon followed, these included Lady Jane, Ravel, Kleptomania, Merc, Irvine Sellars and Mary Quant. And it was the Carnaby Cavern that Pete Townshend walked into one day and informed the shopkeeper that he'd like a jacket made from a Union Jack flag. The Carnaby Cavern agreed, unlike the tailors in Savile Row, who had refused a few weeks earlier.

In 1973 Carnaby Street was pedestrianized and the coloured paving slabs soon followed. By the 1980s many shops had gone and new ones had taken their place, carrying the flame forward and two of the most famous were Shelly's and Melanddi's. Such has been the effect on many dedicated followers of fashion, that the street has even been namechecked in songs by such respected bands as The Kinks and The Jam.

Nowadays, Carnaby Street has not just lost its colourful boutiques and coloured paving stones but it's also lost much of its charm - its history, however, will always remain. In 2005 a Blue Plaque was installed above the entrance where John Stephens' shop once existed. A fitting tribute to one of the most important all time dedicated followers of fashion.

Geoff Harris was an early visitor to the street: 'I used to go to Carnaby Street before it got popular. You could drive up the street then. I would go and have a look to see what John Stephens had in. Often I would go on a Saturday afternoon and return home with a new shirt or a jumper. We had to go to Carnaby Street to try and find different things.

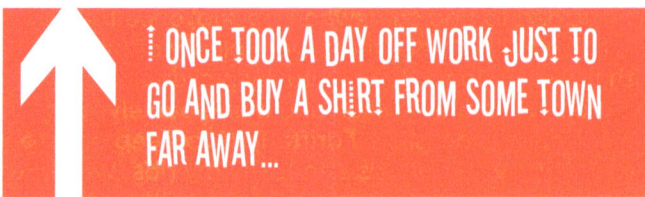

I ONCE TOOK A DAY OFF WORK JUST TO GO AND BUY A SHIRT FROM SOME TOWN FAR AWAY...

We did all sorts of things to try and be different. Another thing I used to do was dye my beige desert boots a different colour. I had one pair that I dyed green so that they matched the full length bottle green suede coat that I owned. My mate, whose scooter I used to jump on the back of, dyed his desert boots blue. We'd do anything to be different. I remember getting some white bowling shoes from a bowling alley in Weston-Super-Mare because very few people had them. I asked Daltrey once where he got a particular item of clothing from. He told me and I ended up driving to the shop in Brighton to get it. I got a white Levi jacket and white Levi jeans; and they were really hard to get a hold of, but Daltrey told me where I could find one. I had to drive to Plymouth. I once took a day off work just to go and buy a shirt from some town far away, just so that I would have something different to everyone else to wear at the next Who gig.'

Peter 'Dougal' Butler, Carnaby Street: 'I left school in 1964 and up until then the places where you had to shop was all grey. The country was run by grey people. It was all grey suits and grey overcoats and everyone shopped in the same places. And then shops like John Stephens introduced us to colour and we started going to buy our clothes in Carnaby Street. Then the hairdressers and more fashion designers started to appear and more and more colour was introduced. It was a very exciting time. There's a bit in Quadrophenia that happened to me in just the same way. I remember being dressed in my desert boots, Levis, Fred Perry shirt and full length mustard coloured suede coat (that I had bought from Petticoat Lane market), crew-cut hair-do and walking down the stairs at home and just about to leave the house and saying to my dad 'ta ta, I'm off out' and he replied 'son, have you seen yourself in the mirror, you look like a Piccadilly ponce'. I simply glanced in the mirror and thought I looked like the dogs bollocks. In those days of being a Mod, every bit of money I earned went on buying clothes, records and going out at the weekend. And then on Monday morning I would be borrowing a fiver off my mum without telling my dad.

Clothes were really important to us and everything spread by word of mouth too. I used to hang around in a group of five. We heard about some shop that was stocking some brand new reefer jackets so we all went and got one. We all went to the Starlite one night wearing exactly the same reefer jackets and we all thought we looked the business. Out of the members of The Who Keith was the one that wasn't fussed so much about clothes. When I started working with him he only owned about four tee shirts, half a dozen pairs of underpants and socks and three pairs of jeans. He just wasn't that clothes conscious. We never had any shopping trips down Carnaby Street, for Keith it would only be an instant buy.'

....

It seems The Who connection to Carnaby Street will never be too far way. On Thursday 27th October 2011 a Quadrophenia exhibition was launched at the Pretty Green flagship store in Carnaby Street. The Pretty Green store, the last shop at the end of the street and directly opposite where John Stephen's shop had once been and where the plaque in his honour is pinned to the brick wall, held the launch on that Thursday evening in the basement of their store.

Many Who fans, Mods and curious punters turned up to marvel at the exhibition, that included some of Pete Townshend's working notes, desk diary and lyric sheets from the original Quadrophenia album and a collection of photographs. There was also a replica Vespa from the film on display. The Oasis front man Liam Gallagher is now the front man for the Pretty Green clothing range, of which the garments have an evident nod to the Mod look of the original wave. Pretty Green even have their own parka and have promotional photographs of Liam wrapped in a large Union Jack flag which is of course is all very the Kids Are Alrightish...and it all works!

The Who played a gig in the St Joseph's Hall, Wembley on 21st February 1965. This was in the familiar area of Keith Moon's childhood and teenage years stomping ground. He would have passed the Roman Catholic Church of St Joseph's on numerable occasions. The site of the church would have been as familiar as the typically large Marks and Spencer's department store in the Wembley High Street. For Moon it would have been only a short journey home after the gig.

The modest St Joseph's Hall hardly compared to the Empire Pool, which both Keith Moon and the St Joseph's Hall existed in the shadows of, and in February 1965 Moon and his band mates could have only had dreamt that one day they may actually perform on the stage of the Empire Pool.

On 14th March 1965, The Who were back playing in the familiar territory of Greenford at the Starlite Ballroom on Allendale Road (they played at the venue again on 27th June, and 29th Oct). Less than two weeks earlier, a smitten Moon had met Kim Kerrigan at a gig in Bournemouth. Kim would become Moon's wife and mother to his daughter Mandy. The other three members of The Who also had reasons to grin like Cheshire cats because only three days earlier they had flown to Manchester to record their debut appearance for Top of the Pops. I Can't Explain was broadcasted that night.

The Starlite had begun life in 1935 as one of the capital's Odeon cinemas but was converted to a ballroom to facilitate dances in 1955. Throughout the sixties, acts like Ben E King, Geno Washington, The Kinks, The Yardbirds and The Hollies all performed at the Starlite. The Who also played again at the Starlite on 13th March and 15th May in 1966 (they were due to play on 16th October 1966 but was cancelled) and on 12th February 1967.

....

Once the hunger for live music died down somewhat in the 1970s, the Starlite turned into a Bingo hall and then a snooker hall before eventually closing its doors. The building has been under threat of being demolished for many years and even has its own dedicated Facebook page trying to save it from what appears to be its ultimate destiny.

....

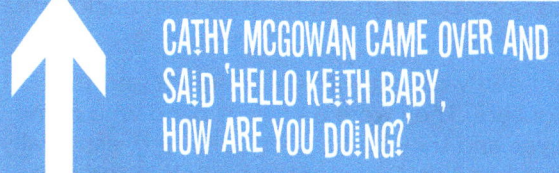

CATHY MCGOWAN CAME OVER AND SAID 'HELLO KEITH BABY, HOW ARE YOU DOING?'

John Schollar shares memories of a particularly amusing night at the venue: 'There were other Starlites, like one in Wembley and another near Crawley Town. I think the Starlite in Wembley had been an old cinema before they turned it into a ballroom. It had a huge stage for the bands to play on. The venue was run by Peter Lindsey, the guy that ran the White Hart in Southall. He didn't own it but he was one of the main band organisers. I went to see The Who and loads of other bands at the Starlite. One night, Keith phoned me up to tell me he was playing down the Starlite and said I should come down. So I went down with Tony, the bass player with the Beachcombers. The Who played a great gig. It was around the time when they were just starting to make hit records and getting known. After the gig, Keith and John came and found us and we went to have a drink at the bar. Whilst we were supping our beers Cathy McGowan came over and said 'hello Keith baby, how are you doing?' Keith looked at her then he looked at me and then back at her and says 'do I know you?' 'Course you do' she says looking all surprised. Keith then looks back at me 'who is she John?' to which I shrugged my shoulders and shook my head. I realised what Keith was doing and played along with it. 'So where do I know you from then?' Keith asks, 'It's me from Ready Steady Go' she replies 'and I'm the presenter here tonight'. 'Ah right' Keith says 'what's your name then?' 'Cathy McGowan' she returns to which he turns to me and says 'its Cathy McGowan…I can't stand her' and starts to laugh before letting her in on the wind up. She was okay with it.'

....

Peter 'Dougal' Butler: 'My interview for The Who took place in the Starlite – well, the pub just below it. I was already familiar with the venue because I had been going to see The Who playing there. It was quite an up to date and modern venue for that period. It was a good size venue too and must have easily crammed in three hundred people. It had an ultra-modern bar that had a large window that overlooked the street that was below. The Starlite was positioned above a row of shops.

I knew Bob Pridden because we had seen each other around the various Mod hang-outs, like Burton dancehall in Uxbridge. We went back to early 1965. Bob was very much into the Mod thing, as was I. I was often jumping on the back on my mate's scooter and we'd go off to Mod clubs like the Marquee, the Flamingo or Le Discoteque. Sometimes we'd get the tube into Soho but then get the milk train back home in the morning.

Bob had been working with Cliff Bennett and the Rebel Rousers. They were a brilliant band who came from Hayes and they had a good following, especially from West London. One night I saw Bob in the pub that was below the Starlite and he told me that he had stopped working with Cliff Bennett and the Rebel Rousers and had started working with The Who. He then told me that the band were just about to go and do a tour around Scotland and would I like to work with them for two weeks. He followed the invitation with a 'and we can pay you fifteen quid', which for me was like winning the lottery because I was only earning five pounds twelve at the time. So I went and did the tour and at the end they asked me to stay on with them and I did. And then it took me weeks to get my fifteen quid off of them because they were so skint.

My job was to drive them around in a Transit van. We had a V6 engine put in it and then I drove them up and down the M1 or a host of A roads. They worked constantly so it felt like I was driving that van all the time. And they were still broke. They had had a couple of hit records but they hadn't broken into America yet.'

Three days after the Who's debut Starlite Ballroom show, they met with photographer David Wedgbury. Wedgbury ushered The Who around various locations in central London, snapping away as he did so.

At some point in the afternoon The Who were photographed on Westminster Bridge, the shot captured Big Ben in the background as Entwistle, Daltrey, Townshend and Moon stared seriously into the camera. Another photograph was taken with Nelson's Column in Trafalgar Square also in the background. After a day spent trudging the streets of London having their photographs taken, the four band members must have felt exhausted, however that night The Who drove to the Ealing Club to play a gig. They did, however, have a rare 'clear' day the following day, so some kind of rest is presumed.

On Thursday 25th March, The Who played at the Blue Opera R&B Club at the Cooks Ferry Inn, Edmonton Marsh. Before The Who played at the venue, it had been a popular jazz club for two decades, and a favourite inn for bargemen since the early part of the nineteenth century. Even when bands like The Who, Alexis Korner and the Graham Bond Organisation played on the stage, in the fairly large hall attached to the Cooks Ferry Inn the Cooks Ferry Jazz Club was still thriving.

....

Peter 'Dougal' Butler: 'The Cooks Ferry was small, very compact. I only went a couple of times and don't recall if there was even a bar there or not. It didn't last for long but all the time it did, we had some brilliant bands play there.'

....

The Cooks Ferry Inn was demolished in the mid-70's following its closure in 1973, to make way for a road widening scheme.

....

The Bromel Club, situated in the Bromley Court Hotel was where The Who played on 31st March (and 28th April).

The venue was a popular hangout for South London Mods. Around the time that The Who first performed, The Animals and Georgie Fame and the Blue Flames were also venturing into Bromley to also play at the venue. Steampacket, which included Rod Stewart, Julie Driscol and Brian Auger, also played at the club in 1965 and before the club closed so had the Jimi Hendrix Experience and Cream.

Geoff Harris visited the club on a few occasions. 'The Who played in the function room that was attached to the side of the Bromley Court Hotel. It was only a single story building and the band played on a low stage. The room was used for weddings, birthday parties and functions like that, when there weren't bands on. I was there one night when Roger turned up in his new Jag. I had heard he had gotten a Jaguar. I expected to see a brand new E Type or something but it was just an old mark two and I made some joke to him as he walked in.'

On Thursday 1st April 1965, The Who played at the Harrow Technical College Students' Rag Week Dance in the Town Hall, Wembley. The other acts included Donovan, Rod Stewart and the Soul Agents and the Five Good Reasons. Donovan was a Glaswegian born young man who had developed his own style of songwriting that blended folk with pop and a splash of early psychedelia. At the time of this performance he was pushing his debut single Catch the Wind, and taking advantage of his recent Ready Steady Go appearance. His debut album What's Bin Did and What's Been Hid was still a month away from being launched.

Rod Stewart had joined the Soul Agents (formerly the Lonely Ones) five months earlier at a time when the band had been breaking into the London R&B scene and playing at venues like the Marquee, 100 Club and Eel Pie Island, and sharing such stages with Long John Baldry and John Mayalls Blues Breakers.

The Welsh Harp, originally called the Harp and Horn when it was built in the late 18th century, was where the Lakeside Scene based itself. The pub rested on the banks of the Brent Reservoir until the early 1970s when it was demolished to make way for the M1 motorway. And it was on 5th April that The Who played at one of the Lakeside Scene nights which hosted the best of the R&B acts doing the circuit. The Detours' old promoter Bob Druce booked bands for the Lakeside Scene.

In the sixties, above the Railway hotel, West Hampstead on West End Lane, was the site of the **Klooks Kleek Club**. It was another popular club where lovers of the British R&B scene could go. Named after the 1956 album 'Klooks Clique' by jazz drummer Kenny Clarke, Dick Jordan opened the clubs doors on 11th January 1961. Jordan was a jazz lover and would have been well aware of the Soho modernist vibe that had been growing in popularity since the mid-50s. Jazz was Jordan's first love but this didn't prevent him from booking Georgie Fame to help usher in the clubs first R&B nights, that began on 10th September 1963 and within months were being held two nights a week. Throughout the club's life (it closed in 1970 but a new club the Moonlight was opened in the late 70s to cater for the emerging punk bands) both jazz and R&B acts shared the club's modest stage. It wouldn't have been unusual to see Tubby Hayes or Sonny Rollins perform one night and then have Brian Auger or Graham Bond on another.

During the club's life, such was its reputation that American artists such as Stevie Wonder and (now relocated to London) Geno Washington also performed. Jimi Hendrix even showed up one night to watch John Mayall play.

Several live albums were also recorded at KlooksKleek, these included albums from Zoot Money, Ten Years After and Graham Bond and would feature some of the cream of the R&B crop on them, like Eric Clapton and Jimmy Page.

Between the 12th and 14th April, The Who camped out in the IBC (International Broadcasting Company) Studios to record a number of tracks with Shel Talmy. Recorded amongst tracks from Bo Diddley, James Brown and Martha Reeves and the Vandellas, The Who also recorded Anyway, Anyhow, Anywhere, which would be released at the end of the following month (21st May).

The IBC had been formed by radio enthusiast Leonard Plugge in the early 1930s (Plugge's home in Lowndes Square was where the film Performance, which starred Mick Jagger, was filmed) and the studios at 35 Portland Place were used extensively in the 1960s to record many of the brilliant acts of the period-The Kinks, Jimi Hendrix, Rolling Stones, Small Faces and even The Beatles. Ex-Animal turned artiste manager Chas Chandler bought the studios in the early 70s and re-named them Portland Place Studios.

On 19th April, The Who ventured into Hayes, the home of EMI (Electric and Music Industries) to play a gig at **Botwell House**. Botwell House, nearby to the Botwell Inn and the Botwell Common, was famous for opening up its grounds each year to host fairs. Sometimes the fairs had themes such as cowboys and Indians, and if a child showed up in a costume they got their entry in for free.

John Schollar recalls: 'Botwell House was part of a large Catholic church. The priest there used to hire the hall out to bands. The Beachcombers supported Shane Fenton there one time. The hall itself was massive and lots of people would get crammed in.'

In mid-May The Who found themselves whisked off to pay a brief visit to the Town Hall in Stratford. During the band's career they didn't visit the East End that often. The East End in the 50s and 60s was a world unto itself. The notorious Kray Brothers ruled the criminal underworld in the East of London and many of the original Mods had come from the area too.

Once the Mod scene was fading away and young people started to wear their hair longer and their clothes even brighter and 'tune in and drop out', much of the East End gathered together defiantly, cut their hair short and stood resolute in their army boots. The 'hard Mods' gave birth to the Skinheads, which in turn evolved into the Suedeheads and, in 1970 the film Bronco Bullfrog, that displayed these East End young people, was filmed in Stratford. The army boot, eventually the Dr Marten air-wear style, would also find their way into Pete Townshend's shoe cupboard by the late sixties.

Stratford's neighbours included Bow, Leyton and Leytonstone, and the impressive Victoria Park. The Who played a gig in the town hall, a beautiful example of Victorian architecture with its 100 foot dome tower, on the 16th May.

....

On Wednesday 2nd June The Who went to Paris. This was the band's first excursion outside of the UK. Back in London by the 5th June they played at the **Loyola Hall, Stamford Hill**. (and again on 7th Aug). Since the late fifties, Stamford Hill had been a lively place and because of this it attracted young people. There was plenty to do. Young people could hang out at any of the several milk bars and cafes, play the pinballs in the amusement arcades such as the 'schtip', eat in the kosher restaurants or in the E&A Salt Beef Bar or go and see a film in the Gaumont Theatre.

In 1959 a Jewish couple named Rita and Benny opened the R&B Record Shop in premises on the Stamford Hill. They were one of the first to introduce Jamaican reggae and Ska into the UK. They would travel to Jamaica and buy tapes from the artists and then release them on their own record label, R&B, and some of these records would find themselves being spun in the various Mod haunts across London by the mid-60s.

Stamford Hill became a sort of Mod stronghold in the early sixties and the Stamford Hill Boys-which included a young Markie Feld (Marc Bolan) and the Stamford Hill Girls-which included a young Helen Shapiro, have since gone down as important players in Mod history. The Stamford Hill cause and its firm setting in the Mod community of London had been furthered when Town Magazine featured Feld in its September 1962 edition, titled The Young Take the Wheel. Feld, standing beside two other Mods, was pictured wearing a three-button jacket (possibly made from a popular tailor that he used, Bilgorri) and a leather waist-coat. Feld was interviewed for the feature too and threw in such comments as 'You've got to be different from the other kids' and 'I mean you've got to be two steps ahead', both very Mod attitudes of the time and ones which Pete Townshend was especially beginning to pick up on too.

On Sunday 6th June, The Who ventured yet again into north London and played at **St Joseph's Hall** in Highgate, and the following day The Who were back at the Marquee playing alongside Jimmy James and the Vagabonds- another act managed by their old friend and manager Pete Meaden.

The Uxbridge Blues and Folk Festival at the Hillingdon Borough Showground on the 19th June was an unusual event for The Who, they certainly

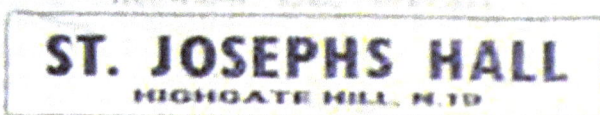

hadn't done anything quite like it before. And some reports from people that were there indicate that it wasn't the most well-attended or enjoyable experience. One person recalled The Who's performance as 'The Who were distinctly lukewarm and Pete Townshend looked really pissed off with the audience'.

The event kicked off at 3pm, and throughout the day the four-thousand strong audience were entertained by Cliff Bennett and the Rebel Rousers, John Mayall's Bluesbreakers, the Spencer Davis Group, the Birds, Marianne Faithfull, Zoot Money's Big Roll Band, Long John Baldry and the HoochieCoochie Men, Solomon Burke and the Ray Martin Group.

The poster advertised the event with the words Weather Good-Open Air, Weather Bad-Under Marquees. The all-day price set at 10/6. For many the main pull was Solomon Burke. The Who played a thirty-minute set that started at 3.45. A small stage was provided upon which Daltrey, Entwistle, Townshend and Moon gathered. Daltrey wore a blue shirt and pin-striped white trousers, Moon a grey sweatshirt and dark glasses. A large Union Jack flag was draped across one of the amps. The Who got paid £150 for their appearance, as evidenced by Christopher Lambert of 84 Eaton Place, London, as signed on the contract.

....

Peter 'Dougal' Butler: 'The Uxbridge Blues Festival was a good day out. The Who and the other bands played outdoors on a stage and behind them a few beer tents had been erected. There didn't seem to be many people watching the bands, I think they preferred to stay in the beer tents. The whole occasion was very good. This sort of event was all very new at the time.'

....

John Mayall's Bluesbreakers played at the Blue Moon Club in Hayes on 7th June, The Who on 20th and the Spencer Davis Group on 27th June. During its mid-60s lifetime, the Blue Moon Club was an important and popular club that also put on The Yardbirds, Manfred Mann, the Birds, Chris Farlow and Ronnie Jones and the Nightimers.

....

Peter 'Dougal' Butler: 'I first saw The Who at the Blue Moon in Hayes. A local guy called Eddie Norman ran the place. He also had the Blue Moon in Cheltenham and the Georgian Inn in Cowley. He put on some good bands like The Downliners Sect, Small Faces and The Yardbirds. Rod Stewart was a regular, and would pop in to the nearby pub for a drink before going to see a band. The Blue Moon was held in one of the bars within the premises of Hayes Football Club. It was a club-house type building, all on one level and there was no alcohol on sale, all you could buy was Pepsi. I knew of The Who but seeing them was great, they were really impressive. What stuck out for me was them playing their version of Heatwave, and everyone shouting out 'do it again, do it again'.

The same year that The Who played at the **Community Centre, Southall** (4th July 1965 and once again on 13th February 1966), local white residents in the area complained about the amount of Asian and black children attending 'their' schools. As a result the Boyle Law was enforced, which stated that no more than 30% of Asian or black children would be accepted into any of Southall's schools. Southall in the sixties and into the next decades would continue a degree of racial tension, and there were episodes when fascist skinheads were witnessed rampaging the streets of Southall demonstrating their racial attitudes.

The Who performed in the community centre regardless. **John Schollar** explains: 'Southall Community Centre attracted some big names like Johnny Kidd and the Pirates and bands like The Beachcombers and The Detours, that were just below them on the rung, would get offered the support slots. The venue was owned by the council and the community hall hosted all sorts of events for the public. Sometimes promoters would hire the hall and put their own events on.'

....

Peter 'Dougal' Butler: 'the Southall Community Centre was a huge venue. Up until seeing The Who there, it wasn't the type of place where I would go and see bands. It had a massive stage and probably had a capacity of four or five hundred people. The night I went, I wore a new suit that I had just had tailor-made and a pork pie hat, that we called Blue Beat hats. But I got into a fight that night and lost my hat.'

On the 29th June, The Who played at the **Burtons Ballroom** in Uxbridge. The following day they drove to Farnborough to play at the Town Hall, and returned to play there again on 6th September and then on 9th March in 1966.

The Who were booked to play at the gala opening of **the Manor House Club** on 7th July. The small club was located in rooms above the Manor House Pub in Harringay. Previously the venue had been the Harringay Jazz Club.

....

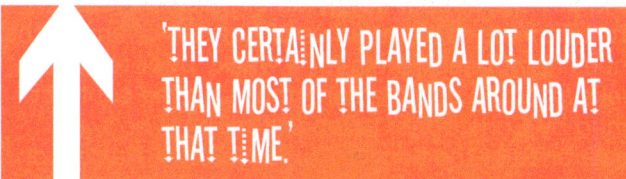

'THEY CERTAINLY PLAYED A LOT LOUDER THAN MOST OF THE BANDS AROUND AT THAT TIME.'

Geoff Harris points out that not all The Who gigs were in big venues: "The Who played in a very small room upstairs at the Manor House. Lots of pubs in London in those days used similar size rooms to host clubs. Some of the rooms weren't much bigger than large living rooms in people's homes. I remember The Who always played very loud. Whenever you walked out of a Who gig your ears would be whistling. It was a deafening experience going to see The Who. They certainly played a lot louder than most of the bands around at that time.'

....

The Pontiac Club, Zeeta House, Putney on 28th July was a short set due to the PA system blowing up. **Richard Cole** (who would go onto to work for The Who) approached Mike Shaw looking for work. Putney, at the time, offered really only two places for live bands to be seen - the St Mary's Hall and the Pontiac. Both The Action and Chris Farlowe and the Thunderbirds had residencies at the club.

....

Geoff Harris: 'I only went to the Pontiac Club once. I used to have a poster from that gig. At one time I used to keep Who gig posters and pin them up in the back of my van. I had a decent collection, which I sold a few years ago. One of the posters from the Marquee was sold for eight thousand dollars by the collector who bought it from me. I had originally taken that poster from inside the Marquee on one of the Tuesday nights. I had a collection of items that I had kept that included tickets, flyers, a Christmas card from The Who fan club and the original letter it was sent in, and even my membership card for the Marquee; a collector bought the lot and has since been selling them on. The Pontiac was a small theatre/cinema type place. I took my girlfriend at the time (who became my wife) and we stood at the side of the stage and watched The Who from there. I remember Pete looked over and said hello to us.'

The Pontiac Club was located in Zeeta House, a four-storey building which was built on the corner of Putney High Street and Upper Richmond Road. Zeeta and Company had been a bakers and confectioners owned by Kensington department store John Barker. During the fifties and sixties, Zeet and Company had stores all over London.

According to the contract offered by the Malcolm A Rose Agency of 35 Curzon Street, Mayfair, 'The artiste shall not, without the written consent of the management, appear at any other place of public entertainment within a radius of 10 miles of any of the venues mentioned herein for 4 weeks prior to and 2 weeks after the engagement' thus said the contract signed by Christopher Lambert for The Who's appearance at the Fender Club in Kenton, Harrow on 30th July. John Schollar remembers that 'the Fender Club took its name after Fender guitars. The Beachcombers played there several times supporting bands like Screaming Lord Sutch and Cliff Bennett. The club itself was run out of a hall in an old social club.'

Two days before the Fender Club gig they had played in Putney (a distance of roughly thirteen miles) and the day following the Fender Club gig they travelled to **Wilton Hall** in Buckinghamshire; so no contracts were breached on this occasion. The contract also stated that the band would get paid £180, guaranteed against 60% of gross door receipts.

During August, The Who made another appearance on Ready Steady Go, but only as a three piece because Daltrey was sick and couldn't make it. They were also filmed for a new youth programme called A Whole Scene Going On. Daltrey did however make himself available for the opening night of **Ready Steady Richmond**. This was the fifth National Jazz and Blues Festival held in the Richmond Athletic Association grounds in Richmond.

The events programme for the event was simple, blue in colour with a few carefully positioned images placed on it, one was of a trumpet resting on a chair as if waiting to be picked up and played. The programme also informed that the event was being sponsored by the Evening News and Star.

The National Jazz and Blues Festival had been started by Harold Pendelton in 1961. Such artists as Chris Barber and Johnnie Dankworth performed on that occasion. By 1963 the attendance was in the region of 27,000 people, which swelled to a staggering 33,000 in 1965 when The Who performed. Such was the increased capacity of the festival that by 1966 it was prevented from returning.

While the festival ran, many of the new and upcoming acts appeared. The Rolling Stones played at the festival in 1963 and got paid only £30. They returned to be top of the bill the following year and negotiated a much higher fee (50% of the night's takings). Other artists that played at the festival included Memphis Slim and Mose Allison-a personal favourite of Pete Townshend.

During their set, The Who played My Generation, Daddy Rolling Stone, Shout and Shimmy, I Can't Explain and Anyway, Anyhow, Anywhere. Some of the other acts joining The Who at the three day festival in 1965 were The Yardbirds, the Moody Blues, Georgie Fame, Manfred Mann, Kenny Ball, Chris Barber, Ken Collyer, The Animals, the Spencer Davis Group and Long John Baldry. It was certainly an event that was worth every penny.

On 14th August The Who visited Cowley, a small town on the edge of Greater London's boundary, to play at the **New Georgian Club**. It was a one-off visit.

Going into September, The Who continued to work hard and travel around the UK. They also flew to Holland and Scandinavia and Denmark to play concerts. It was also in Denmark that Daltrey got fired following an incident that also included Keith Moon. Within three days Daltrey was back in The Who and they continued to tour, visiting Scotland, playing at the legendary **Twisted Wheel Club** in Manchester, zipping down to Cornwall, dropping into the **Cavern Club** in Liverpool and more gigs and more travelling before falling into November to play in the more familiar surroundings of the **Marquee Club**. The gig was billed as the 'Return of The Who'. They hadn't played at the club for four months - their London fan base surely must have missed them.

On the 17th November The Who played at **Queen Mary College, Stepney**. On this occasion they did breach a contract they had with the London Student Carnival Ltd (which was also in association with Radio Caroline and Immediate Records) and their performance due at the Glad Rag Ball on the 19th.

On the evening of the 19th The Who appeared at the **Glad Rag Ball**, which was being held in the Empire Pool, Wembley. Cathy McGowan was present performing her duties as compere and three thousand young people watched on. The Stamford Hill 'ace face' Mod Mark Feld, now calling himself Marc Bolan, also performed alongside and amongst several more acts Donovan, The Merseybeats, The Hollies and the incredible Wilson Picket.

The day after the Glad Rag Ball, the Who drove down to Brighton, scene of many a Mods and Rockers confrontation and where they had built a good following up with the Mods in the area by playing in the Florida. That night The Who were banned from playing in the **Aquarium** ever again because their fans caused extensive and expensive damage to the venue. In some ways this marked the end of The Who's Mod Brighton connection; something that had certainly helped put them on the map, only the summer the year before when they played at the 'All Nite Raves'.

'If they press any harder they'll come through as chips' said John Lennon when The Beatles played on the small wooden stage at the Wimbledon Palais on Merton High Street, Wimbledon two years before The Who. Lennon's comical remark related to the cage-like fence that was erected around the stage upon which The Beatles played in an attempt to protect them... and the stage.

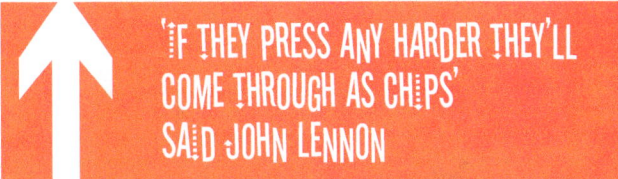

'IF THEY PRESS ANY HARDER THEY'LL COME THROUGH AS CHIPS' SAID JOHN LENNON

The Wimbledon Palais had a spell in the sixties of hosting live music, and the same year that The Who played, the Melody Maker was holding its annual National Beat Contest there. A large banner saying 'Wimbledon Palais Welcomes You To Beat Time' hung behind the bands as they competed for the prize. Radio London and one of their star disc jockeys Pete Brady also held regular nights in the Palais too. The Who played at the venue on 26th November and returned again in 1966 on the 11th February and 13th May. The venue was closed in 1967 and later demolished.

The Who only performed a handful of gigs until they played at the **White Lion Hotel** in Edgeware High Street on 5th December and then at the **Eltham Baths** in Eltham, south London on 6th December (and on 28th February 1966). However, the days in between their Wimbledon Palais gig and the Eltham gig had been certainly eventful.

The band's debut album My Generation was released, the single reached an encouraging number two in the charts, there was another appearance on Ready Steady Go and Top of the Pops, and in amongst all the celebrations and accolades, Keith Moon got whooping cough. Starting at the Eltham Baths gig he had to miss some shows. Moon's temporary replacement was Viv Prince, who had been playing drums in The Pretty Things.

Eltham Baths, located on Eltham Hill in the Borough of Greenwich, had opened in 1938. The building housed two swimming pools, the largest of which could be floored over to allow people to stand on it whilst shows were hosted. This was a popular practice for many swimming baths, especially during the winter months. It was a good way of generating revenue for such swimming pools around London. Since the 1940s, boxing had been a regular feature at the baths and in the sixties other bands like The Kinks, The Yardbirds and The Pretty Things also played.

Eltham Baths were sadly closed in 2008 and the building demolished in 2011.

The Who played one more of their regular Tuesday nights at the Marquee on 21st and then to sign off 1965, on New Year's Eve they went to the television studios located in Kingsway and performed My Generation and I Can't Explain for another Ready Steady Go.

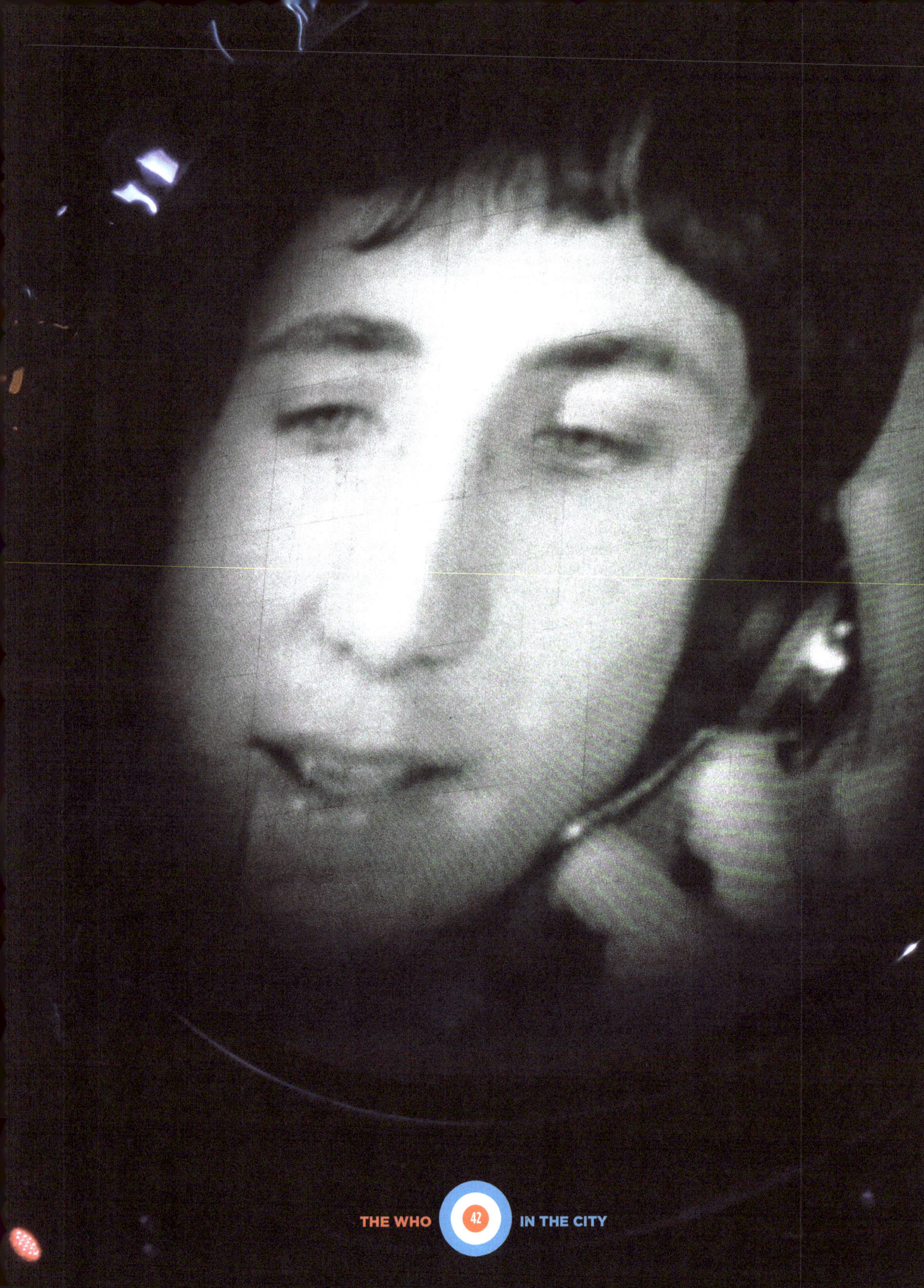

THE WHO 42 IN THE CITY

CHAPTER FOUR
1966 - A QUICK ONE, WHILE HE'S AWAY

The Who played twice on 15th January 1966. The first was at the Big Beat Club held in the premises of the Two Puddings Hotel, Stratford. Eddie Johnson took over as landlord at this notoriously tough East End establishment in 1962. Such was its reputation for having 'blood spilt' it earned itself the name the butcher's shop. Many bands played at the Two Puddings and it was even the site of Britain's first ever disco.

The second performance of the night was in nearby Hackney at the **In Crowd Club** night. The club night drew its inspiration from the song written by Billy Page and recorded and released by Dobie Gray in December 1964, and then by the Ramsey Lewis Trio in May 1965.

The legendary **Astoria /Rainbow Theatre**, Seven Sisters Road, Finsbury Park. Throughout the 1920s and 1930's the Astoria had been used as a cinema. It had first opened on 29th September 1929 with a Greta Garbo film called The Kiss. The venue was one of four Astoria Theatres in London built by Arthur Segal.

It wasn't until the early 1960s that the current owners of the theatre made the venue available for live music and before The Who played there on 4th February 1966, there had been appearances by such jazz greats as Miles Davis, Sarah Vaughan and Dave Brubeck and then it was the turn of the likes of The Rolling Stones, The Beatles, Chuck Berry and even Frank Sinatra. One of the most famous performances was delivered by Jimi Hendrix on 31st March 1967. This was the night he first set his Fender Strat on fire.

In the early 70s the venue was briefly closed, but when it was re-opened The Who were the act that ushered in a new era of live music on the 4th November 1971 (and returned on the 5th and 6th). 'Down at the Astoria the scene was changing' was the opening line from The Who's song Long Live Rock, which was an obvious nod to the legendary venue.

For the next decade, the Rainbow remained one of London's most favourable live music venues before it closed for good in 1981. But during the time that the Rainbow's doors were openPink Floyd, Queen, Genesis and Bob Marley and the Wailers all played there. The Who played two shows at the Rainbow as a fundraiser for the Stars Organisation for Spastics. More than £10,000 was raised. Paul McCartney paid £1000 for five tickets.

The Who's other dates at this venue include:
4th, 5th Nov and 6th Nov 1971, 9th December 1972, 13th December 1973,14th April 1974, 2nd May 1979, 3rd and 4th February 1981.

The day before The Who played at the **Ram Jam Club**, 390 Brixton Road, Brixton on 10th March, Substitute had entered the charts at number 19. The club had only been opened a few months earlier by brothers Rik and John Gunnell. The brothers decided on the name, taking it from Geno Washington's backing band the Ram Jam Band. Geno and his band appeared at the club several times. The club played a mixture of soul, Ska and reggae music and attracted popular artists such as The Skatallites, Nina Simone, Mary Wells and even Otis Redding with his fourteen piece band.

Going into April marked the first London High Court hearing relating to Shel Talmy's claim for the exclusive recording rights to The Who's material. Until the matter was resolved The Who were restrained from doing any further recordings. The Who simply continued to travel the country and do what they did best-perform. The Who set off on their second British Package tour on 14th April, joined by the Spencer Davis Group.

On 14th April, The Who were in Southampton, then on

the 15th at the **Fairfield Halls, Croydon**. The site of the Fairfield Halls had originally hosted fairs in the 19th century and then the actual building was opened in 1962. The Beatles played in the halls in April 1963 and after them came many more acts such as Chuck Berry and Pink Floyd. The Fairfield Halls have also been used to record live albums by Traffic and The Nice, and continue to this day to host an assortment of musical and theatrical productions. The Who returned on 21st September 1969 and played for nearly two and a half hours. Their set contained most of Tommy.

The Regal Cinema on the corner of Fore Street and Silver Street, Edmonton was opened in March 1934. It had been built by A E Abrahams and the architect was Clifford Ash, who also designed the Regal's sister cinema in Marble Arch. The cinema and theatre area included an impressive forty foot deep stage, a huge size by any theatre's standards. There was also seating for three thousand people and a standing area for a further thousand. During the building's lifetime The Beatles, Frank Sinatra and T. Rex played at the venue and The Who on 17th April.

Going into the seventies, The Regal became a disco, then a music venue again, then a bingo hall before eventually being demolished in the mid-80's. A supermarket now stands on the original Regal site.

The month before The Who played at the **Witch Doctor** on 28th April there had been a fatal shooting, stemming from a gangland confrontation that involved members of the Richardson gang. The Richardsons and the Krays were the two most well-known gangs of the London criminal underworld. The actual Witch Doctor Club was located above the Savoy Rooms at 75 Rushey Green, Catford. There was a casino called Mr Smith's below, and that was where the shooting incident had taken place.

The Witch Doctor had opened late in 1965. In the same year that The Who played so did The Herd, The Lonely Ones, The Fleur De Lyes and The Mark Four, which included guitarist Eddie Phillips, who, that same year, would form The Creation.

Tiles was a basement club in Oxford Street located opposite the 100 Club on the corner of Chapel Street and that's also where the entrance was. The club opened its doors as **Tiles** in March 1966 after a stint under the ownership of Alexis Korner, who had had it since 1964, when it had been called the Beat City Club. Jeff Dexter was one of the house DJs who presented his popular 'Jeff Dexter record and light show'. Other DJs that served up their sounds were Clem Dalton and Mick Quinn from the Juke Box Jury show. John Peel also ran his Perfumed Garden show from the club just before it closed in September 1967. Other bands that performed at the venue other than The Who include The Eyes, Manfred Mann, David Bowie, Otis Redding, Pink Floyd and Sugar Pie Desanto.

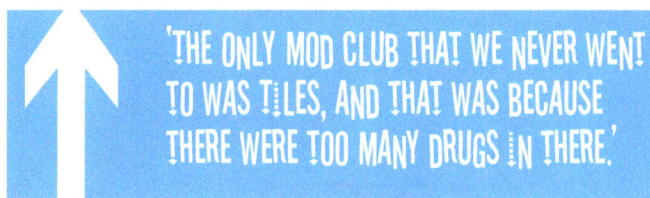

'THE ONLY MOD CLUB THAT WE NEVER WENT TO WAS TILES, AND THAT WAS BECAUSE THERE WERE TOO MANY DRUGS IN THERE.'

On the 29th April, the first night that The Who performed, such was the interest that the venue quickly reached its full capacity and hundreds of fans were left milling around Oxford Street considering an alternative option. Meanwhile, in the club below, fans surged towards the stage, interrupting The Who's performance and leaving the band no option other than to cut their set short and abandon the gig. The Who returned for a second time on 29th July. But as popular as Tiles was, it was gathering momentum at a time when 'the London scene' was changing and it wasn't to everyone's taste, as original Mod female Janice Beckett points out: 'The only Mod club that we never went to was Tiles, and that was because there were too many drugs in there.' Naturally this wasn't an experience or opinion shared by all.

On 1st May 1966 The Who paid their second visit to the **Empire Pool, Wembley** for the NME Poll Winners event. The Who, alongside an impressive list of other acts that included The Beatles, The Rolling Stones, The Walker Brothers, Roy Orbison, Dusty Springfield, The Yardbirds, the Spencer Davis Group, Sounds Incorporated, The Overlanders, the Alan Price Set, The Seekers, The Fortunes, Cliff Richard and the Shadows, Herman's Hermits, Crispian St Peters, Dave, Dee, Dozy, Beaky, Mick and Tich and The Small Faces, played to 12,000 people. Naturally The Beatles headlined, followed by the Stones and then The Who, who performed My Generation and Substitute.

It was to be another eventful summer for The Who. They travelled the length and breadth of the country and had various fallings out and confrontations. Keith Moon even left the band for a week. They also performed in Sweden, Germany and Denmark and returned to the IBC Studios to record some new material that included Disguises, So Sad About Us and I'm a Boy. I'm a Boy was released by Reaction Records in August, the same month Pete Townshend flew over to New York with Andrew Loog Oldman to discuss a new recording contract with Allen Klein. The other members of the Who were not privy to the 'real' reason for the meeting. In October The Who also booked some recording time in the CBS Recording studios at 104 New Bond Street. They laid down versions of Don't Look Away and Whiskey Man.

One of the most popular clubs that opened in London in 1966 was **The Speakeasy** at 48-50 Margaret Street (just off of Regent Street). The club had a coffin as the counter where the guest paid their few pennies before stepping down into the main area. The club opened in December 1966 and was popular amongst local and touring musicians. During its life, the Speakeasy hosted many an impromptu jam session and on occasion these included Jimi Hendrix. It was also the venue where Track Records launched themselves.

Kinks drummer **Mick Avory** points out: 'I saw Keith do some stupid things in the Speakeasy, but the management never threw him out; if anything they expected those behaviours.' It was in the 'Speak' that in 1969 Deep Purple made their debut. It was also in the club that Pete Townshend also befriended Paul Cook and Steve Jones of the Sex Pistols. That night he was attending a John Otway gig in the club.

Not too far from the Speakeasy was another popular drinking hole. **The Ship**, 116 Wardour Street was often frequented, amongst many other rock musicians, by Keith Moon. It was also in the Ship that George Harrison invited Peter Frampton to play on his debut solo album All Things Must Pass. The Ship has always been a convenient meeting point before heading off to any number of the nearby clubs that have existed across the decades.

This area of Soho had long been a popular gathering point. Just around the corner from the Ship in Broadwick Street there is another pub, the Bricklayers Arms, which served a similar function to the Ship (in the 50s and 60s – it closed as a pub in 1964), and it was in the room above this pub that Brian Jones formed The Rolling Stones in 1962.

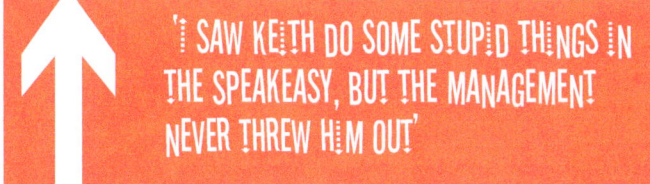
'I SAW KEITH DO SOME STUPID THINGS IN THE SPEAKEASY, BUT THE MANAGEMENT NEVER THREW HIM OUT'

Just a short walk from the Ship was the old **Roundhouse** pub, 83-85 Wardour Street. It was at these premises that the London Skiffle Club was opened by Cyril Davies in 1952. Soon Davies teamed up with Alexis Korner to form the London Blues and Barrell House Club, which helped create a British buzz around such blues artists as Muddy Waters.

The music introduced and enjoyed at the London Skiffle Club would go on to have a huge influence on all the members of The Who and contribute to their own unique playing styles. Pete Townshend had a flat on the fifth floor in 87 Wardour Street (and on the corner of Brewer Street), the premises he moved into following his departure from an address in Old Church Street, Chelsea. Townshend employed a carpenter to build areas that would house his growing record collection and musical recording equipment, and the flat soon turned into a den that Townshend would often invite friends back to, to smoke some grass and play some records.

When Townshend wasn't entertaining at his flat he would sometimes frequent the Wheelers restaurant or the Colony Club located on the first floor at 41 Dean Street. The club had been run by Muriel Belcher since the late forties and had a reputation for attracting the 'creative types'. Francis Bacon was one of the names that liked to frequent the club.

Near Wardour Street and Dean Street was Old Compton Street and the premises of the 'world famous **2i's coffee bar** - home of the stars' (59 Old Compton Street) which first fired up its coffee machine in 1956. Whilst the machine hissed away and churned out mouth-watering aromas, the basement area below hosted Marty Wilde, Adam Faith and Cliff Richard. It was also in the basement of the 2i's that record producer Shel Talmy auditioned The Who before taking them into the studio to record a demo of I Can't Explain. Track Records, owned by The Who's management, also had their offices in Old Compton Street. The entrance was exactly opposite the 2i's.

Just off Old Compton Street and into Frith Street, there was another famous coffee house called the **Bar Italia.** The premises, where Bar Italia has made its home since 1949, actually has an intriguing previous history. It was on this location, that on the 26th January 1926 John Logie Baird provided the first public demonstration of the television. Nowadays, there is a blue plaque reminding the world of this great achievement, and in Bar Italia today there is a television nailed to the wall at the back of the long narrow bar, that repeatedly shows all manner of Italian related sports and news channels.

However, it was in 1949 that Lou and Caterina Polledri opened their coffee bar at 22 Frith Street. They already owned a café in Covent Garden, but saw an opportunity to open a second in Soho, which was growing increasingly popular with Italians. The Polledris installed a Gaggia machine and nearly sixty years later it's still there, supplying regular customers like Paul Weller, Martin Freeman and Kevin Rowland with their espressos.

Little has changed regards the interior of the bar. The original tiles on the floors and walls still remain, there are stools and mirrors that run along the length of the bar and on any day it will be full of people sipping away at their coffees. The bar Italia has been a popular meeting place since the day of the coffee bar culture modernists of the 50s, the Mods of the 60s and the rock n rollers of the 70s, 80s and 90s; Pulp even wrote a song about the bar which was included on their 1995 album Different Class.

Today the Bar Italia remains 'the place' to be seen and have a meeting, and it even has its own scooter club- the Bar Italia Scooter Club, who meet frequently and park their stylish Vespas and Lambrettas outside of the bar. It's a wonderful sight to behold that evokes fond memories of the 50s and 60s Mod scene.

Opposite the Bar Italia is **Ronnie Scott's** at 47 Frith Street. Jazz musician Ronnie Scott had been one of the faces in the ranks of the first wave of the Soho Modernists. He was included in the line-up that formed the Club Eleven (41 Great Windmill Street), along with other London jazz big-hitters John Dankworth and Tony Crombie. Following Club Eleven, Scott opened another club in Gerrard Street, but then moved that to the Frith Street address in December 1965. By 1968 he had converted the upstairs space into an area that could also cater for live music, and this area attracted such rock bands as The Who in 1969 and The Jam nearly a decade later. The upstairs area was also where Jimi Hendrix joined Eric Burdon on stage for a jam. This was the last time that Hendrix performed live to an audience. Two days later the world was informed that Jimi Hendrix was dead.

It had also been in a restaurant in Frith Street where Pete Meaden had once worked in the kitchens but also accepted the £500 from Chris Stamp for him to take over the management of The Who.

Back in London on 7th July, The Who played at the **Locarno Ballroom** on Streatham Hill, Streatham. They returned again on 15th December, which also happened to be the first time that Bob Pridden was used as the band's soundman. This relationship continued for many years thereafter. The Locarno Dance Hall had been opened by bandleader Billy Cotton in 1929 and by the sixties was a popular venue for live music. In 1969 it became the Cat's Whiskers, in 1984 the Studio, in 1990 the Ritzy and in 1994 it was the home of Caesars Night Club which it remained as until it closed in 2010.

The Who remained in London and on 9th July The Who's live performance at the **Technical College** in Westminster was filmed by a Canadian television company for a programme called Take Thirty.

On 24th August The Who played at the **Orchid Ballroom** in Purley. Purley fell inside the boundary of Greater London. (the band returned to the Orchid on 18th January 1967).

On 6th September The Who ventured out again into the Greater London town of Ilford to play a show at the **Palais**. Essex would go onto become a Mod stronghold in the later years of the next decade.

On 12th November, at the Duke of York Barracks, Chelsea, The Who were filmed again, this time for American television. On this occasion The Who performed five songs. By this time the area of Chelsea had become much more fashionable than it had since The Who last visited the area. Earlier in the year a new boutique selling clothes that reflected the psychedelic and changing times, called Granny Takes a Trip, was opened at number 488 in the fashionable Kings Road by Nigel Weymouth, his girlfriend Sheila Cohon and their friend John Pearse. It became a Mecca for the swinging kids of London and for many members of the rock music fraternity, including the likes of The Rolling Stones, who were still encamped in the surrounding area and drinking in places like the Worlds End.

A few days before Christmas, The Who were at the **Upper Cut Club** in Forest Gate.

Small Faces author **John Hellier** describes the club that he sometimes frequented: 'The Upper-Cut Club was right near the railway station and the Princess Alice pub. The club really was fabulous. Previous to being the Upper-Cut it had been a rolling skate rink, it was a big venue. It was bought out by a famous boxer at the time called Billy Walker. That's how the club got its name -Upper-cut because of the boxing. I went there about late 1966 and it was only open for about a year or so, but boy was it a good night out.

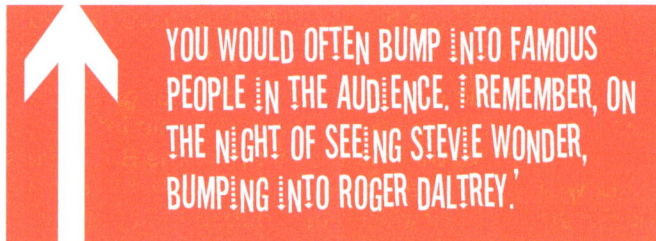

The capacity was perhaps 1500 people. So yeah, you walked down this alleyway and would be faced by this very impressive building.I saw the Small Faces there, also Stevie Wonder. It was a really popular club. You would often bump into famous people in the audience. I remember, on the night of seeing Stevie Wonder, bumping into Roger Daltrey.'

Following their set on the 21st December, Keith Moon peeled away from his band mates to spend the remainder of his night elsewhere, whilst Roger, John and Pete travelled over to a respectful night club haunt in Kensington called Blaise's to see for themselves what some new act in town called the Jimi Hendrix Experience was all about. Townshend for one was completely knocked out.

The Roundhouse in Chalk Farm, Camden, would have been the place to go on a hot summer's night in London's psychedelic sixties. The Middle Earth Club began its life at the venue and was a natural continuation from the UFO club which had existed for a short period in Covent Garden. The crowd was pretty much made of the same smiling faces.

The Who played alongside The Move, and the darlings of the London psychedelic scene Pink Floyd, on New Year's Eve in 1966, which was promoted as the *Giant New Year's Eve Freak Out All Night Rave*. There were equipment difficulties on the night, but it didn't prevent the 'psychedelic ravers' achieving their acid drenched hazy dream like states. However, Townshend was observed putting some extra zest into his smashing up his guitar performance at the end of their set.

After the Middle Earth Club ceased, the Roundhouse was taken over by the **Implosion Club**. This was a psychedelic rock step up from the sounds of the previous two years. The Implosion Club nights ran on Sundays and during the club's life, such big hitters as Deep Purple and Frank Zappa performed. The Roundhouse continued to host live music for many years to come and the list of rock legends is endless. For a period of time the venue closed, but has since been refurbished and now a much plusher Roundhouse exists and once again hosts live music, although it looks nothing like it did at the time of the Implosion Club.

> LSD WAS A VERY NEW DRUG TO MANY PEOPLE IN 1966, THERE WAS STILL VERY LITTLE KNOWN ABOUT THE EFFECTS...

Apparently Pete Townshend only took LSD on four occasions and one of those was at the Roundhouse on that New Year's Eve 1966. The Who played the same night, albeit about 3am. Lysergic Acid Diethylamide, better known as LSD, was a very new drug to many people in 1966, there was still very little known about the effects and it certainly wasn't everyone's choice of drug, but it was a huge factor and influencer in much of the music that was churned out during this period and, this included The Who. Six days after the Roundhouse trip, Townshend went to the UFO Club to see Pink Floyd, who really were the darlings of, and at the epicentre of, the emerging London psychedelic acid scene.

Peter 'Dougal' Butler: 'I have a few memories of the Roundhouse and one is of Viv Prince of The Pretty Things coming back stage. He was wearing a German tin helmet and was out of his fucking tree and because he was being a pest I had to kick him out. He knew the band and had even drummed for them at the Eltham Baths gig a couple of years earlier.

The Roundhouse is a nicely done up building now, but back then it was a just a big basic venue. It had a big stage that had been built up of old timber and I remember Pete telling me that he thought the sound was good in the venue. On the whole it was just a cold, dark and dismal place. It was circular and had been originally used to turn the trains around.

The Who played at the Roundhouse a number of times in the late sixties. A lot of things had gone psychedelic by then. That whole scene wasn't something that I personally brought into. I never wore any of that Indian garb or burnt joss sticks. I was really still a Mod at heart, as were a lot of people of my age and who had been Mods since the beginning.

A lot of the sort of people that wore that hippy, flower power and psychedelic stuff hadn't come out of the Mod thing. Mostly the only people I knew who dressed in that 'swinging way' were those that played in bands. When you went down the Kings Road or passed I Was Lord Kitchener's Valet there would be some people buying their clothes, like all that military stuff.

But by and large that look didn't take off with The Who's audience. The crowds of the Jimi Hendrix Experience and Pink Floyd dressed like that though, but they were made up of younger people who hadn't been into the Mod thing.'

Other roundhouse dates The Who played included: 5th October and 15th and 16th November 1968, 23rd February 1969 and 20th December 1970.

CHAPTER FIVE
1967 - I CAN SEE FOR MILES

The Who opened the New Year by returning to the Orchid Ballroom in Purley, where they had first played back in the Summer of 1966. On the 29th January 1967 The Who played two shows (6.00 and 8.30) at the Saville Theatre, Shaftsbury Avenue (they also returned later that year on 22nd Oct). The Who were joined by the Jimi Hendrix Experience, The Thoughts and The Koobas. On 31st January The Who drove out to Ilford to play at the Palais Des Danse.

The Beatles' manager, Brian Epstein, had been the theatre's leaseholder since 1965 and he collaborated with Robert Stigwood to put on a series of Sunday night concerts in the theatre. On the night that The Who played in January they gave a debut performance of A Quick One (While He's Away), which was witnessed by Paul McCartney and John Lennon.

The Saville Theatre at 135 Shaftsbury Avenue had opened in 1931 with the play For the Love of Mike. The 1400 capacity venue suffered bomb damage in the Second World War and in 1955 had a complete refurbishment. By the sixties, bands were appearing in the theatre and The Beatles even shot their promotional film for Hello Goodbye in it. The Rolling Stones played in December 1969-that same month the Saville Theatre closed. It reopened the following year as an ABC Cinema and has remained a cinema (now an Odeon) ever since.

In the spring, Track Records signed Jimi Hendrix - it was a huge coup for them. Not long after, in April, The Who released Pictures of Lily. And then, as the warmer weather approached and Britain's youth embraced wafty clothing, hashish and mind expanding drugs like LSD, the Summer of Love happened. In June The Beatles released their Sgt Pepper's Lonely Hearts Club Band album and the world changed forever. The previous year the Beach Boys had released Pet Sounds, which was well received by most (excluding Keith Moon), but the Sgt Pepper album was a whole new something and The Who responded with The Who Sell Out. Pete Townshend was also spending time more of his time hanging out with like-minded people in the UFO Club.

Towards the end of March, The Who flew to America to make their debut live performance on the Murray the K Show, which was filmed in New York. Wilson Picket and Cream also appeared on the same show. This was The Who's first step into this brave new world and they followed those tentative steps up with many more confident ones. The Who returned to London for a brief visit and recording session of Pictures of Lily, before jetting off again to play some concerts in Germany.

> **THERE WAS EVEN A HELTER-SKELTER RENTED FOR THE NIGHT AND ALL THIS AGAINST A WISH WASH OF PSYCHEDELIC LIGHT SHOWS AND THE AROMA OF HASHISH.**

The 29th April 1967 was a special date for the psychedelic subscribers of the Summer of Love year. It was the occasion of the 14 Hour Technicolour Dream, held in the lavish surroundings of the Alexandra Palace. The Who were listed as one of the bands due to perform but they didn't. However, Pete Townshend did attend the event. There were many acts that performed at the event and these included the Crazy World of Arthur Brown, The Pretty Things, The Move, The Soft Machine, The Creation and Pink Floyd who headlined. There were also poets, artists, jugglers and dance outfits such as the Tribe of the Sacred Mushroom. There was even a helter-skelter rented for the night and all this against a wish wash of psychedelic light shows and the aroma of hashish.

The Alexandra Palace, the 'People's Palace' was built in 1873 and over the next hundred and fifty years served many functions. In the 1930s it was the headquarters for the BBC Television Station and, as the blue plaque informs it was the place where 'the world's first regular high-definition television service was inaugurated on 2nd November 1936'.

The venue has also hosted many bands and club nights. There have been many remarkable events held at the 'Ally Pally' (as it was nicknamed by Gracie Fields), the 14-Hour Technicolor Dream, then four months later on 29th July there was the Love-In

concert, which began at 9pm and finished at 9am and cost just £1 to get in. By this time Londoners had a taste for all night raving, something they would still be doing forty years later. On that night of the Love-In, some of the cream of 1967 performed - Pink Floyd, Julie Driscoll and the Trinity, Eric Burdon and The Animals and the Crazy World of Arthur Brown.

The Who were back in America throughout the summer, playing concerts in venues like the Fillmore in San Francisco and also appearing at the Monterey International Pop Festival, an event held between 16th and 18th June. The Who performed on the 18th and shared the bill with the likes of Ravi Shankar, Hendrix and the Grateful Dead.

A few days after the Monterey International Pop Festival, Keith Moon found himself sitting in on a session with The Beatles in Abbey Road Studios. Mick Jagger, Marianne Faithful and Eric Clapton were also present to contribute backing vocals on the chorus to All You Need is Love. The event was broadcast live to 400 million people in 25 countries and the song released the following month.

On 3rd November, The Who played at the **Granada Cinema** in Kingston-Upon-Thames. The following day on the 4th November they played two shows at the Granada Cinema, Walthamstow. They hadn't played this venue before. The venue located in Hoe Street had been an arts centre since 1887 before being taken over by Granada Cinemas in 1930. However, when it had been an art centre, films were being shown as far back at 1886, some of the earliest screenings in cinematic history.

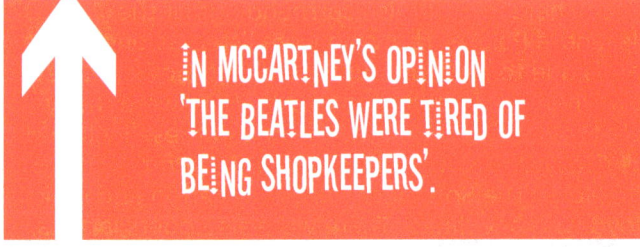

IN MCCARTNEY'S OPINION 'THE BEATLES WERE TIRED OF BEING SHOPKEEPERS'.

Walthamstow had come under the county of Essex, but in 1965 it became incorporated into Greater London. It contributed to housing London's ever-growing working class population and its industry to employ them. The area of Walthamstow was heavily bombed during World War Two and had been undergoing extensive refurbishments since the late 50s.

Ian Dury, one of the leading acts in the pub rock scene of the mid-70s, studied at Walthamstow Art College and Blur's Damon Albarn's father Keith, who had a spell managing Soft Machine, also taught there during the 1960s. Plus pop art artist Sir Peter Blake was a local resident. The Who played again at the Granada in Walthamstow on 8th November 1968.

In mid-November, The Who returned to America. Whilst there they performed at the Festival of Music in Cow Palace, San Francisco and at the Festival of Music at the Hollywood Bowl in Los Angeles. I Can See For Miles had recently been released in the States and was doing well. Before returning to England on 3rd December they had also played several more concerts across America that also included a visit to New York City.

On 7th December Keith Moon and his wife Kim (maiden name Kerrigan) attended the opening of The Beatles' Apple Boutique store on the corner of Baker Street. Marijke Koger and Simon Posthuma, also known as The Fool, had been handed £100,000 and asked by The Beatles to design a boutique for them and their ideas. The intention, according to McCartney, was to provide 'a beautiful place where you can buy beautiful things'. The boutique sold clothing and jewellery that reflected the psychedelic times that The Beatles were helping to drive along. Lennon and Harrison were the only Beatles able to attend the launch party.

During the Apple Boutique's brief existence, the wall that faced Paddington Street was painted in psychedelic shapes and colours that included a giant image of the face of a Red Indian. However, by the following summer, local tradesmen supplied the council with a petition demanding that the 'art work' be removed, and it was. Within only a few months the boutique had hemorrhaged money through either frequent shoplifting or bad management, and on the 30th July the Apple Boutique liquidated itself. It had been open less than a year. In McCartney's opinion 'The Beatles were tired of being shopkeepers'.

The Who's final London gig of 1967 was billed to be at the Olympic Grand Hall, Kensington on 22nd December. An all day and night event called Christmas Peace on Earth included the Jimi Hendrix Experience, The Move, Traffic, Soft Machine, Eric Burdon and the Animals and Pink Floyd.

Sadly The Who missed this event.

CHAPTER SIX
1968 – YOU'RE ALL FORGIVEN

Before The Who were flown out to Australia and New Zealand to play several concerts, they played their first London gig of the new year on the 12th January at the Royal Ballroom, Tottenham.

The venue had begun life in 1910 as an ice skating rink before being turned into a ballroom called the Tottenham Palais in 1925. The Mecca Leisure Group took over ownership of the venue and renamed it the Tottenham Royal. Many bands played at the venue during the 1950s and 1960s. At the end of the 1960s the Tottenham Royal hosted soul and reggae club nights that were popular amongst London's new emerging youth sub-culture group called Skinheads. In 2004 the building was demolished to make way for new houses.

Towards the end of February The Who embarked on a six-week tour of America and Canada. One week after landing back in the UK they were back playing in the Marquee with the Bonzo Dog Doo-Dah Band. Their drummer Leggs 'Larry' Smith would forge a strong friendship with Keith Moon and the two would be often been seen drinking around the most fashionable clubs in London, the Speakeasy was a particular favourite of theirs.

The Who returned to play at the Marquee on only a few occasions during 1968, they also returned to the London College of Printers in June.

....

Super Who fan **Dermot Bassett** had his first experience of seeing The Who at the Marquee. It was to be the first of many more over the next fifty years.
Dermott: 'I had seen The Who twice in Rochester and twice in Maidstone in the mid-60s but the first London gig was at the Marquee in 1968. When I went to see them they hadn't played at the Marquee for quite a while. There are some people that consider 1968 to be the lost Who year. To some extent the hits had dried up and it was as if the band didn't have much idea of the direction in which they were heading. I think to play the Marquee again was good for them.

On the night I saw The Who, there were two support bands, Jethro Tull, who were soon to start their own residency at the club, and then there was The Gun, who had a hit record called Race With The Devil. Jon Anderson, who went on to play in YES, was playing keyboards with The Gun that night.

It was a full house at the Marquee, you couldn't move. My mate was getting a bit itchy, worrying about the time because we had to catch the last train back to Kent. He wanted to look at his watch, but to do so he had to drag his arm up through the crowd and I had to push his sleeve back with my mouth just so that he could read the time. Yes it was a very full house.

On the night The Who played a mixture of songs, a bunch of their hits alongside numbers like Summertime Blues and, I think, Shakin' All Overtoo. They were sort of building up a set that they would include in the Tommy shows that began the following year.

I saw The Who twice in 1968 but the gig in December was like seeing a different band from the earlier part of the year. There were very evident changes and certainly in Roger Daltrey, not only had he grown his hair, he had also grown in stature and it was marvellous to see. Before 1968 I always thought Roger looked a bit awkward and a bit unsure of himself, but then by the end of 1968 we were seeing Roger Daltrey the rock God. And then the following year was just massive for him and The Who.'

....

On 2nd March The Who played a one-off gig at the **New Edmonton Gardens**, Edmonton. They had played in Edmonton before but it wasn't a place that they visited often.

In May, Pete Townshend had married his long-term girlfriend Karen Astley and four days later, on the 24th they played at the City University, Clerkenwell. Kit Lambert had also booked The Who into Advision Recording Studios, 83 New Bond Street. This was one of only a handful of London studios that offered an eight-track recording facility.

In June The Who were back touring America and Canada. This pre-occupied them for nine weeks, returning on 1st September. Magic Bus was released in July (in the States and October in the UK) and reached number twenty-five in Billboard. Two days before Magic Bus was released in the UK a traditional green London bus set off from BBC's Lime Grove studio. Joining members of The Who on the bus were a lion and a young elephant. The promotional 'magic' bus made its way through the streets of London, passing along Oxford Street, Regent Street and Shaftesbury before heading off towards the Kings Road in Chelsea.

On Friday 18th October The Who were booked to perform at the Brunel University Students Union 'Midnite Rave' event held in the **Lyceum**. The magnificent Rococo style building with its tall pillars on Wellington Street, just off of the Strand, had been a theatre since 1756. Built and re-built several times since then, it has hosted the English Opera House, the first exhibition of waxworks from Madame Tussauds, and many of the world's biggest and favourite bands like Queen, Led Zeppelin, Genesis and The Clash. The Lyceum had become a Mecca Ballroom 1951 and during the early sixties was another Mod stronghold. This was partially due to the music that got played but the beautiful wooden dance floor was also a massive pull. On 15th December 1969 Keith Moon found himself playing drums alongside Eric Clapton, George Harrison, Yoko Ono and John Lennon in the Plastic Ono Band on the Lyceum's stage.

East of Eden (who as yet hadn't released their debut album, Mercator Projected), Proteus and David Booth joined The Who for their gig on 30th October at Eel Pie Island, Twickenham. For decades Eel Pie Island, situated on the River Thames, could only be reached by boat and then in 1957 the first bridge was erected. The Eel Pie Island Hotel had been built in the late nineteenth century and in the fifties jazz musician Brian Rutland started to draw in the cream of the jazz and blues crop. Before Eel Pie Island closed in 1967 and became a hippie commune in 1970, the likes of Ken Collyer, Alexis Korner, Cyril Davis, The Rolling Stones, Yardbirds and Pink Floyd had all played there. Pete Townshend bought the nearby Boat House and built the Eel Pie Studio (Oceanic Studio), where many a great song was then written and recorded.

At Stonebridge House Studios, Wembley on 11th December The Who joined The Rolling Stones for their The Rolling Stones' Rock and Roll Circus. Included in the filming was also John Lennon and Yoko Ono, Eric Clapton, Marianne Faithful, Mitch Mitchell, Jethro Tull, Taj Mahal, Ivry Gitlis, Julius Katchen and black American model Donyale Luna. Keith Moon, embracing the event, dressed like a clown and with full make-up. The film wasn't actually released until 1996.

....

The Who's last London gig of the year was at the Marquee. Yes supported The Who at 'The Who's Xmas Party'

CHAPTER SEVEN
1969 - I'M FREE

For many who had come-of-age in the sixties, 1969 would bring the colourful decade to an unexpected and abrupt end. For many, things just weren't turning out to be the way they had hoped they would. In the January, the USA and North Vietnam met in Paris to engage in peace talks. In the meantime the Vietnam War continued to rage on. In November John Lennon returned his OBE in protest of the UK's support for the war. In December the first posters of 'War is Over! If You Want It - Happy Christmas From John and Yoko' began to appear.

The build up to this point-the closure had seen Led Zeppelin release their debut album in the States, Cream perform their last gig in the Royal Albert Hall, Jim Morrison was arrested for exposing himself at a concert and then arrested again for drunkenness on an aeroplane, George and Patti Harrison were found with 120 cannabis plants growing in their home, Concorde made its virgin flight, the notorious Kray Twins were found guilty of murder and imprisoned for life, The Beatles released Abbey Road and their days as the world's greatest band were numbered, and Brian Jones mysteriously died on 3rd July. Two days later The Rolling Stones played a concert in Hyde Park. And whilst hundreds of cabbage white butterflies were released into the air and Jagger recited parts of poetry from Shelley in tribute for Jones, people could feel the changes coming.

Change however favoured The Who and their popularity continued to grow. In May they released their rock opera masterpiece *Tommy*. Tommy was The Who's fourth studio album and offered up brilliant songs like Amazing Journey, the Acid Queen, I'm Free and Pinball Wizard.

The Who's success, particularly in America was impacting on the amount of shows that they could play back in the UK. But they didn't completely desert their fans and on 25th January they played at the New Year's Ball at the **Middlesex Borough Road College**, Isleworth.

Then on 8th February they played at the **Regent Polytechnic**, Portland Hall, Little Titchfield Street. The venue had been hosting bands since the student union had formed in 1965. It was in this venue that Jimi Hendrix made his debut UK appearance when he joined Cream live on the stage. Other acts like Pink Floyd, Fleetwood Mac and blues man Howlin' Wolf also played at the Regent Polytechnic. The Who's support on the night they played were Family. Family were a band formed from the ashes of an R&B outfit called the Roaring Sixties. By 1969 they were playing a mixture and fusion of rock, folk, psychedelia and jazz. Jenny Fabian, author of the novel Groupie, drew inspiration from Family, although in her book, also published in 1969, she called the band Relation.

On 1st May, a few days before The Who set off for another American tour, they performed *Tommy* upstairs at **Ronnie Scott's** in Frith Street to a crowd mainly made up of the press. At first there was some jeering from some 'drunken' members of the press and a heavy sense of being judged. By the end of the night the Who had won the press over.

....

Peter 'Dougal' Butler was there: 'I thought Ronnie Scott's was a great place to have the launch for Tommy. It was in the smaller room upstairs. There was a free bar put on for all the journalists and there was also a fair bit of banter going on between them and the band members just before the band played. By the time The Who started to play, the journalists were swimming in booze. The thing was, no one had heard Tommy-this so called opera before. This meant the band were quite nervous, and so were the journalists to some extent. I've read that there was some abuse being thrown at The Who before the performance but I didn't hear any. Once they had downed a few beers they were quite enthusiastic.

The gig itself was spot on. The Who were fantastic and bearing in mind they had only played it in rehearsals they did such a brilliant job. I had only ever heard the songs played in rehearsals, so to hear them all being played in the correct order and as one piece of music, an opera, was just fantastic.

I had been present when they had recorded the songs, but when they had recorded the songs it had been done like a jigsaw puzzle, there were songs all over the place. And as time went by you could see Keith, Roger and John starting to 'get' what Tommy was all about and it all started to come together. And when they played Tommy at Ronnie's it was just perfect and it all made sense. At the end of the show I think 99% of the journalists were blown away by what they had heard.

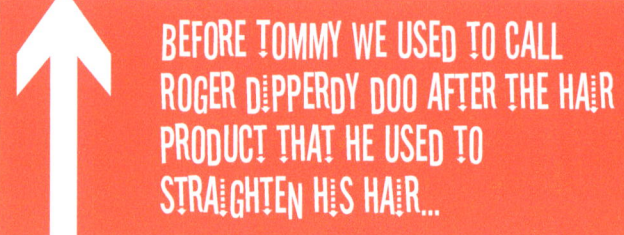

BEFORE TOMMY WE USED TO CALL ROGER DIPPERDY DOO AFTER THE HAIR PRODUCT THAT HE USED TO STRAIGHTEN HIS HAIR...

Tommy helped Roger's career no end. He became Tommy. He became a rock icon after Tommy. Something changed in Roger. I witnessed it. Because of Tommy, Roger became the focal point of The Who at that time. He was the figure that sang Tommy's story. He looked fucking great and he carried off the part superbly. With Tommy, everything about The Who clicked into place. Before Tommy we used to call Roger dipperdy doo after the hair product that he used to straighten his hair, we also called Moonie Barney after Barney Rubble from out of the Flint Stones, but after *Tommy* and Roger had that long hair we didn't anymore.'

It wasn't until the 5th July that The Who were back playing in London, and when they did it was at the Pop Proms held in the **Royal Albert Hall**. Chuck Berry was also on the bill and both bands wanted to headline. The matter was eventually resolved by both acts closing one of the two shows on the day. There were many Rolling Stones fans sitting beside The Who fans on the occasion, because The Who's concert had been held on the same day as the Stones' Hyde Park concert; their first performance without Brian Jones.

Dermot Bassett had been to Hyde Park earlier in the day but had left because he had tickets for The Who concert and, remembers the events that unfolded all too well: 'I was at the Royal Albert Hall in 1969 on the night the fight broke out. Both The Who and Chuck Berry were playing that day. There were two shows organised; one in the afternoon and one in the evening, I went to both and for each the two acts shared the headline slot. It had been agreed that Chuck Berry would headline the afternoon show but when The Who were playing their set they were getting grief from some of the Teds in the audience.

Many of us Who fans had already been thinking it was odd to see these Teds; people who were in their early thirties at the same concert as us. I think one Ted either threw something or said something to Roger and he reacted. Up until that point, Pete had been trying to calm things down by saying things like 'come on we're all fans of Chuck Berry aren't we?' But it wasn't really having much effect. Roger's reaction was to swing his microphone and I saw it swing in the direction of some Ted. I don't know if it actually made contact with him but I saw his head jerk backwards.

And that was the trigger because then all hell broke loose. There were people climbing onto the stage, The Who got ushered off, Roger was the last and you could see he was more intent in swinging his microphone at the Teds.

The trouble went on for a while but eventually cooled down and sorted itself out, and The Who returned to the stage and finished their set. The seats in the first front rows had been completely destroyed in the violence and the place was a mess. The atmosphere had been absolutely electrifying.

Funnily enough, the second show in the evening went off without a hitch. The concerts had also taken place on the same day that The Rolling Stones had played their famous concert in Hyde Park. They had been releasing white butterflies into the air whilst The Who had been involved in a punch up. It said it all.'

In August, The Who were back in America for the Woodstock Festival and sharing the legendary festival with the likes of the Grateful Dead, Janis Joplin and Jefferson Airplane. Although The Who were due to play their set at 10pm it wasn't until 4am that they actually got onto the stage. Only a few hours earlier the band's drinks had been spiked with acid.

At the end of August, Keith Moon broke his ankle after he fell down some stairs. However he still managed to drum for The Who at the 2nd Isle of White Festival held on the 30th August. The Who's fee for performing was £900 and an additional £200 for expenses and they arrived in style via helicopter.

There were no London gigs until 21st September until The Who were back at the **Fairfield Halls, Croydon**. They played for nearly two and a half hours and their set contained most of Tommy.

The Who then spent the majority of November back in the USA before returning home to play on the 14th December at **The Coliseum**, St Martin's Lane. The Coliseum was the home of the English National Opera and, on the night The Who performed, the 2500 capacity venue was a sell-out.

Dermot Bassett was there:'I went to see The Who at the Coliseum but it felt very strange being in some plush opera house. The band were great and the

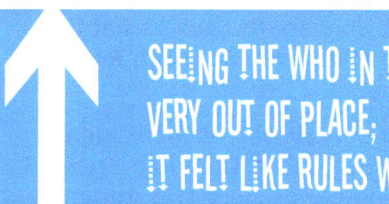

SEEING THE WHO IN THE COLISEUM FELT VERY OUT OF PLACE; IT FELT LIKE RULES WERE BEING BROKEN.'

songs sounded brilliant, but I wasn't used to seeing them in that style of venue. I had only seen The Who in halls and clubs and seeing The Who in the Coliseum felt very out of place; it felt like rules were being broken.'

The Coliseum concert was to be The Who's last performance in London of the decade. The sixties had provided every possible opportunity for a gang of young musicians. Certainly pop music would never be same after the sixties and The Who had contributed to this. Since 1962 they had been playing in their own back garden of London relentlessly, they had been called The Detours, The High Numbers and The Who, they had released four albums My Generation, A Quick One, The Who Sell Out and Tommy and although the number one spot had eluded them they had also released the singles Zoot Suit, I Can't Explain, Anyway, Anyhow, Anywhere, My Generation, Substitute, A Legal Matter, The Kids Are Alright, I'm A Boy, La La La Lies, Happy Jack, Pictures of Lily, Whisky Man, The Last Time, I Can See For Miles, I Can't Reach You, Call Me Lightening, Dogs, Magic Bus, Pinball Wizard and I'm Free.

They had been Mods, they had been there, at the epicentre. The Who had lived through the Mod years, as they and their music evolved into the psychedelic years and, then into the rock years. And they had conquered America, an achievement not every rock band could claim to have done. And next they had the 1970s to deal with, and the seventies was going to throw at The Who a whole bunch of different challenges.

The seventies was going to include another chapter of sex, drugs, rock and roll...and death!

© Ernie Stortini

© Ernie Stortini

© Ernie Stortini

© Ernie Stortini

THE WHO 56 IN THE CITY

Chapter Eight
1970 - SEE ME, FEEL ME

The year didn't start well for members of The Who, especially Keith Moon. On 4th January 1970 Moon's driver and friend Neil Boland had been killed in an accident involving Moon's Bentley. This incident, the circumstances, and the loss of Boland had a huge effect on Moon, but the band had to continue to work and over the next weeks returned to do some studio work and, play concerts in Europe. In the spring the band found themselves recording in Townshend's Eel Pie Studios as well as the IBC Studios.

On Valentine's Day The Who recorded their concert at the University of Leeds. The band's first live album, called Live at Leeds was then released on 16th May. There had been thirty three songs on the set list on the original night of recording, not all could be included on the album, but such songs like Summertime Blues, Young Man's Blues and Substitute did make the final cut.

In late May, The Who spent a few days rehearsing in the Granada Theatre in Wandsworth, they hadn't been back to the venue since November 1968. Then they left for another American tour on 7th June - their seventh American tour, visiting the states of Columbia, Illinois and Texas.

In August, The Who returned to perform at their third **Isle of Wight Festival**. The Doors performed on the same day. Throughout September The Who were back touring in Europe and it wasn't until 18th October that The Who were back playing in London at the **Odeon Cinema, Lewisham**. In all of the years that The Who had played in London they hadn't played in this particular Odeon. The Beatles had in 1963 and the Bay City Rollers would in 1974. The Who wouldn't return until February 1982. What had started as the art deco style Lewisham Gaumont Palace in 1932 was long past its heyday, and not long after The Who played the building was closed and demolished.

The Who then played only one more time in London, at the **Hammersmith Palais** on 29th October, before closing their year with their **Roundhouse** concert. Although The Who would go onto play the Hammersmith Odeon on several occasions, they only played at the Hammersmith Palais the once.

Lovers of rock music seemed to be in a constant state of mourning in 1970, in April Paul McCartney had announced that he was quitting The Beatles, and in the weeks that followed, the most popular band ever disintegrated. And then, on 18th September, Jimi Hendrix was found dead in his home and Janis Joplin joined him in some bar in rock and roll heaven a few weeks later on 4th October. If the dying months of 1969 had closed the door tightly on the most significant decade for popular music, then 1970 certainly shut the lid on a very special era.

The remainder of the seventies would also take the lives of Jim Morrison, John Bonham and ultimately Keith Moon. The seventies handed a cruel blow to some of the most important pioneers in rock music.

But this wasn't the end (as Jim Morrison had once sung) of rock music, far from it, because on the 20th December 1970 The Who returned to the **Roundhouse** in Camden. Elton John, America, Patto and a fifty strong Salvation Army choir joined The Who at this 'Implosion' fund raising concert.

CHAPTER NINE
1971 - WHO'S NEXT

Rehearsals for The Who's Lifehouse project and concerts began at the Young Vic Theatre in Waterloo on 4th January (and 14th Feb, 15th Feb, 1st March, 26th April, 5th May). Only a limited number of tickets were made available, so those who were at the Young Vic Theatre concerts were indeed privileged. It was only on the date scheduled for 22nd February that The Who failed to appear; Thunderclap Newman stood in for them.

The Lifehouse project kept The Who busy throughout the beginning of the year, but in April they booked themselves into Olympic Sound Studios in Barnes to record some new material that would contribute towards Who's Next. Also in April, Townshend's daughter Aminta Alice was born and in July Keith Moon bought Tara House-an entire book could be devoted to the tales of parties and motor car incidents at this home alone.

In the summer, The Who were back touring America and their next London appearance wasn't until 18th September at the Oval Cricket Ground, Kennington. It was during this concert that the ever-ready to have a laugh Keith Moon decided to play his drums using a cricket bat that he had grabbed off of Jeff Dexter (once he was finished he tossed it into the 31,000 strong crowd). The Who played most of their Who's Next album to 35,000 people. The Who were joined by The Faces on the day, Kenney Jones bashing away on the drums.

The Who's next London engagement was on 4th November where they were booked to open up the Rainbow Theatre in Finsbury Park - they returned again for further shows on 5th Nov and 6th Nov. It had been 1966 when the Who last played at the venue; only back then it was the Astoria Cinema.

After the Rainbow Theatre concerts, The Who flew to America again and spent the remainder of the year out there. They didn't return to England until mid-January 1972.

CHAPTER TEN
1972 - JOIN TOGETHER

The Who played just one concert in London in 1972 and that was back in the Rainbow Theatre, Finsbury on 9th December where they performed *Tommy* on a stage designed to look like a huge pinball machine.

They each spent time engaging in various projects and activities that interested them. Townshend flew to India to be closer to Meher Baba, Entwistle's son Christopher Alexander John was born and he finished his second solo album *(Whistle Rymes)*. Daltrey also had a new addition to his family when his daughter Rosie Lea was born in October, and Moon continued to party, often joining the band Sha Na Na wherever they happened to be playing and being filmed for the movie *That'll be the Day* and as a band the Who spent time recording in Olympic Studios - songs like Long Live Rock and Relay, they also went on a short tour in Europe.

CHAPTER ELEVEN
1973 - I WOKE UP IN A SOHO DOORWAY

Similar to the previous year, The Who played only a handful of times in London during 1973 and when they did it wasn't until the closing weeks of the year. They played the Lyceum on 11th, 12th and 13th November and on 13th December at the Rainbow Theatre, Finsbury.

Tommy was presented, however, the only Who member to be involved with this was Roger Daltrey, but he was joined by a cast of actors including amongst other characters from the Tommy show - David Essex, Elkie Brooks and Bill Oddie, and they were backed by the London Symphony Orchestra.

Adam Porges, who had only recently become a teenager, was at one of the Lyceum concerts: 'It was November 1973, and coming to the end of the Quadrophenia tour. On the approach to this I had read that the band had been having terrible problems with all sorts of things and at one point Townshend had even attacked one of the road crew on stage too.

I was only thirteen and had by that time had already seen Slade and Roxy Music. I then found out there was going to be some Who concerts at the Lyceum in London and I decided that I wanted to go. I loved my rock music and although I had sort of heard of Mods, I really didn't know very much, or the real connection to Quadrophenia.

On the day the tickets went on sale, I got up very early and got the tube to the Lyceum. I strolled out of Holborn tube station at the crack of dawn and headed for the Lyceum. And then I saw this endless queue that stretched all the way along by the side of the theatre and round the block. The queue was full of people with long hair, wearing sheepskins and some were sprawled out over the pavement, either asleep or just chilled out. It was evident that many had been outside the Lyceum most of the night; or at least from the very, very early hours of the morning.

Now, being slight of build and a bit of a little urchin, I simply jumped in the queue near the front. And the best bit was, absolutely no one said a word. I don't know whether they just hadn't noticed or just thought, cheeky little monster, and allowed me to get away with it. I still had to wait almost four hours until the box office actually opened. But I got my Who ticket and one for my friend.

My memory isn't completely clear on this one, but somehow I ended up sitting in really good seats up stairs. I know I walked around down stairs too. I found out after the concert that the sound and the view downstairs was really terrible. But anyway, I found myself upstairs in the front row of a small area that had several tables with lamps on them. I wondered if it was the area reserved for press. Like I had with the queue outside, I just shuffled in and found a great spot with the most fantastic view, and no one challenged me.

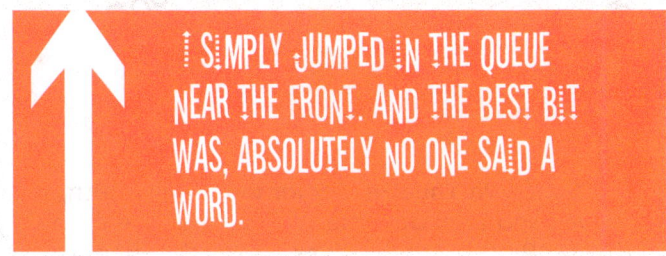

> I SIMPLY JUMPED IN THE QUEUE NEAR THE FRONT. AND THE BEST BIT WAS, ABSOLUTELY NO ONE SAID A WORD.

Watching The Who from the vantage point that I had was amazing to say the least. And one of the best bits was that I could get a clear view of Keith Moon. He had the most enormous drum kit; I had never seen anything like it. Moon was also wearing his headphones. Watching him play those drums left me speechless. He just kept going round and around his drums with such power and such speed. It blew me away. He had so much energy. Moon was immense.

During the concert they played virtually all of *Quadrophenia* but I believe they had dropped a couple of songs because they simply hadn't worked live on stage. And then the last part of the set they played a bunch of their monsters. They were all superb throughout the entire concert; Daltrey swung his microphone around, and at times it looked like it might even reach where I was sitting in the balcony, Townshend just played amazingly and Entwistle, as usual, stood still looking very cool.'

Dermot Bassett was also at the Lyceum: 'As much as I love Quadrophenia, those shows at the time were a bloody shambles; which sort of detracted from it. It was as if they just couldn't capture the great live feel that they had done around 1970/71. I went to the Lyceum shows and they had problems with the tapes and this meant the whole Quadrophenia thing just wouldn't work live. The shows just didn't live up to the album. However, the Quad shows of 2014 at the O2 were fantastic. The album was performed in a way it simply couldn't have had been back in 1973. At the O2 they had extra musicians, staff, equipment and sound systems that they couldn't have imagined back in the 1970s.

On the day that the tickets went on sale for the Lyceum, for whatever reason I didn't get there early enough. The queue stretched almost back to Charing Cross Station. My brother in law and me jumped the queue; something I had never done before. We got a few looks but nobody said anything. I've since heard that quite a few people did the same as us, I spoke to Who writer Matt Kent, and he told me that he had bunked off school that day and also had jumped the queue.'

> 'AS MUCH AS I LOVE QUADROPHENIA, THOSE SHOWS AT THE TIME WERE A BLOODY SHAMBLES; WHICH SORT OF DETRACTED FROM IT.'

At the **Sundown Theatre, Edmonton** on 18th, 19th, 22nd Dec and 23rd Dec The Who played 'The Who's Christmas Party'. Babe Ruth served as the support. The Who had played this venue back in 1966 when it was called the Regal. In 1968 the venue changed its name to the Sundown Theatre.

This was the year that The Who camped out in Ramport Studios to record *Quadrophenia*. Ramport Studios, at 115 Thessaly Road in Battersea, were built within premises that had once been a church hall. The Who had decided it best to create their own studio, something that would meet their recording needs, so they purchased the building and installed a 16-track recording desk. **Georgiana Steel-Waller**, the band's friend and one time Moon's girlfriend, ran the place while The Who went about their business.

Georgiana: 'When I got back we took to hanging out in places like the Speakeasy Club. There was a crowd of us that included Wiggy and Cy (Langston). It was great. During one of the conversations something came up about needing someone to run Ramport studios and I got the job. There were a bunch of girls that would hang around outside the studio and we got friendly too.'

During the studio's life other bands like Supertramp, Thin Lizzy and Judas Priest also used it. The four tall chimneys of Battersea Power Station (made famous on the album cover of Animals by Pink Floyd) could be seen from the windows of Ramport and in the streets surrounding the studio a young Mod (someone Townshend had met outside the studio) was photographed posing and riding around on a scooter. These photos were used in the inner-sleeve of the *Quadrophenia* album.

Peter 'Dougal' Butler: "Ramport Studios was in an old church hall. In fact when The Who took it over they had to have it deconsecrated...and then exorcized afterwards because of what went on in there! When the band were recording Quadrophenia and I was working for Keith, I spent a lot of time in there. The band got let down with the recording equipment and ended up having to use Ronnie Lane's mobile studio.

A typical day at Ramport would include getting there about two in the afternoon, sit around and have a chat, maybe listen to some of Pete's demos or have a run through something, then we'd often go for a drink down the pub that was just along from the studios, then we would return about three hours later and the band would work on something and then we'd be heading back off down to the pub, stay there until closing time at 11 o'clock and then go and spend the remainder of the night down the Speakeasy. I would then get home around five in the morning, go to bed, then get up and do it all again.

To see the band working together in Ramport was phenomenal. To witness Pete produce one of his demo tapes and share with those present what was on it was unbelievable. And then I would watch the band put it all together and produce the song. It was just brilliant. It was genius. It was incredible. For me, sitting behind that big glass window in the mixing recording booth was like 'fucking hell'. And I saw a lot of that and even after all the years that I was with Keith and The Who, I never lost the feeling that I was around something special and amazing. It was the same for the live shows, at the end of the night, back stage in the dressing room after having heard songs like Won't Get Fooled Again or My Generation, the hairs would still stand up on the back of my neck.

And as a band they put everything into their live performances. They would come back stage afterwards and be totally physically fucking exhausted. And they would be on a high too, not a drugs high, a natural high. I've seen a lot of bands in my time but no others touch them; and I'm not just saying that because they were my band and I had been a Mod. As a rock band they were terrific all the time.'

> AS A BAND THEY PUT EVERYTHING INTO THEIR LIVE PERFORMANCES. THEY WOULD COME BACK STAGE AFTERWARDS AND BE TOTALLY PHYSICALLY FUCKING EXHAUSTED.

I'm Free was released in July and 5.15 in October the same month The Who decamped to Shepperton Studios to rehearse for their forthcoming tour of the UK. Shepperton, Surrey, boasts some of the most outstanding areas of natural beauty that the Home Counties has to offer. Therefore, it's not surprising that some of the most affluent members of society have chosen Surrey as their home. Apart from its lush green slopes and leafy valleys, the M25 and London are not too far away, and this has been a desirable pull for anyone that needs to get into London for work, or to simply have an evening out. And for those that have needed to venture out of London to visit Shepperton, it can be done with very little drama.

In the mid-17th Century a manor house was built in Littleton village in the borough of Spelthorne and just two miles from the River Thames. It was named Littleton Park House and had beautiful black and white marble flooring and impressive ornate fireplaces. In 1931 Littleton Park caught the attention of a Scottish businessman called Norman Loudon. Loudon was looking for premises in the South of England that would make a suitable home for his new business venture called Sound Film (also known as Sound City). Loudon built his studios on the site, and by late 1932 he was already making his first short films.

During the Second World War filming movies ceased in the studios. Instead they were used to store sugar. After the war the studio's ownership changed to British Lions Films and by the time The Who gathered in their studio space (which they had bought the previous year) for the day on Thursday 25th May 1978, the studios had become Shepperton Studios, and had been the location in which such great films such as 2001: A Space Odyssey, the Omen and Star Wars had been made.

The reason The Who were filming and recording that day was a second attempt of capturing material for their *The Kids Are Alright* film. The first attempt, at the Gaumont State Theatre in Kilburn on 15th December 1977, had only produced a small amount of quality material that was deemed suitable for usage.

A version of *My Wife* and a few words from Pete Townshend was pretty much all that was kept, whilst the rest of Jeff Stein's work was discarded.

But quality material that reflected The Who as they currently were was still required. The film producers had decided that The Who should be seen as the strong and successful band that they still were. For many, the music industry was at the dawn of a new era, and one that many music lovers would have difficulty understanding. Punk and New Wave had exploded with such a bang that even the heavyweight acts that had dominated the sixties and seventies couldn't fail to notice. In 1977, for example, an angry young three-piece band from Woking in Surrey, called The Jam, had been signed to Polydor Records and released their debut album called In the City. The Jam's songwriter Paul Weller stood out and slightly away from his Punk peers. Instead, Weller dressed and played his guitar more like one of his idols-Pete Townshend. The Jam were an example of what was new and what a large portion of the young music buying public wanted. For many, there were evident links between Weller's Jam and The Who.

Not only did The Jam have a song and album called *In the City*; they also did cover versions of the Batman Theme and would go on to record further versions of *Disguises* and *So Sad About Us*. But with bands like The Jam, The Clash and the Sex Pistols stealing some of the thunder from the seventies rockers, it certainly didn't mean that The Who were done and dusted. Far from it, but certain events were destined to change the course of The Who's history and ultimate direction. And there would be nothing that they could do about it.

However, a date for the second attempt was agreed and their space in the Shepperton Studios organised. On 25th May (Paul Weller's birthday) The Who crashed through many songs that included *Magic Bus, My Generation* and *Summertime Blues*, but only versions of *Baba O Reilly* and *Won't Get Fooled Again* made the final cut of the Kids Are Alright film. Only after the final song had been played and the amplifiers turned off, did the members of The Who join a collection of invited fans and friends in the grounds of Shepperton Studios for some tea and a selection of fresh sandwiches. For those present on that day in May, it would have been the last that they would have seen Keith Moon sitting behind his drum kit, playing along with the band that he had been an integral component in for fifteen years. Keith Moon would die four months later.

....

In November and December The Who embarked on their US and Canadian Quadrophenia tour and it was also in 1973 that Bill Curbishley, an employee of Track Records, effectively took over the management of The Who from Lambert and Stamp. Two years later Trinifold was formed.

CHAPTER TWELVE
1974 – LONG LIVE ROCK

Going into 1974, Townshend was busy working on extra music for the film score of *Tommy*, Moon was wrapping himself in *Stardust* (the sequel to That'll Be the Day) and packing his bags so that he could move into a beachfront address on the Pacific Coast Highway in Santa Monica. John Lennon, Ringo Starr and Harry Nilsson hung out a lot and were engaged in recording with Nilsson. The Who also ventured into France for more shows before Townshend returned to perform his first ever solo set on 14th April at the Roundhouse, Chalk Farm, Camden. It was a benefit concert fundraising for the Camden Square Community Play Centre.

Filming for *Tommy* was also well underway and then on 18th May The Who played a concert at the Charlton Athletic Football Ground - it was the first time that a football stadium was used to host a rock concert, again another demonstration of how innovative The Who could be. The supports were Humble Pie, Lindisfarne, Lou Reed, Bad Company, Maggie Bell and Montrose. The event was filmed by the BBC and an estimated 80,000 fans squeezed themselves in the terraces and across the pitch.

....

Children's book illustrator Richard Schaller was just one Who fan in the Charlton crowd on that day:
' I certainly remember the excitement at the prospect of at last seeing my favourite rock band The Who perform live. They would top the bill at the Summer of 1974 Festival at The Valley, home of Charlton Football Club, and it was an opportunity not to be missed!

It was college times and money was in short supply. So quite often I would choose to spend it going to Stamford Bridge more than going to gigs. But when we could manage it, me and some buddies would often go to the Kursaal in Southend-on-Sea to see bands such as Hawkwind and Humble Pie. The Dagenham Roundhouse would sometimes be a venue on a Saturday night where we would see bands such as Status Quo and Manfred Mann's Earth Band.

But The Who would always stand out for me on radio or on album. When I played my Who's Next album for the first time three years earlier the music hit me like a bolt of lightning. A vibrant mix of rock and storytelling that made me think for the first time about the life we were facing and the land we were living in. I was still at school then as well.

Well, thinking back forty years is not that easy when some of it is blurred at the edges but the performance of The Who that late spring afternoon and early evening at Charlton would always be indelible on the memory. In addition there was a list of support acts on the day that made the whole experience amazing value for money at £2.50! And a crowd of 80,000 plus would add to the atmosphere.

© Richard Schaller

Firstly, I remember a group of us from college went, and split up when we got there for some reason. Myself and buddy Trevor Morgan put a stakehold down on an area on the huge terrace bank which was directly opposite the stage at half a distance away but with a great view of the acts. The stage was set up beneath the main football stand. If I remember we had beer which was in the form a big party seven type can and we managed to hold back having a pee for the whole day as there was not that many loos available and it would also take ages to get to them anyway.

It rained quite hard when we got there early afternoon, but as the acts began the sun suddenly burst through and within minutes we were bone dry as the temperature shot up and the sun gave us its full force for the rest of the day. By the time the show was done we both had sunburnt backs to take home with us.

As for the show, the impressive line-up began to unravel as the afternoon wore on. No need to go through them in detail, other than to remember how good heavy rock band Montrose were and also Glasgow's very own Janis Joplin, Maggie Bell was impressive. But the performance of Stevie Marriot's Humble Pie was the highlight of the show before The Who hit the stage. The Small Faces were the first band I liked when at school years earlier. Then, Stevie Marriot was the original mod icon. By 1974 Humble Pie had been playing the circuits for five or so years and, playing mainly hard rock originally, were now reverting back to Stevie Marriot's R&B and Soul roots. Marriot's voice was vibrantly unique. I remember 'I Don't Need No Doctor' being brilliantly performed with the crowd totally into it.

> 'THE LATE SPRING DUSK SKY MIXED IN WITH THE STAGE LIGHTING... A GREAT BACKDROP FOR THE BAND TO PLAY AGAINST.'

The Who would perform a two-hour set during which the sun finally set behind the stand that the stage was set in the front of. This added to the atmosphere as the late spring dusk sky mixed in with the stage lighting. A great backdrop for the band to play against. And boy did they. I cannot compare to them any other band whose members had their own unique style of body language and performance. Pete Townshend would often do his windmill guitar playing while jigging along the stage.

Roger Daltrey would march on the spot while belting out his songs, holding up his mic towards the sky above his head with his outstretched arms while Townshend played his solo. And then John Entwistle- his body motionless apart from all his fingers, one set whizzing up and down the fret of his bass guitar while his other set would tap ferociously on the bass strings. At the same time Keith Moon would be performing his brilliant drum sequence in his indomitable style of wide-eyed animal behaviour and manic high energy. His massive drum kit would include two huge gongs behind him.

I remember clearly, still to this day, how wonderfully The Who performed *'Baba O' Riley'* as the sun set behind. The whole crowd was one with the song. I loved Keith Moon's singing part (if you can call it that!) in *Bell Boy* which was from their then recently written *Quadraphenia*. My all-time favourite Who song *Won't Get Fooled Again* was performed brilliantly. To hear this for the first time live was a bit special for me! It was a cracking day forty years ago.'

....

Throughout the remainder of the summer the filming of *Tommy* pushed forward and Entwistle worked on the *Odds and Sods* project (it was released in October). Daltrey signed the Steve Gibbons Band to the record label, Goldhawk, that he and Bill Curbishley had set up. The Who's old manager Pete Meaden ended up co-managing them, along with Curbishley.

Pete Meaden died from a barbiturates overdose at his parents' home in Edmonton on 29th July 1978. The importance of his life and what he had done and meant for The Who hadn't gone unnoticed - The Who paid for Meaden's funeral service costs. Meaden also left behind what is possibly the most famous quote explaining what Mod is - 'Mod living is an aphorism for clean living under difficult circumstances'.

Many an inspiring young Mod has since embraced and armed themselves with this insight.

CHAPTER THIRTEEN
1975 – DREAMING FROM THE WAIST

The Who's film *Tommy* was released in March and nobody could deny Roger Daltrey's status as a rock and roll superstar. He had pulled off the role of the 'deaf, dumb and blind boy' perfectly. Not one for wanting to be left out, in April Moon released his debut solo album *Two Sides of the Moon*. And then on the 3rd October The Who's next album *The Who By Numbers* was released.

In mid-October, a few days before flying off to play some concerts in Europe, The Who played again at the Empire Pool, Wembley on 21st, 23rd and 24th October. In November The Who flew out to tour the US again and then they were back playing at the Odeon Hammersmith on 21st, 22nd and 23rd December for the shows titled 'Merry Xmas From the 'Orrible 'oo'.

It was at one of the Hammersmith shows where Daltrey wore a tee shirt with the words 'George Davis is Innocent' written across it. Daltrey was one of many who voiced their feelings regards the imprisonment of George Davis. Davis had been convicted earlier in the year for his involvement in an armed robbery against the London Electricity Board. He had been administered a twenty year prison sentence, but many believed him to be innocent. For several years, many walls across London had been daubed with the words 'George Davis is innocent' or 'Justice for George Davis'. More often than not the graffiti remained on the walls until either nature or the local council intervened.

In May 2011 at the Court of Appeal three judges quashed the raid on the London Electricity Board. On 23rd September 1977 George Davis pleaded guilty to his part in a raid on the Bank of Cyprus on Seven Sisters Road. He was released from prison in 1984.

Peter 'Dougal' Butler:
'I saw several bands at the Hammersmith Palais, but The Who only once. It was quite a grand place really, with balconies.

Me and my mates would go up to the balconies and survey the crowd below. We'd pick out the girls that we fancied and then go down and talk to them.'

CHAPTER FOURTEEN
1976 – THE PUNK AND THE GODFATHER

This would be the year that changed everything. This was the year that the British public got its first whiff of Punk rock. Thousands of members of the British public woke up on 2nd December to be confronted by the front line headlines of the Daily Mirror. 'The Filth and the Fury' reported the newspaper, making reference to the appearance of the Sex Pistols and members of the Bromley Contingent on the Bill Grundy Today show, aired at a time when most people were sitting comfortably in the front rooms scoffing their teas in peace.

> PUNK OF 1976 WAS REALLY JUST A VEHICLE THAT TOOK SOME PEOPLE TO SOME NEW PLACE. THE WHO WATCHED FROM A CAUTIOUS DISTANCE...

They had no idea that the Sex Pistols were about to invade their private space with their foul language and verbal attack 'you dirty bastard' and 'you dirty fucker' on the very British Bill Grundy. Who are these Punks? The Daily Mirror asked and out of the members of The Who, it was Pete Townshend who was especially interested. He, unlike many of his peers, didn't dismiss the scruffy, gobbing, swearing, and spotty young men out of hand; but then he had written the song The Punk and the Godfather for the Quadrophenia album three years earlier.

The Sex Pistols continued to tear their way through the music industry, some of the biggest record labels and a whole new generation of youth were born. Over the next three years they were joined by other punk bands like The Clash, The Jam, The Slits, The Damned and The Buzzcocks, but in reality the initial Punk explosion had only lasted a handful of months before it too got sucked into the commercial machine that even the scruffiest couldn't resist.

Because of Punk some good records were churned out, and many people that had never even considered being in a band or even get the opportunity to play on a stage or appear on television did get the chance, and some went on to have very lucrative and successful careers. Punk of 1976 was really just a vehicle that took some people to some new place. The Who watched from a cautious distance, Moon ventured into clubs like the Roxy to see what all the fuss was about, but of course wasn't accepted as one of their own. Punks were young people who hummed Anarchy in the UK and White Riot, their bands played in shitty clubs and their audiences danced strangely; they had nothing in common with an old band from the 1960s who their parents owned records by.

Punk wasn't a new thing for America. They had already seen its genesis in the bands that played at CBGBs in New York-the Ramones, Blondie and Johnny Thunders and the Heartbreakers. The Brit Punk bands did little to shock or shake their world. In fact Rolling Stone even voted The Who 'the Best Band of 1976'.

The Who could only do what they did best - they toured The Who By Numbers album and on 31st May they went back to perform again at the Charlton Athletic Football Ground. For this 'Who Put the Boot In' concert The Who were supported by Little Feat, the Sensational Alex Harvey Band, the Outlaws, Chapman- Whitney's Streetwalkers and Widowmaker. It rained hard all day and there were several violent outbreaks.

The Who did, however, manage to get themselves into the Guinness Book of Records as the 'World's Loudest Pop Group'.

CHAPTER FIFTEEN
1977 - THE KIDS ARE ALRIGHT

In July The Who were to be found camped out in Shepperton Studios, into part of which they had recently invested a considerably sum of money (£350,000). They did this so that they could use it whenever they wanted to, and their most current project was filming *The Kids Are Alright*.

In May, the Sex Pistols released *God Save the Queen* - it was banned from virtually every radio station. A few months on later 16th September, one of the original shakers and shockers of the 70's - Marc Bolan, died tragically in a car accident.

He was two weeks away from his thirtieth birthday.

On the morning of 15th December, Capitol Radio announced The Who would be playing that evening in the Gaumont State Theatre, Kilburn. Over 800 people showed up to see the band. Jeff Stein, who had been making The Kids Are Alright, filmed the event, intent on using some of the footage in his film (no footage actually made the final cut).

Peter 'Dougal' Butler: 'We went to the Gaumont State to film for *The Kids Are Alright*. The Gaumont was a lovely venue. It was all art deco and fabulous inside. They couldn't use the footage though because it wasn't good enough. Keith had played pissed and it wasn't good. The Who had managed to keep the concert quiet but had announced it the day before. And because they had announced that it was free to get in, it was packed. At the concert we had eight cameras filming, which was a lot of cameras and a lot of money.

I had been with Keith backstage and he had been getting more and more pissed and more and more silly. And then The Who went on stage and they played, but Keith kept going out of time. After the concert Pete and the others looked at the footage and realised that they couldn't use it. They knew it would cost a fortune but they had to re-shoot it. That was when they went to Shepperton Studios.

I was there that day and that was Keith's last gig with The Who. I wasn't working for Keith by that point; I had stopped working with him but I was working on the actual film with Jeff Stein.'

THE WHO 67 IN THE CITY

CHAPTER SIXTEEN
1978 – NOT TO BE TAKEN AWAY

The 25th May 1978 at Shepperton Studios, Middlesex was to be Keith Moon's last live performance with The Who. After this date The Who would never be the same again. How could they? On that May date, The Who played a few numbers, which included Won't Get Fooled Again, in front of a selected amount of fans and friends. The event was the idea of Jeff Stein, who was having a second attempt at trying to capture some good footage to be included in *The Kids Are Alright*.

On 7th September Keith Moon died. Naturally this was a sad and confusing time for the members of The Who and its management, and everyone that knew Moon. Keith had died at his flat in Curzon Place.

Peter 'Dougal' Butler: 'Even after I stopped working with Keith I carried on seeing him. I remember going around to his flat in Curzon Place, we had a good chat and he told me that he had given up this and that; but I had my doubts. I knew the flat well because for a time I lived there with him and Harry Nilsson. It was a fantastic place, two bedrooms and very ultra-modern. Pete Townshend ended up buying the flat off of Harry Nilsson.

I even saw Mama Cass dead in that flat. There was a period when Keith and I moved out and at the time she was in London doing some shows and it was arranged that she would stay there. She used the master bedroom, the one that Keith used, and in that room was an area that was used as a wardrobe. During a visit back to London I had to return to the flat to pick up some of Keith's clothes that he needed. I phoned Mama Cass management and explained to them what I needed to do and it was arranged that I could go round there. When I walked in there was someone there from the management with another person. I was told that Mama Cass was still in bed and still asleep. The thing was, I didn't have time to hang around so I asked if I could tiptoe into the bedroom and just gather up the clothes quietly and I was told yes. I pushed open the door and walked into the semi-dark bedroom. I couldn't help but notice Mama Cass hanging half out of the King size bed; everything was hanging out. I didn't think too much about it and as quietly as I could, grabbed Keith's clothes and left the bedroom, said my goodbyes and jumped in the Rolls Royce that Keith had at the time. I popped into the office and then headed out to see my parents who lived near Hayes. I was driving with the radio on and this newsflash comes on announcing that Mama Cass had died in her bed in the flat she was staying at. Fuck me! I nearly crashed the motor. I couldn't believe that only a few hours earlier I had seen Mama Cass in her bed and she had been dead all the time.

Mama Cass was great. Keith and me had met her a few times. We had all hung out in Laurel Canyon in the early seventies with people like John Sebastian of the Lovin' Spoonful and people from that scene. We had a fantastic time with that lot.'

Some suspected that would be the end of The Who and maybe for a brief moment so did Townshend, Daltrey and Entwistle, but to the words on the back of the *Who Are You* album 'not to be taken away' meant more than just Moon's departure. The Who weren't going anywhere either.

Who Are You was The Who's eighth studio album and was released in the UK on 18th August. Keith Moon died twenty days later. In May The Who had filmed a promotional video for the release of the double A-side of *Who Are You* and *Had Enough*. The Who were filmed in a studio playing the song. Moon wore a bright red tee shirt with Keith written in white on it. He blew and puffed his way through the song, often bouncing on his drum stool, twiddling his drum sticks and grinning away like a Cheshire cat. That energy unique to Moon and the chemistry special to his relationships with Townshend, Daltrey and Entwistle is displayed loud and clear. The Who are a rock band and in the video, a band of brothers who are demonstrating what they do best.

Other than on that day in Shepperton, it would be the last time they would be seen in that spirit.

CHAPTER SEVENTEEN
1979 – WHO'S NEXT

Even though Daltrey was initially resistant to the idea of having Kenney Jones take over the drumming duties for The Who, both Townshend and Entwistle were able to convince him that their old friend, whom they had known and hung out with since their 1960s Mod days, was the best choice. So Kenney Jones joined The Who and the next phase of the band began.

Having caught the 'bug' for being involved in film making throughout 1979, The Who included themselves in the making of *Quadrophenia*. Based on the band's album from six years earlier, and taking them back on a nostalgic trip to 1964, the film was about the story of a young Mod named Jimmy Cooper and follows him as he rides around London on his scooter, falling in and out of Mod clubs, relationships and confrontations with the Mods' rivals the Rockers.

Quadrophenia, released in September, was directed by Franc Roddam and produced by Bill Curbishly and Roy Baird. It also included a bumper cast of young people who were relatively new to the film industry but who would go on to carve out successful careers in the 'biz'. The likes of Phil Daniels, who played the main character Jimmy, Leslie Ash, his love interest Steph, Ray Winstone, his friend but a Rocker, and Sting who played the Ace Face, all have since become household names. What was more, *Quadrophenia* has gone down as being the greatest youth culture film ever, and rightly so. In 2014 a book about the making of *Quadrophenia* was written by Simon Wells and published by Countdown Books. The book had been waiting to be written for a long time and it was well received. The book was a fitting testament to the deep meaning of the film, what it represented and what its soundtrack meant to so many people.

Although the soundtrack to *Quadrophenia* included many great Who songs such as *5.15*, *I'm The Face*, *I Am The Sea* and *Love Reign O'er Me*, there were also many brilliant songs from back in the day when the first wave of Mods roamed the streets of London - *Green Onions* by Booker T and the MGs, *Night Train* by James Brown and *Louie Louie* by The Kingsmen had been great in the days of the Scene and the Flamingo Clubs and still sounded good over a decade later.

What the film also did was introduce a whole new generation to the Mod music from the sixties. The year before *Quadrophenia* was released there had been 'rumblings' in the East End of London from a small gathering of young people, helped on by the foresight of a young West Ham supporter called Grant Fleming, who were starting to dress like the bands they were discovering from the 60s. Small at first, but quickly gathering pace, the second wave of Mod was on the verge of exploding into something very influential. A three-piece band from Woking, called The Jam, led by angry and energetic front man Paul Weller, were spearheading the revivalist Mod scene. They were quickly joined by other bands like Secret Affair, Purple Hearts and the Merton Parkas. Without a doubt, *Quadrophenia* helped introduce Mod to the masses and it got very big and left behind a legacy that remains to this day.

The Who's first concert of 1979 with Jones was at the familiar Rainbow Theatre, Finsbury Park. Dermott Bassett attended the shows: 'I went to all three nights of the Rainbow's opening. It was The Who's first shows with Kenney Jones and the last thing that me and my mates wanted was a Keith Moon wannabe. There were plenty of conversations where people would say Moon's replacement should have been so

> **WHAT THE FILM ALSO DID WAS INTRODUCE A WHOLE NEW GENERATION TO THE MOD MUSIC FROM THE SIXTIES.**

and so, or there could only be so to do the job because they play like Moon; but I would retort, no one else can play like Keith, absolutely no one. That first night at the Rainbow was very emotional. I had spent the night lying on the pavement waiting to get my ticket for that concert but I'm glad I did because seeing The Who at those Rainbow gigs were like seeing The Who starting all over again. They were a different band, they were like a new band and I didn't mind that. I was just pleased that they were carrying on, because after I had heard that Moon had died, like most people, I thought the band would finish. I think by the time The Who were playing those Rainbow concerts they were at their peak. The years of 1970 and 1971 they were just incredible. Their performance was superb, they had great energy; they were just from a different world at that point.'

....

Peter 'Dougal' Butler: 'I had seen The Who rehearsing with Kenney and it was a bit strange seeing Kenney playing up on the stage with them, but I thought they were good. It was great to see Kenney and it was sad at the same time. At the time I didn't see it as being a 'new' Who. I don't know if Kenney was the right choice but that's what happened. And then years later Simon Phillips took over and he was a very good drummer. But you cannot compare any of them to Keith-they are all different. I think I only really started to think of The Who as being an outfit with an identity of its own after John died. John was such a powerful force in The Who-you can really tell that he isn't there anymore. And then I think the inclusion of Zak is the best thing that has happened to them since Keith. Zak plays very close to Keith's style and when they go into what they call free-fall, it's like Keith all over again. When they were in free-fall it didn't matter how drunk or drugged up Keith was - he would watch Pete and John like a hawk; they used to read each other so well. I don't think any of the other Who drummers have been able to do that, except for Zak. And that's not knocking any of the other drummers, that's just what I've seen. Keith was the natural drummer for The Who, he couldn't have played drums in, say, The Faces.'

On 18th August The Who played Wembley Stadium. The doors were opened at 2pm and the event went through until 10pm. 80,000 people filled the impressive stadium that had hosted so many great events from football (England beat Germany in the World Cup in 1966) to rugby and even stock car racing since it had built for £750,000 in 1923. On that summer's day,

The Who were supported by the Stranglers, AC/DC and Nils Lofgren. Tickets were £8 in advance and £8.50 on the day and the promotional poster depicted a large ferocious lion wearing a red tee shirt which said 'The Who and Friends Roar In'.

In early December, while The Who were on tour in the States, tragedy struck. At their concert in Cincinnati eleven people were trampled on and crushed in the stampede as thousands of concert-goers tried to access the venue. The Who cancelled their next two shows at the Riverside Coliseum but did play at the Pontiac Silverdrome before returning to the UK. The whole experience painfully affected all the members of The Who and their management.

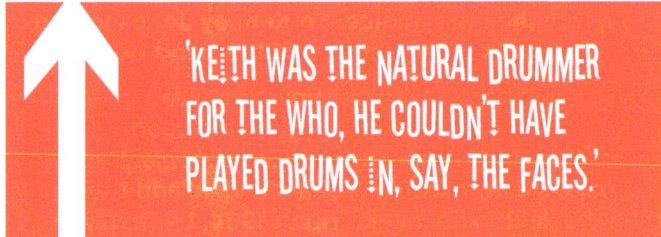

'KEITH WAS THE NATURAL DRUMMER FOR THE WHO, HE COULDN'T HAVE PLAYED DRUMS IN, SAY, THE FACES.'

Across four nights in December, Paul McCartney organised fund raising concerts to help victims of the Cambodian war. The 'Concerts For The People Of Kampuchea' were held in the Hammersmith Odeon. Queen kicked off the events on the 26th, then on the 27th Ian Dury and the Blockheads, The Clash and Matumbi, on the 28th it was The Who, The Pretenders and The Specials. Included in The Who's set was *Substitute, I Can't Explain, 5.15* and *Behind Blue Eyes*.

On the final night on the 29th Wings performed alongside Elvis Costello and the Attractions, Rockpile and Rockestra.

CHAPTER EIGHTEEN
1980 - WHOOLIGANS

The Who didn't play any concerts in London at all in 1980, they did however tour North and West America, finishing up at the Exhibition Stadium in Toronto.

Townshend finished his solo album *Empty Glass*; he also found a new home on the Kings Road which he would stagger back to after spending boozy nights in various clubs around London like the New Romantics' exclusive hideaway club run by Steve Strange 'Club For Heroes' (one particular night Townshend took heroin, something that almost killed him).

Around this time, alcohol and cocaine also became constant features in Townshend's day to day activities. Daltrey on the other hand continued to engage in a more healthy living lifestyle and promoting the latest film that he was the main character in, called McVicar, and Entwistle and Jones got on with their lives, and they certainly weren't the types to abstain from a good night out.

CHAPTER NINETEEN
1981 - YOU BETTER YOU BET

A twenty-seven date tour of the UK, with John 'Rabbit' Bundrick on keyboards as a constant addition, was organised for 1981, the first London dates on 3rd and 4th February were at The Rainbow, Finsbury Park and these were quickly followed by playing at the Odeon Theatre, Hammersmith on 8th and 9th February.

The Rainbow concerts had been charity events for battered wives. Dogged by technical problems Daltrey threw his microphone down and walked off, announcing there'd be no encore; an encore was however delivered to an expectant audience. Townshend admitted to having played the gig 'pissed'.

In February The Who's latest single *You Better You Bet* was released. In March the album from which the single had been lifted *Face Dances* was released.

The album had been recorded the previous year in Odyssey Recording Studios in London. The studios, located in Marble Arch, had only opened in 1979. Daltrey would also record his solo album *Under A Raging Moon* there and so would other great albums like In Our Lifetime by Marvin Gaye and Alf by Alison Moyet.

On 9th, 10th and 11th March The Who performed in what had now been renamed Wembley Arena.

CHAPTER TWENTY
1982, 1983 AND 1984 – IT'S HARD

The Who played no concerts in London during 1982, 1983 and 1984. During some of these years Townshend battled with his drug abuse and spent weeks at a time in a drug withdrawal programme in Los Angeles.

His next solo album *All The Best Cowboys Have Chinese Eyes* was released, and he did what he could to improve his family life. Daltrey released an album called *Best Bits* in America and Europe but not in the UK.

As a collective, The Who were presented with an Ivor Novello Award for Services to the Rock Industry. They had been contributing to the music industry for over two decades by this point. The Who had managed to maintain their place in a music industry that had been going through changes since the days when they played in small clubs like the Paradise or the Scene. The early eighties were to be no different and The Who had their own pressures and played their Farewell Tour and released *The Who's Last album* as bands like Madness, Ultravox, Spandau Ballet and ABC dominated the British charts. For a while it even felt that bands that played 'real' instruments, other than just synthesizers, was to be a thing of the past.

During these years Townshend's Eel Pie Island's related projects and resources suffered financially and cuts were made; his Magic Bus Bookshop closed.

And in the April of 1983 The Who's old manager and friend Kit Lambert died. 'Without Kit there would probably not have been The Who' was one comment from Townshend.

CHAPTER TWENTY-ONE
1985 – WHO'S LAST

Going into the mid-80s The Who certainly appeared all but finished; they sold off their investments in both Shepperton Studios and Ramport Studios. And then, as the British summer started to unfold, The Who had were contacted by Bob Geldof.

For years, Ethiopia had been suffering from droughts and a cruel and intense civil war that had already killed thousands of people. In November 1984 Bob Geldof and Midge Ure decided they could help and organised the Band Aid event, which included getting together a list of musicians to record the song Do They Know It's Christmas. The song was a huge hit and raised eight million pounds. Realising that a few million pounds would only make a small dent in an increasingly desperate situation, Geldof and Ure organised the Live Aid events.

On 13th July 1985 77,000 people crammed into Wembley Stadium and nearly 90,000 into the John F. Kennedy Stadium in Philadelphia. The intention was to raise much more cash and bring the tragic events that were happening in Ethiopia to the attention of the world. It did just that, and on Saturday 13th July, over an estimated billion people watched the televised events.

Status Quo kicked off the event at Wembley Stadium at noon, they were followed by The Style Council, which included Steve White on drums, the youngest person to perform on the day (White would perform with The Who a few years down the line). The remainder of the day saw other such as Ultravox, U2, Dire Straits, David Bowie, Elton John and Paul McCartney, amongst many others, all take to the stage. The Who, sandwiched between David Bowie and Elton John, played an impressive set. It was their first live appearance since 1982. 'Rough but right' Rolling Stone Magazine described The Who's set and the band couldn't argue with that.

1986 and 1987 No London concerts

CHAPTER TWENTY-TWO
1988 – WHO'S BETTER WHO'S BEST

The Who had been very much present during the First Summer of Love, but twenty years down the road, much of Britain's youth was being swept along by the second. The music of the Second Summer of Love was full of sounds and beats that would have been unimaginable to the psychedelic subscribers of the late sixties.

By the time D-Mod released They Call It Acid and the call of accceeeddd could be heard virtually everywhere and Mr Fingers had declared 'and this is fresh', the underground Rave scene was well established and had produced anthems of its own such as Your Love by Frankie Knuckles, NRG by Adamski and Voodoo Ray by a Guy Called Gerald. Ravers had taken their music out of a handful of clubs in London, like Shoom, and were descending on warehouses and countryside fields near to the M25 to hold their illegal parties. It took the Police and the authorities a couple of years to catch on to what was happening, but when they did they took stern action.

For a solid two summers, Ravers had been wearing tee shirts with smiley faces on them, sipping their favourite choice of fluids - water or Lucozade - and had been dancing at the all-night raves whilst popping E's (ecstasy) with manes like Burgers and dropping acid with names like Microdots and Strawberry Fields. The organisers of the raves gave their parties names like Back to the Future and A Mid-Summer's Night Dream, and they depended on a network of pirate radio stations such as Centre-Force and Sunrise to help promote them. It was the most significant event in youth culture since punk, which had been over ten years earlier; for this 80s generation, Rave was their Punk.

Whatever the Who felt about this new electronic music and its scene, and about playing live again, they wouldn't do so in London again until 8th February 1988; and when they did it was in one of their favourite old stomping grounds - the Royal Albert Hall.

CHAPTER TWENTY-THREE
1989

Thankfully not every record in the charts or being played in the homes of the music buying public was 'dance' music. There were a few bands that were still able to break through.

Leading from the front, with obvious influential echoes from the past, were the Stone Roses and the Happy Mondays. This was also the year when someone took a large sledgehammer to the Berlin wall and it was the year that The Who embarked on their 25th Year Anniversary Tour.

The Who had now introduced several extra musicians, such as a percussionist and backing singers; something Daltrey initially rejected before being talked around. The tour kicked off in Toronto on 24th June with their new drummer Simon Phillips. The

Who's 25th anniversary tour ended back home in London playing at Wembley Arena on 23rd, 24th, 26th and 27thOctober.

Jed Bere was there on one of the October nights: 'I caught a coach up from Kent to Wembley Arena for The Who concert. One of the local newspapers used to put coaches on for events in London. Simon Phillips was on drums during that time. I had good seats on the ground level and just to the right of the stage, so the view and the sound was really good.

I kept my ticket stub too. It was a big deal seeing the band for the first time, a band that had meant so much to me since my Mod days in the early eighties.'

To close the year, The Who performed *Tommy* at two charity shows on 31st October and 2nd November at the Royal Albert Hall. In 1989 an estimated two million people had seen The Who play live; an awesome achievement for a bunch of ageing rockers.

CHAPTER TWENTY-FOUR
1990,1991, 1992, 1993, 1994 - NO LONDON GIGS

In 1990 The Who were inducted into the Rock and Roll Hall of Fame. Keith Moon' daughter Mandy was present to accept the award on behalf of her father, whom she had lost twelve years earlier.

The ceremony was held at the Waldorf Astoria Hotel in New York. As Mandy accepted the award she said 'It's fitting that I be here to accept for my dad. He would never have been able to get into this hotel. He was banned from the Waldorf', the audience laughed.

Although The Who were buzzing from their 1989 tour it wasn't to last. Townshend decided he didn't want to continue because he had other ventures that he wanted to pursue. Again each band member went their separate ways, for a period that would last until 1995.

CHAPTER TWENTY-FIVE
1995

When The Who resurfaced again, the musical landscape of the UK was in the grip of Brit Pop. The rise of a new scene in Britain had happened quickly.

As if from out of nowhere, four young men from Manchester who played in a band called Oasis, were confidently taking over the world. To many they represented rock and roll's last stand; they had it all: charm, anger, character, arrogance, but above all a collection of great songs, almost anthem-like, and they played real instruments. Oasis made guitar bands fashionable again.

Oasis also passionately shared their influences-The Beatles, The Jam, The Who. They even wore similar clothes to the ones that their influences had worn: button down shirts, crew neck jumpers and desert boots; only they put their own spin on it. As Brit Pop caught on, more and more kids rediscovered or were introduced to the music and clothes from the 1960s and Vespas and Lambrettas became sought after items again. A new type of Mod had appeared. For a period between the mid-90s and the end of that decade, music was interesting again.

On 16th September 1995 there was a Who convention held in the Bottom Line, Shepherds Bush. Roger Daltrey and John Entwistle performed a fantastic show to a grateful and appreciative audience.

CHAPTER TWENTY-SIX
1996

'It's like going to the dentist. It's good once you've done it' Daltrey told a reporter as he and The Who approached The Who Tour 1996-1997. It was the first time that the founding three members of The Who shared a stage again together as a band.

A show where *Quadrophenia* was to be performed was decided and the reason wasfor a Princes Trust event. The concert was held in Hyde Park on 29th June. On the day,The Who were joined by Phil Daniels (*Quadrophenia*'s Jimmy Cooper) who provided the narration, Gary Glitter provided the role of the Rocker, Ade Edmondson the Bell Boy and Stephen Fry the hotel manager. And on the day, Pink Floyd's Dave Gilmour joined The Who to play *Love Reign O'er Me* and *Dirty Jobs*.

Daltrey, Townshend and Entwistle's new Who included Zak Starkey on drums and Pete's brother Simon Townshend on guitar, plus a brass section and keyboards. Soon after the Hyde Park concert, The Who flew into New York and reproduced the show for six nights at Madison Square Gardens. The Who's new tour, that would stretch into 1997 and take them through Europe and North America, was well and truly underway. And back in London at the end of '96 The Who played two concerts at Earls Court on 6th and 7th December.

....

Johnny Bance: 'I saw The Who in Hyde Park, June 29, 1996. It was a huge gig with the whole of *Quadrophenia* played, and support was from Alanis Morrissette, Bob Dylan and Clapton (they were boring!). I remember that it was an overcast day, lots of different ages of people that cut right across the generations. Phil Daniels was superb and received huge cheers as "the narrator" doing the Jimmy bits of the story. Daltrey was on fire-fit and healthy and belted out the words with passion. He had a "mod target" bandage over one of his eyes after being accidentally hit by Gary Glitter in rehearsals with a microphone. We were in the middle of the park with good views, huge screens helped to capture the atmosphere perfectly.'

Bassist Paul Moss was also in the audience on the 29th, 'It was a genuine surprise to hear in April 1996, not only that The Who would be performing in Hyde Park, but no less than *Quadrophenia* in its entirety, something not attempted since the rock opera's 1973 release. *Quadrophenia* has consistently been one of my favourite albums of all time since I first heard it in the early eighties and has always felt like a 'London' album. I purchased my first copy in a Camden Record Shop, I listened to it endlessly in either my Leytonstone home or on the tube, most of the story is set in London; so it only seemed fitting that this was going to happen in the capital.

> THE RUMOUR AT THE TIME WAS THAT PRINCE CHARLES HIMSELF CHOSE THE ACTS, ALTHOUGH IT SEEMS UNLIKELY THAT HIS ROYAL HIGHNESS IS AN ALANIS MORRISETTE FAN...

The Hyde Park event was put on by The Princes Trust, and the rumour at the time was that Prince Charles himself chose the acts, although it seems unlikely that His Royal Highness is an Alanis Morrisette fan, Jools Holland's Big Band and Bob Dylan's appearance was just enough to keep this idea alive.

The Hyde Park experience has certainly changed, and more recent events have more of a festival feel to them - back in 1996 I recall that stalls were sparse, a couple of burger vans, one T-shirt stall and a few program sellers. Worst of all, there was a strict 'no booze' policy for this event, you couldn't bring or buy any alcohol. It didn't stop a group of young Mods that I found myself standing next to, although what they were drinking was having quite an effect on their perception of reality, their claims that they tunnelled in to the event so they could get drink in seemed doubtful due to their spotless clothes, that despite trying to be Mod suits, were clearly fashioned in the early 70s. They seemed obsessed by two subjects, the first being Zak Starkey's ability to play Keith Moon's drum fills, the second being that The Merton Parkas were reforming for this event and would be on after Bob Dylan. (The Merton Parkas weren't and to my knowledge, never have reformed.)

After Bob Dylan's set, the stage was clearly being set

for The Who, with the exception of the Merton Parkas fans by me, and despite the lack of alcohol in the audience, the excitement level and the shoving for the front grew exponentially. Digital multimedia had come a long way from the dark times of the early seventies. The old tapes that played *I Am The Sea* or the orchestrated sections of *Love Reign O'er Me*, had frequently broken down or come in at the wrong time. Keith had kept time with them by means of a click track played through his headphones, along with his own recorded instructions "Middle eight coming up, 1-2-3-4." John Entwistle thought it was hilarious when at one show these were played through the PA by mistake.

....

By 1974 most of *Quadrophenia* had been dropped from the set, however by 1996 a lot had changed. Digital backing was more reliable, and working with click tracks had become the industry standard - it was also possible to synchronise this in with a video "multimedia" screen. So, after Jools Holland announced The Who's *Quadrophenia*, instead of listening to Keith Moon's drumming instructions, *I Am The Sea* played over the sound system while the screen showed a video of the Sea.

> **JOHN'S BASS PART DURING THE INTRO WAS IN HIS OWN WORDS "PLAYING A SILLY BASS PART AND THAT'S THE ONE THEY LIKED."**

As The Who launched into The Real Me the real sound of "The Oo" became apparent. For those of us that were unfortunate enough not to experience the band in the sixties or seventies heyday, or those of us that grew up listening on cheap record or cassette players, there is a whole sonic netherworld that you may never have heard before, for the "Real Who", it's all about the bass.

So for sure, those familiar lines John Entwistle plays on record were spot on, but you didn't just hear them, you felt them. John's bass part during the intro was in his own words "playing a silly bass part and that's the one they liked." But this is the melodic intro to this song, the counterpoint to Daltrey's verses and underpins the frustration of the chorus. That afternoon, the bass washed over me, as always John's performing made it look effortless and cool, his gold maxima strings gleaming in the sun, his custom Buzzard bass guitar that went through a myriad of processors and amps, thunder-fingers made this band sound like The Who.

Fast-forward ten years and I'm back again in Hyde Park to see The Who. Much has changed; Pete has come out from behind his acoustic and is windmilling on a fender Stratocaster, Roger looked more like a Shepherds Bush Mod and less like a Greek god, and in a relaxed, enlightened 2006, you can even buy a beer. One thing is sadly missing, John's passing in 2002 has left more than just a huge hole in the lives of his family and friends, it's the difference between watching a storm on TV or watching a real storm.

Back in '96 we are feeling the Ox Thunder during *5:15*, John's bass solo using his "tapping/typewriter" technique was raising cheers from all over the park - over the next six years, John would expand this solo, but in the moment we all thought that this would probably be that last Who show we would ever see. It's increasingly difficult to remember an age where we were not informed on every bit of information. Some had said that Phil Daniels might be playing Jimmy, but no one could be sure that was happening until we saw him on stage. Being joined by Adrian Edmonson, Stephen Fry and Trevor McDonald was an extra surprise and a joy. It wouldn't be until the following day I would learn about the upcoming dates at Madison Square Garden and the North American Tour. So as the final strains of *Love Reign O'er Me* rang around Hyde Park, and it was clear that there would be no encore, none of us could be sure that there would be another show by The Who.

As the crowd and myself wisely moved away from the stage before Eric Clapton's lifeless acoustic slot, the 70s Mods were nodding approvingly about Zak Starkey, commenting he'd got most of Moon's drum fills right and were getting to the front of the stage to see The Merton Parkas. "I bet you a hundred quid they start with *You Need Wheels*…"

I'd see John with The Who again, later that year at Earls Court. This was *Quadrophenia* with an expanded multimedia show and some hits in the encore. Whilst these shows and subsequent ones sounded more polished, they lacked the edge, uncertainty and excitement of Hyde Park.'

> **AS THE FINAL STRAINS OF *LOVE REIGN O'ER ME* RANG AROUND HYDE PARK, AND IT WAS CLEAR THAT THERE WOULD BE NO ENCORE, NONE OF US COULD BE SURE THAT THERE WOULD BE ANOTHER SHOW BY THE WHO.**

CHAPTER TWENTY-SEVEN
1997

Having spent the earlier part of 1997 on tour, The Who did return to play at Wembley Arena on Sunday 18th May. For an admission price of £27.50 The Who fan got to hear *Quadrophenia* performed again.

By this time P J Proby was joining The Who to perform *The Punk and the Godfather* and *I've Had Enough*. *I Am The Sea*, *The Real Me* and *Quadrophenia* opened the show while *Behind Blue Eyes*, *Substitute* and *Who Are You* closed it.

The Quadrophenia tour was initially going to be called TED In The Shed (Townshend, Entwistle, Daltrey). However, the title was considered rubbish and it was dropped.

1998 No London concerts

CHAPTER TWENTY-EIGHT
1999

In 1999, The Who played only seven times-five of which were in America. One of the shows in October was filmed, and a DVD of the show, called The Vegas Job, was released. The Who had appeared at the Pixelon launch event held in Las Vegas on 29th October.

The Who's concerts at the House of Blues in Chicago on 12th and 13th November, and at the Shepherds Bush Empire on 22nd and 23rd December, were recorded and the songs contributed to The Who's live album called Blues To The Bush. On the Shepherds Bush nights the set included *I Can't Explain, Substitute, Pure and Easy, I'm A Boy, Magic Bus* amongst many other familiar and well-loved tunes. While Townshend, Daltrey and Entwistle continued to be joined by Zak Starkey and John 'Rabbit' Bundrick (they had dropped the brass section and backing vocals) their newest live album included such tracks as *Pinball Wizard, Pure and Easy, Boris The Spider, Won't Get Fooled Again* and a nine-minute version of *My Generation*. This was also the year that the Who re-introduced *Anyway, Anyhow, Anywhere* into their set; they hadn't been performing it live since 1966.

Writer Stuart Deabill remembers Townshend being on form on one of the Bush nights, 'it was an intimate gig in their, and my, old manors, and I wasn't going to miss that. Fantastic night, grown men weeping at being that close to the band rather than the usual arena / stadium shows and the band were enjoying themselves as well.

My abiding memory of the night was when, halfway through the gig, in-between songs Pete asked the audience if there was anyone in from the Bush, me and a couple of others cheered and then some geezer down the front shouted 'Norwich!' Pete in his aggressive manner replied - Norwich? Norwich ain't in Shepherd's Bush you cunt!'

Dermot Bassett also shares one fond memory too: 'Something that always struck me was Roger's face when he walked onto the stage. He broke into a smile, literally, like a really happy and excited child meeting Santa. I had never seen it before and haven't since.'

CHAPTER TWENTY-NINE
2000

The Who tour of 2000 would be the last that John Entwistle would play. The Who kicked off their tour at a charity event in New York on 6thJune. Zak Starkey couldn't make it, so Simon Phillips stepped in for a one-off gig. The Who then spent most of July, August and September touring the States before returning to the UK in October.

At the Docklands Arena on 13th November, The Who played a set that lasted over two hours. Joe Strummer and the Mescaleros provided the support. The Docklands Arena, sometimes known as the London Arena, had been opened in 1989, eventually closed in 2005 before reopening as the o2 Arena, and has since become one of London's most popular live music events venues. On the 15th and 16th November The Who played at the Wembley Arena. And then on 27th November The Who were back at the Royal Albert Hall for a Teenage Cancer Trust event. Paul Weller and Noel Gallagher also performed at the event. This particular concert will remain a memorable one for **Melissa Hurley**: 'I was at the Royal Albert Hall concert when Pete fell off the stage and his guitar hit me. I have the scar to prove it.'

The Teenage Cancer Trust was founded in 1990 with the intention to offer young people with cancer the best care and support that could be afforded. Roger Daltrey is a patron of the TCT and was instrumental in bringing to life the music events that have now established themselves in the annual diary.

Daltrey said 'Over the years, I have met many young people with cancer and like the Teenage Cancer Trust I believe that they should not have to stop being teenagers just because they have cancer' and has since helped to get the support of, and engineer performances from, the likes of Paul Weller, Paul McCartney, Kasabian and Oasis.

2001 No London gigs

CHAPTER THIRTY
2002

John Entwistle, 'the OX' bass player with one of the world's greatest ever rock bands, played his last shows with the band he had been in for over forty years on the 7th and 8th February 2002 at Royal Albert Hall.

John Entwistle died on 27th June, found dead in his hotel room in Las Vegas. The Who were due to begin their American tour on the 28th. 'The OX has left the building-we've lost another great friend', said Peter and Roger.

2003 No London gigs

CHAPTER THIRTY-ONE
2004

In 2004 The Who played eighteen times. It was their first shows without the OX, instead Pino Palladino took over the bass duties and played alongside Daltrey, Townshend, Starkey, Rabbit and Simon Townshend.

The first shows were at the Forum in Kentish Town (it had been many years since The Who had found themselves in that part of London) on 22nd, 24th and 25th March. Each set opened with *Who Are You*, before other established favourites like *Substitute* and *I Can't Explain* were revisited.

Dermot Bassett recalls: 'I was at the Forum for the first show after Townshend's arrest. The Who opened with *Who Are You* and when they got into the guitar break it was almost as if the band faded into the background and every spotlight hit Townshend. You could hear, feel and see the months of frustration. I think I cried.'

And then, on 29th March, The Who returned for another Teenage Cancer Trust event at the Royal Albert Hall (supported by the Coral and the Bark) before heading off to America for a few dates, coming home to play some UK dates and again appearing at the Isle of White Festival, and then in July they went to perform their first ever concerts in Japan, and in the same month they returned to Australia, where they hadn't visited since 1968.

CHAPTER THIRTY-TWO
2005 LIVE8 CONCERT

On 2nd July 2005 The Who took part in the Live8 benefit concerts organised by Bob Geldof. The London concert was held at Hyde Park and also included Pink Floyd, U2 and Paul McCartney.

The Who performed two songs: Won't Get Fooled Again and Who Are You. Steve White, the respected drummer who had played with the Style Council and then in Paul Weller's solo band for many years, provided the drumming duties for The Who on that day.

Steve White: 'I was doing some recording with Paul Weller at his Solid Bond Studios in London when Pete Townshend came in and asked Damon Minchella and me if we were up for doing it. We said we were. Pete then gave us a list of five songs and asked us to learn them. And then we didn't actually get together to rehearse the songs until one or two days before the concert. On the day of Live8 the two songs to be played were *Won't Get Fooled Again* and *Who Are You*.

We got together for one rehearsal, and I took along my Premier red sparkle kit. Pete arrived quite late. He literally picked up his guitar and we launched into the

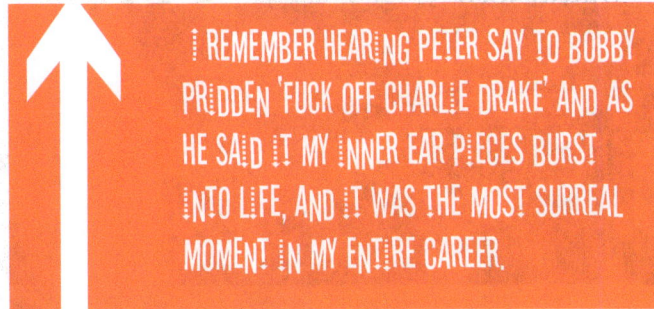

I REMEMBER HEARING PETER SAY TO BOBBY PRIDDEN 'FUCK OFF CHARLIE DRAKE' AND AS HE SAID IT MY INNER EAR PIECES BURST INTO LIFE, AND IT WAS THE MOST SURREAL MOMENT IN MY ENTIRE CAREER.

first song. At the end he turned to Roger and said "I think we'll do the two songs the other way round on the day".

Then, just before he left, Pete came over to my drum kit and looked at it. My kit was a replica of the kit Keith Moon used back in 1966. Pete leaned out his hand and gave it a gentle touch and said 'red sparkle. I like red sparkle.' And then he disappeared.

On the day of the concert I plugged in my in-ear monitors (which I hate) but they weren't working. And at that point no one seemed to want to take responsibility to get them working. To say the world dropped out of my bottom was an understatement. I mean I was on stage with The Who and my ear monitors are not working.

Thankfully, the comedian Peter Kay was given thirty seconds to do a bit on the stage and introduce The Who. I had met Peter via my wife previously so I knew there'd be no way he would stick to just thirty seconds. And he did over run and in that time I managed to get the ear monitors working. The sound engineers turned in the frequency and I remember hearing Peter say to Bobby Pridden 'fuck off Charlie Drake' and as he said it my inner ear pieces burst into life, and it was the most surreal moment in my entire career.

During *Won't Get Fooled Again* I remember dropping down to the part where it's just the keyboard sequencers and looking up to the sky and thinking "Keith - If you're up there, give me a heads up on this one buddy". I was shitting myself because I had been told that if Roger likes what's happening he will do the scream at the end, but if he isn't feeling it, he won't. But he did the scream and it was fucking great.'

CHAPTER THIRTY-THREE
2006

A blistering hot Sunday on 2nd July found The Who performing again in Hyde Park for the Hyde Park Calling event. The previous day, Roger Waters had taken to the same stage to perform the Dark Side of the Moon.

On the day The Who played, Zak Starkey wore a target tee shirt. It was an obvious nod to his godfather. The Zutons and Razorlight were the supports on the day. The Who then played one more time in London, on 29th October they were back at the Roundhouse in Camden.

CHAPTER THIRTY-FOUR
2007

The Who played another Teenage Cancer Trust event at the Royal Albert Hall on 31st March before heading to play two concerts at Wembley Arena on 26th and 27th June.

Jed Bere was at the Wembley Arena gig on the 26th: 'The second time that I saw The Who, Zak Starkey was on drums for them. It had been almost twenty years since I had last seen them and it was brilliant to hear all the great songs from their albums again. It was at this gig that I went to the merchandise stall to buy a tee shirt, but the one that I wanted had all sold out in my size, it was a tee shirt from one of their late seventies Canadian tours and I really wanted one. I was gutted and had to settle for another tee shirt that I wasn't that keen on but bought anyway. Then a few nights later, I went to the Brickmakers, my local pub, and it turned out that Bob, who worked behind the bar had an uncle that supplied The Who tee shirts at the concerts. I told Bob that I tried to get the Canadian tour tee shirt and he said 'leave it with me'.

I was propped up at the Brickmakers bar the following week and Bob appears with a bag he hands to me and says 'there you go Jed, you can have them'. I opened it up and he had managed to get me one of each of the tee shirts that had been on sale at the Wembley gig, including the Canadian tour one. I couldn't believe my luck, thank you Bob. I wore those tee shirts until they turned to dust.'

CHAPTER THIRTY-FIVE
2008

On 13th April, The Who were back at the Royal Albert Hall, where Daltrey and Townshend performed an acoustic set that included Let's See Action (from the Endless Wire album that The Who were promoting), Behind Blue Eyes, Two Thousand Years (Simon Townshend joining in playing mandolin), Mike Post Theme, Won't Get Fooled Again and Tea and Theatre.

And then on 14th, 15th and 17th December The Who played their Christmas concerts in the Indigo O2. This was a smaller (almost 3000 capacity) live music venue within the o2 complex. The audience were delighted to hear Slip Kid get its first run out in over three decades.

....

Dermot Basett: 'I saw the three shows at the Indigo in 2008. The Indigo is the smaller venue in the O2. It was very tight to get in, you had to bring photo ID and evidence to prove who you were; it was meant to be a gig for the proper fans. On the same night that The Who were playing, Coldplay were in concert in the main arena. I remember the looks on the faces of people who passed us as we were queuing. They thought we were going to see some Who tribute act. They had no idea we were there to see the real Who.

During the performances, The Who were very relaxed and joking about. People from the audience shouted out requests and they would do them, someone kept shouting 'play *Tattoo*' and eventually Roger said 'oh go on then'. And then the band had to have a discussion on stage about what key they should play it in. At one point Pete chipped in with "My god it's just like the old days again". Those Indigo shows were certainly some of my favourites from the more recent years. They were fantastic, absolutely fantastic.'

CHAPTER THIRTY-SIX
2009

The Who played another Teenage Cancer Trust benefit concert on 21st May. The venue for this occasion was the Emirates Stadium; the new home of Arsenal Football Club.

The audience were treated to three acoustic versions of *The Kids Are Alright*, *Who Are You* and *Won't Get Fooled Again*.

CHAPTER THIRTY-SEVEN
2010

The 30th March saw The Who returning to the Royal Albert Hall for another Teenage Cancer Trust event. They performed *Quadrophenia*, the last time had been back in 1997. Tom Meighan of Kasabian and Eddie Vedder of Pearl Jam were invited to help out with some of the vocal parts.

The Who only performed two more times in 2010, in February they had played five songs at halftime at the Super Bowl XLIV game in Miami.

CHAPTER THIRTY-EIGHT
2011

Since 2009, Daltrey had been touring *Tommy Reborn* with his band known as the Roger Daltrey Band, or No Plan B.

On 24th March the band played at the Teenage Cancer Trust event in the Royal Albert Hall. Scott Devours was the band's drummer and Pete Townshend joined the band on stage to play along with *The Acid Queen* and *Baba O' Reilly*.

On the 21st and 24th July the band performed *Tommy Reborn* at the Indigo o2.

CHAPTER THIRTY-NINE
2012

The closing ceremony of the Summer Olympics was held on 12th August. Countless events had been held in the Olympic Park located in Stratford on the lead up to the closing event.

The Who performed *Baba O Reilly*, *See Me, Feel Me* and *My Generation*. At the time, the Who had been touring America and Canada with their *Quadrophenia and More* Tour.

CHAPTER FORTY
2013

On 15th and 16th June the Who were back in the O2 but playing in the Arena. The Who's final show of their 2013 tour was held on 8th July at Wembley Arena. The concert was recorded and released as *Quadrophenia Live in London*. It reached number 28 in the British album charts.

> DALTREY KIND OF BLEW HIM A KISS AS KEITH'S IMAGE FADED TO NOTHING. IT WAS A STRANGE FEELING TO THINK THAT SOMEONE WHO HAD BEEN DEAD FOR SO MANY YEARS WAS BEING PART OF THIS MASSIVE SHOW.

Johnny Bance was at the concert: 'I went to see The Who at the O2 in June 2013; it was when they were doing Quadrophenia. I remember that it was a gorgeous hot summer's night. The atmosphere outside the O2 was building, and there was a strong feeling of anticipation hovering in the air. The age range was right across the board; there were young kids wearing Who T-shirts, middle age men and women and people clearly in their seventies too. There were plenty of families there for the occasion.

The actual event was incredible and fortunately we had some really good seats, where we could see the band and get a good view of the large screens. It was a proper show from start to finish. The band performed the whole *Quadrophenia* album from beginning to end and there was no talking in between songs. There were sound effects like the waves of the sea and rain; it was just brilliant.

And, bearing in mind both Daltrey and Townshend were into their old age, they played a superb show.

The vibe was really good which was great because I didn't really know what to expect. Before the gig I had read some reviews that said stuff like Roger Daltrey's lost his voice and it's too weak now; but I didn't witness anything like that, they were all just great and Daltrey's vocals on *Love Reign O'er Me* were outstanding. And to hear the songs from *Quadrophenia*, which is my favourite Who album, meant a lot to me. I had seen The Who once before at the Birmingham NEC but I was only young and didn't really appreciate it; but at the O2 gig I did.

There were large screens at the O2 too, and they showed footage of Keith Moon and John Entwistle, it was really moving actually, especially when the image of Moon faded because Daltrey kind of blew him a kiss as Keith's image faded to nothing. It was a strange feeling to think that someone who had been dead for so many years was being part of this massive show. The audience gave the moment a huge round of applause. It was special.'

CHAPTER FORTY-ONE
2014

The 17th and 18th December 2014 concerts, scheduled to be played at the O2 Arena, were cancelled the day before due to Daltrey being unwell.

There had been reports from fans and the media that Daltrey had been suffering with his health (throat) on the last few concerts leading up to the London shows. Naturally the fans were disappointed.

The O2 concerts were postponed until 22nd and 23rd March 2015.

CHAPTER FORTY-TWO
2015

The Who played on 22nd and 23rd March at the London O2.

Peter 'Dougal' Butler: 'I don't like the O2 as a venue, but I think it's great that The Who are still playing and I think they are still fantastic. They are in demand and so they have to play these big venues, but I still want to see them in a small venue, say like somewhere in Shepherds Bush. At the end of the day they are a different band but they are still The Who and I know Keith and John are not here to say so but I think they would both feel proud that Pete and Roger have kept going.'

Katie Town: 'Last night (22/3/15) I saw The Who at the O2 arena. I wasn't sure what to expect as I'd never seen a band as big as The Who or been to the venue. It was fantastic. The atmosphere was brilliant, everyone was really into it. Even 50 years on, the amount of energy Pete and Roger have on stage is unreal. Simon and Zak were also brilliant. In-between some of the songs Pete talked about why he wrote them which was really interesting. One of my favourite songs they played was *Love Reign O'er Me*. The atmosphere was amazing when that came on. It was certainly the best concert I've ever been to and I would do it all over again.'

On 26th March The Who played at the Royal Albert Hall for the fifteenth Teenage Cancer Trust. Wilko Johnson was the special guest on the night.

Author: 'Within five minutes of being escorted through the basement corridors inside the belly of the Royal Albert Hall, I had seen Roger Daltrey, Bill Curbishly, Bob Pridden and Simon Townshend. I only managed a brief exchange with Roger before several official and concerned people grabbed him and ushered him off into some room. The room happened to be next to Wilko Johnson's dressing room.

Seeing dozens of people rushing around tending to their chores and maybe some even just trying to look busy because they were on The Who's payroll was insightful. Some of the urgency may have been because The Who were only fifteen minutes away from doing their soundcheck. I had been allowed to sit in on the band's soundcheck because Pete Townshend's PA, Nicola Joss, and The Who's tour manager Rex had organised it for me. They knew I had done the Keith Moon book and was gathering material for this book. Both Nicola and Rex were extremely helpful.

Rex pointed me in the direction of a closed door. On the other side was a narrow passageway that led out into the floor area of the Royal Albert Hall. I have been to several gigs at the venue but never actually been this close to the stage. With my notebook and pen in hand I positioned myself in a chair ten rows from the stage. I looked around to see who I was sharing the Royal Albert Hall with and counted less than ten people. I only recognised two people - Robert Rosenburg and Alan McGee of Creation/Oasis fame of all people.

> 'WITHIN FIVE MINUTES OF BEING ESCORTED THROUGH THE BASEMENT CORRIDORS INSIDE THE BELLY OF THE ROYAL ALBERT HALL, I HAD SEEN ROGER DALTREY, BILL CURBISHLY, BOB PRIDDEN AND SIMON TOWNSHEND'.

A few roadies and techy types scuttled back and forth on the stage, picking things up, putting them down, moving things, then moving them back. I found it quite amusing to watch. Bob Pridden joined them and things seemed to fall into place.

Zak then appeared on the stage and got behind his see-through drum kit, he was wearing a colourful stripy tee shirt; he'd still be wearing it during the gig later that night. Then Roger appeared, dressed in black jeans, black shirt and a stylish looking black waist-coat. And he had his glasses on. The rest of the band also appeared and took up their positions. Also a large projection of a target with the words Who 50th appeared behind them. There were also visuals and banners promoting the Teenage Cancer Trust carefully placed around the stage and venue.

Roger found what he had been searching for and several bursts of harmonica filled the Royal Albert Hall. It sounded good to me, but after a few seconds

THE WHO 86 IN THE CITY

Roger stopped and called out to the people manning the sound desk 'too much top side'.

The harmonica issue having been dealt with, Roger then picked up an acoustic guitar and began to strum *I Can See For Miles*. Zak and Palo joined in but it didn't last long because Roger was onto his band to test the backing vocals. The band responded and jumped in singing their BV parts to *I Can See For Miles*. Roger seemed happy with the sound and exchanged some jolly banter with his bandmates.

> PETE'S LAST WORDS WERE 'WELL IT SOUNDS GOOD TO ME UP HERE.' I WANTED TO SAY 'PETE AND IT DOES OUT HERE TOO.'

And then Pete Townshend walked onto the stage wearing a black hat, dark glasses, jeans and grey blazer. 'Hi Pete' said Roger. Within seconds Pete, not known for his willingness and patience for soundchecks, had strapped his red and white Fender Strat around himself. Before he strummed it he commented favourably on the TCT banners and Who visuals that were projected behind him. He appeared to be in a happy relaxed mood as he launched into playing *Who Are You*. The rest of the band joined in, creating a fantastically awesome sound. And Pete got right into playing the song; he even threw in a few of his trademark arm windmills too and danced around the stage a bit. It was superb to watch. At the end of the song he picked up a mug of tea and took sips from it as he talked with Roger.

Pete, Roger and Frank then had a lengthy discussion about the amount of bars that they had been playing in *Eminence Front*. Pete wanted to make changes and play it differently for the concert that they'd be doing in about three hours time. The band briefly rehearsed the changes, before moving onto the next song which happened to be *I'm One*.

Pete was now playing an acoustic. Bob Pridden walked onto the stage and casually stood in the centre of it, hands relaxed inside his pockets. Then he strolled off again. Pete was still playing and singing *I'm One*. Hearing this thrilled me because *Quadrophenia* is my favourite Who album.

At the end of the song Roger, who had been playing his harmonica, stepped up to the microphone and said 'this place always sounds boomy when it's empty.' He then turned to one of the crew and jokingly said 'what did you wash these harmonicas in- Persil?'

Before the soundcheck was over, the band had also gone through some of *Magic Bus* and *My Generation*. And then the soundcheck was complete. Pete's last words were 'well it sounds good to me up here.' I wanted to say 'Pete and it does out here too.'

The concert that night was a medley of some of The Who's much-loved hits. There were plenty of visuals too, and even some bursts of unseen footage from *Quadrophenia* and Mods dancing in the audience at the Railway Hotel gig, which Lambert and Stamp filmed fifty years earlier.

The sell-out audience was a mixture of young, middle and old aged people. Pete and Roger were in good form-two seasoned warriors of the stage, with enough experience of rock music to write a hundred books between them, and there was plenty of banter between them and members of the audience. Pete occasionally talked about how a particular song came about, which was interesting. There were also reminders as to why the concert was happening and I'm sure the Teenage Cancer Trust were most appreciative. The band sounded great - they were having fun and enjoying the gig, and that was clear. The Who had started with *I Can't Explain* and topped the night off with a brilliant performance of *Won't Get Fooled Again*.

...

Full set list-
I Can't Explain, Substitute, The Seeker, Who Are You, The Kids Are Alright, I Can See For Miles, Pictures Of Lily, My Generation, Magic Bus, Behind Blue Eyes, Join Together, You Better You Bet, I'm One, Love Reign O'er Me, Eminence Front, Mini-Opera, Amazing Journey, Sparks, Pinball Wizard, See Me Feel Me, Listening To You, Baba O' Reilly, Won't Get Fooled Again.

...

On the 26th June 2015 The Who played Hyde Park along with Paul Weller, Kaiser Chiefs and Johnny Marr of The Smiths.

...

Dermot Basset: 'I fell in love with The Who the very first time I saw them on the television in 1965 and fifty years later I still love them and still go to see them live. I have no idea how many times I have seen them on stage over those fifty years. Since I saw them on the TV they have always been 'my' band.

The Who's music has always been important; but there's something much bigger going on too. It's something that I find very difficult to put into words, but it's as if it's almost an attitude. I've grown up with The Who and fifty years is a long time, and I'll always go to see them.

CHAPTER FORTY-THREE
THE WHO LONDON CONCERTS
1962-2015

1962

1st July 1962. Paradise Club, Peckham
1st September 1962. Acton Town Hall

1963

11th January 1963. Fox and Goose Hotel, Hanger Lane, Ealing

19th January 1963. C.A.V Sports ground, Northolt. (and 6th April)

17th February 1963.
Douglas House, Bayswater.
(and 24th Feb, 10th March, 17th March, 24th March, 31st March, 7th April, 14th April, 21st April, 28th April, 5th May, 12th May, 19th May, 26th May)

17th February 1963.
White Hart Hotel, Acton.
(and 24th Feb, 25th Feb, 3rd March, 4th March, 11th March, 18th March, 25th March, 1st April, 8th April, 15th April, 22nd April, 29th April, 5th May, 9th May, 26th May, 6th June, 9th June, 23rd June, 30th June, 7th July, 14th July, 21st July, 11th Aug, 15th Aug, 18th Aug, 25th Aug, 1st Sept, 8th Sept, 15th Sept, 22nd Sept, 29th Sept, 24th Nov, 29th Dec)

21st February 1963.
Oldfield Hotel, Greenford.
(and 22nd Feb, 23rd Feb, 28th Feb, 7th March, 9th March, 14th March, 21st March, 28th March, 4th April, 11th April, 13th April, 18th April, 25th April, 27th April, 30th April, 11th May, 18th May, 23rd May, 28th May, 1st June, 8th June, 15th June, 20th June, 27th June, 29th June, 4th July, 6th July, 11th July, 18th July, 20th July, 23rd July, 25th July, 10th Aug, 17th Aug, 20th Aug, 22nd Aug, 27th Aug, 29th Aug, 5th Sept, 7th Sept, 19th Sept, 26th Sept, 28th Sept, 3rd Oct, 10th Oct, 12th Oct, 17th Oct, 24th Oct, 26th Oct, 7th Nov, 9th Nov, 14th Nov, 21st Nov, 28th Nov, 5th Dec, 12th Dec, 14th Dec)

13th March 1963.
Mazenod Church Hall, Kilburn.

29th March 1963.
The College of Distributive Trade.

17th May 1963. Park Hotel, Carnival Ballroom, Hanwell.
Townshend describes including some 'funkier R&B' tunes in the set at this performance.

7th June 1963.
Goldhawk Social Club, Shepherds Bush
(and 5th July, 12th July, 16th Aug, 6th Sept, 25th Oct, 8th Nov, 22nd Nov, 29th Nov)

14th June 1963.
G.E.C Pavilion, Wembley.

22nd June 1963.
Myllet Arms, Perivale.

26th July 1963. Club Durane, Notre Dame Church Hall.
(and 30th Aug, 27th Sept)

9th September 1963.
St Mary's Hall, Putney.
(and 6th Oct, 17th Nov, 1st Dec, 8th Dec, 15th Dec, 22nd Dec).

13th September 1963.
Glenlyn Ballroom, Forest Hill.
(and 4th Oct, 11th Oct, 1st Nov, 6th Dec, 20th Dec).

15th November 1963.
Feather's Hotel, Ealing.
(and 13th Dec)

26th November 1963.
Town Hall, Acton

30th November 1963.
Railway Hotel, Greenford.

1964

2nd January 1964.
Oldfield Hotel, Greenford.
(and 11th Jan, 14th Jan, 16th Jan, 18th Jan, 21st Jan, 23rd Jan, 25th Jan, 30th Jan, 6th Feb, 13th Feb, 20th Feb, 22nd Feb, 27th Feb, 5th March, 17th March, 19th March, 26th March, 2nd April, 16th April, 23rd April, 30th April, 7th May, 14th May, 28th May)

3rd January 1964.
Glenlyn Ballroom, Forest Hill.
(and 24th Jan, 14th Feb, 16th March, 23rd March, 3rd April, 6th April, 10th April, 20th April, 24th April, 4th May, 11th May, 15th May, 18th May, 21st May, 25th May, 1st June, 8th June, 15th June, 22nd June, 29th June)

5th January 1964.

St Mary's Hall, Putney.
(and 26th Jan, 31st Jan, 2nd Feb, 9th Feb, 23rd Feb, 1st March, 8th March)

12th January 1964.
White Hart Hotel, Acton.
(and 19th Jan, 15th March, 5th April, 12th April, 26th April, 31st May, 26th July)

7th February 1964.
Goldhawk Social Club, Shepherds Bush.
(and 28th Feb, 6th March, 27th March, 11th April, 17th April, 8th May, 31st July)

29th February 1964.
Evershed Sports Pavillion, Brentford.

7th March 1964.
Old Oak Common Institute, Shepherds Bush.

7th March 1964. Mead Hall, Ealing.

13th April 1964.
100 Club, Oxford Street.
(and 27th April)

2nd May 1964. Venue unknown.

4th June 1964.
White Hart, Southall.
(and 11th June, 18th June, 25th June, 6th Aug)

26th June 1964.
The Refectory, Golders Green.

30th June 1964.
Railway Hotel, Harrow and Wealdstone.
(and 4th July, 7th July, 14th July, 21st July, 28th July, 4th Aug, 11th Aug, 18th Aug, 25th Aug, 8th Sept, 15th Sept, 22nd Sept, 29th Sept, 6th Oct, 20th Oct, 2nd Nov)

22nd July 1964.
Scene Club, Soho.
(and 29th July, 5th Aug, 12th Aug, 19th Aug, 26th Aug, 2nd Sept)

15th August 1964.
Thomas Riverboat Shuffle, London

23rd August 1964.
Town Hall, Greenwich.
(and 30th Sept, 14th Oct, 28th Oct).

2nd October 1964.
Shandon Hall, Romford

21st November 1964.
Ealing Club, Ealing Broadway.
(and 27th Dec)

24th November 1964.
The Marquee Club, Soho.
(and 1st Dec, 8th Dec, 15th Dec, 22nd Dec, 29th Dec)

12th December 1964.
Harrow Technical College.

14th December 1964.
The Red Lion, Leytonstone.
(and 21st Dec, 28th Dec)

19th December 1964.
London College of Printer's, Elephant and Castle.

1965

2nd January 1965.
Ealing Club, Ealing Broadway.
(and 9th Jan, 30th Jan, 11th Feb, 18th Feb, 25th Feb, 4th March, 10th March, 17th March, 24th March, 26th March)

4th January 1965.
The Red Lion, Leytonstone

5th January 1965.
The Marquee, Soho.
(and 12th Jan, 19th Jan, 26th Jan, 2nd Feb, 9th Feb, 16th Feb, 23rd Feb, 2nd March, 9th March, 16th March, 23rd March, 30th March, 6th April, 13th April, 20th April, 27th April, 25th May, 7th June, 13th July, 2nd Nov, 21st Dec)

9th January 1965.
Club Noreik, Tottenham.
(and 23rd Jan, 13th March, 24th April, 26th June)

15th January 1965.
Technical College, Chelsea.

21st February 1965.
St Joseph's Hall, Wembley

12th March 1965.
Goldhawk Social Club, Shepherds Bush.
(and 20th March, 16th April, 3rd Dec)

14th March 1965.
Starlite Ballroom, Greenford.
(and 27th June, 29th Oct)

25th March 1965,
Blue Opera R&B Club at the Cooks Ferry Inn, Edmonton

31st March 1965.
Bromley Court Hotel
(and 28th April)

1st April 1965.
Town Hall, Wembley.

3rd April 1965.
The London College of Printing.

5th April 1965.
Lakeside Club, Hendon.

10th April 1965.
The Cavern Club,
Notre Dame Church Hall

19th April 1965.
Botwell House, Hayes.

16th May 1965.
Town Hall, Stratford.

5th June 1965.
Loyola Hall, Stamford Hill.
(and 7th Aug)

6th June 1965.
St Joseph's Hall, Highgate.

19th June 1965.
The Uxbridge Blues Festival.

19th June 1965.
The Cavern Club,
Notre Dame Church Hall.

20th June 1965.
The Blue Moon, Hayes.

24h June 1965.
Town Hall, Greenwich.

29th June 1965.
Burtons Ballroom, Uxbridge.

30th June 1965.
Town Hall, Farnborough

4th July 1965.
Community Centre, Southall.

7th July 1965.
The Manor House, Harringay.

28th July 1965.
The Pontiac, Zeeta House, Putney.

30th July 1965.
The Fender Club, Kenton, Middlesex

6th August 1965.
The Jazz and Blues Festival,
Athletic Ground, Richmond.

14th August 1965.
The New Georgian Club, Cowley.

6th September 1965.
Town Hall, Farnborough

17th November 1965.
Queen Mary College, Stepney.

19th November 1965.
Glad Rag Ball, Empire Pool, Wembley.

26th November 1965.
Palais, Wimbledon.

5th December 1965.
The White Lion Hotel, Edgeware.

6th December 1965.
Eltham Baths, Eltham.

1966

15th January 1966.
Two Puddings Club, Stratford.

15th January 1966.
The In Crowd, Hackney.

21st January 1966.
Glenlyn Ballroom, Forest Hill.

4th February 1966.
Astoria Theatre, Finsbury Park.

11th February 1966.
Palais, Wimbledon
(and 13th May).

13th February 1966.
Community Centre, Southall.

28th February 1966.
Eltham Baths, Eltham Hill.

9th March 1966.
Town Hall, Farnborough.

10th March 1966.
Ram Jam Club.

11th March 1966.
The Cavern Club,
Notre Dame Church Hall .

13th March 1966.
Starlite Ballroom, Greenford.
(and 15th May)

15th April 1966.
Fairfield Halls, Croydon.

17th April 1966.
Regal Cinema, Edmonton.

28th April 1966.
Witch Doctor Club, Catford.

29th April 1966.
Tiles Club.
(and 29th July).

1st May 1966.
NME Poll Winners,
Empire Pool, Wembley.

7th July 1966.
The Locarno Ballroom, Streatham.

9th July 1966.
Technical College, Westminster.

24th August 1966.
The Orchid Ballroom, Purley.

6th September 1966.
Palais, Ilford

12th November 1966.
Duke of York Barracks, Chelsea.

15th December 1966.
Locarno Ballroom, Streatham.

21st December 1966.
Upper Cut Club, Forest Gate.

31st December 1966.
The Roundhouse, Camden.

1967

18th January 1967.
The Orchid Ballroom, Purley.

29th January 1967. Savile Theatre.
(and 22nd Oct)

31st January 1967.
Palais Des Danse, Ilford

12th February 1967.
Starlite Ballroom, Greenford.

2nd March 1967.
The Marquee Club, Soho.

29th April 1967.
14 Hour Technicolour Dream,
Alexandra Palace.

3rd November 1967.
Granada Cinema,
Kingston-Upon-Thames.

4th November 1967.
Granada Cinema, Walthamstow.

22nd December 1967.
Olympic Grand Hall, Kensington.

1968

12th January 1968.
Royal Ballroom, Tottenham.

2nd March 1968.
New Edmonton Gardens, Edmonton.

15th April 1968.
The Marquee Club, Soho.
(and 23rd April, 17th Dec).

24th May 1968.
City University, Clerkenwell.

15th June 1968.
The London College of Printers.

5th October 1968.
The Roundhouse, Camden.
(and 15th Nov, 16th Nov).

18th October 1968. The Lyceum.

30th October 1968.
Eel Pie Island, Twickenham.

8th November 1968.
Granada Theatre, Walthamstow.

11th December 1968.
Stonebridge House Studios, Wembley.

1969

25th January 1969.
Middlesex Borough College, Isleworth.

8th February 1969.
Central Polytechnic.

23rd February 1969.
The Roundhouse, Camden.

1st May 1969.
Ronnie Scott's, Soho.

5th July 1969.
Pop Proms, Royal Albert Hall.

21st September 1969.
Fairfield Halls, Croydon.

14th December 1969. The Coliseum.

1970

18th October 1970.
Odeon Cinema, Lewisham.

29th October 1970.
Hammersmith Palais.

20th December 1970.
The Roundhouse, Camden.

1971

4th January 1971.
The Young Vic Theatre, Waterloo.
(and 14th Feb, 15th Feb, 22nd Feb, 1st March,
26th April, 5th May).

18th September 1971.
Oval Cricket Ground, Kennington.

4th November 1971.
Rainbow Theatre, Finsbury Park.
(and 5th Nov, 6th Nov).

1972

9th December 1972.
Rainbow Theatre, Finsbury.

1973

11th November 1973.
The Lyceum.
(and 12th Nov, 13th Nov).

13th December 1973. |Rainbow
Theatre, Finsbury.

18th December 1973.
Sundown Theatre, Edmonton.
(and 19th Dec, 22nd Dec, 23rd Dec).

1974

14th April 1974.
Roundhouse, Chalk Farm, Camden
(Pete Townshend solo performance).

18th May 1974.
Charlton Athletic Football Ground.

1975

21st October 1975.
Empire Pool, Wembley.
(and 23rd Oct, 24th Oct).

21st December 1975.
Hammersmith Odeon.
(and 23rd December).

1976

31st May 1976.
Charlton Athletic Football Ground.

1977

15th December 1977.
Gaumont State Theatre, Kilburn.

1978

25th May 1978.
Shepperton Studios, Middlesex.

1979

2nd May 1979
The Rainbow, Finsbury Park.

18th August 1979.
Wembley Stadium.
77,000 capacity and supported by AC/DC and
Nils Lofgren.Tickets £8 in advance and £8.50
on the day.

28th December 1979.
Hammersmith Odeon

1980

NO LONDON GIGS

1981

3rd February 1981.
The Rainbow, Finsbury Park

4th February 1981.
The Rainbow, Finsbury Park

8th February 1981.
Odeon Theatre Hammersmith

9th February 1981.
Odeon Theatre Hammersmith

9th March 1981. Wembley Arena

10th March 1981. Wembley Arena

11th March 1981. Wembley Arena

1982, 1983 and 1984

NO LONDON GIGS

1985

13th July 1985.
Wembley Stadium. LIVE AID

1988

8th February 1988.
Royal Albert Hall

1989

23rd October 1989 Wembley Arena
24th October 1989 Wembley Arena
26th October 1989 Wembley Arena
27th October 1989 Wembley Arena
31st October 1989 Royal Albert Hall
2nd November 1989 Royal Albert Hall

1990, 1991, 1992, 1993, 1994

NO LONDON GIGS

1995

16th September 1995.
The Bottom Line, Shepherds Bush

1996

29th June 1996. Hyde Park
6th December 1996. Earls Court
7th December 1996. Earls Court

1997

18th May 1997.
Wembley Arena

1998

NO LONDON GIGS

1999

22nd December 1999.
Shepherds Bush Empire

23rd December 1999.
Shepherds Bush Empire

2000

13th November 200 Docklands Arena
15th November 2000. Wembley Arena
16th November 2000. Wembley Arena
27th November 2000.
Royal Albert Hall.

2001

NO LONDON GIGS

2002

7th February 2002. Royal Albert Hall
8th February 2002. Royal Albert Hall

2003

NO LONDON GIGS

2004

22nd March 2004. The Forum
24th March 2004. The Forum
25th March 2004. The Forum
29th March 2004. Royal Albert Hall.

2005

2nd July 2005. Hyde Park

2006

2nd July 2006 Hyde Park
29th October 2006. The Roundhouse

2007

8th February 2007. The Hospital
31st March 2007. Royal Albert Hall
26th June 2007. Wembley Arena
27th June 2007. Wembley Arena

2008

13th April 2008. Royal Albert Hall
14th December 2008. Indigo o2
15th December 2008. Indigo o2
17th December 2008. Indigo o2

2009

21st May. London Emirates.
Teenage Cancer Trust event.

2010

30th March 2010. Royal Albert Hall

2011

24th March 2011. Royal Albert Hall
21st July 2011. Indigo o2
24th July 2011. Indigo o2

2012

12th August.
The closing ceremony of the Summer Olympics

2013

15th June. O2 Arena
16th June. O2 Arena
8th July. Wembley Arena

2014

17th December 2014.
O2 Arena.
Cancelled and postponed until 22nd March.

18th December 2014.
O2 Arena.
Cancelled and postponed until 23rd March

2015

22nd March. O2 Arena
23rd March. O2 Arena
26th March. Royal Albert Hall.
26th June. Hyde Park.

THE WHO IN THE CITY

CHAPTER FORTY-FOUR
GOING MOBILE
LOCATIONS FOR THE WHO TOUR OF LONDON

PART 1: WEST LONDON

GOING MOBILE START
ACTON TOWN HALL

The Detours continued to rehearse up their set and add extra songs as they approached their next live performance, booked for Saturday 1st September at the Town Hall in Acton. But on that Saturday night in September, under the name The Detours Jazz Group, they supported the Ron Cavendish Orchestra at the grand re-opening of the town hall. The band's future promoter Bob Druce was in the audience that night, and although not completely 'blown away' by what he witnessed, he must have seen enough to arrange for them to audition for him a short while after at the Oldfield Hotel in Greenford.

GOING MOBILE TWO
THE WHITE HART, ACTON

A few months on from the Acton Town Hall occasion, The Detours would return to Acton to play again and the venue, the White Hart, would become one of the band's most important launch pads to take their careers further. It was at the White Hart Hotel in Acton's High Street where The Detours first manager Helmut Gorden would see and hear the band.

GOING MOBILE THREE
THE GOLDHAWK CLUB, SHEPHERDS BUSH

The first time that The Detours played at the Goldhawk Social Club, Shepherds Bush was on 7th June 1963. By the end of 1963 one of the Mods' anthems, Green Onions by Booker T and the MG's was being included in the set.

The Detours returned to the Goldhawk Social Club many more times in 1964 just as Mod was really picking up momentum. It was from the loyal fan base that gathered in the Goldhawk that the '100 faces' a group of hard core Mods originated. On 16th November 2014 a blue plaque was erected at the site of the Goldhawk Club, thathad been so important in The Who's early career.12th March 1965.

GOING MOBILE FOUR

THE FEATHERS HOTEL, EALING

On the 15th November 1963 the Detours played at Feather's Hotel, Ealing Broadway, Ealing - they returned the next month on 13th December, to perform at the Evershed and Bignoles Apprentice Association Social Club Dance. The 'Feathers' had a large basement area where bands played. Several years after The Detours played there, the Pink Floyd and Jeff Beck also played there too.

Ealing, and what was bubbling away in the area would have been familiar to the various members of The Detours, and unknown to them at the time other key figures that would shape the direction in which popular music was destined to head also lived in the area; these included Dusty Springfield (she also worked in Squires Record Shop on Ealing Broadway), Mitch Mitchel (who would go on to play alongside Jimi Hendrix in the Experience) and Alexis Korner, who in 1962 co-founded the Ealing Blues Club with Cyril Davies.

GOING MOBILE FIVE
THE EALING BLUES CLUB

The Ealing Blues Club, which opened on 17th March 1962, had previously been the Ealing Jazz Club, established in early 1959. The club became the birthplace of what evolved into the British R&B scene and was the epicentre of everything that a select group of young people desired. It was in this club that Mick Jagger and Keith Richards first met their future bandmate Brian Jones.

The club was situated at 42a The Broadway, below the Aerated Bread Company and accessed by carefully navigating one's steps down a narrow alleyway that led towards Haven Place. The basement area wasn't massive and at the very most only held 200 people. But those that were fortunate to attend the club and perhaps even contribute to it went on to help develop a scene and pave the way for other R&B clubs such as the Crawdaddy and Eel Pie Island to be established.

On the 17th March 2012, fifty years to the date after the Ealing Blues Club first opened, a blue plaque was unveiled. It read 'The Ealing Club, 17th March 1962, Alexis Korner and Cyril Davies Began British Rhythm and Blues on This Site'.

GOING MOBILE SIX

11th January 1963. Fox and Goose Hotel, Hanger Lane, Ealing advertised The Detours arrival on their poster with 'Jiving and Twisting Fridays Featuring the Dynamic Detours'. Surely the young musicians, so new to the 'biz' must have been thrilled with such a welcome and advert; and all for the admission price of 4/-. The Detours played their set in the modest, licensed Fox and Goose Hotels' ballroom to an appreciative crowd.

GOING MOBILE SEVEN

The Myllet Arms, Perivale. Saturday the 22nd June 1963- The Detours played at a wedding in the Mylett Arms, Western Avenue in Perivale, Greenford.

GOING MOBILE EIGHT
OLDFIELD HOTEL, GREENFORD

The Detours managed to get an audition for local promoter Bob Druce of Commercial Entertainment Ltd. Druce booked bands to play the circuit that the Detours were desperate to get on, to get noticed and make some regular money. The audition took place at the Oldfield Hotel, Greenford. 21st February 1963.

And then one night at the Oldfield a young man wearing a ginger suit joined them on stage for a few numbers; his name was Keith Moon. The first song that Keith, Pete, Roger and John played together was Roadrunner. Dougie Sandom had recently left the group. In his absence The Who had auditioned several drummers, Mitch Mitchell amongst them, but none had fitted in. Keith Moon was something different and almost cut from the same cloth, as is often the case with the unique way a band 'comes together'.

GOING MOBILE NINE

On 14th March 1965, The Who were back playing in the familiar territory of Greenford at the Starlite Ballroom on Allendale Road (they played at the venue again on 27th June, and 29th Oct). Less than two weeks earlier a smitten Moon had met Kim Kerrigan at a gig in Bournemouth. Kim would become Moon's wife and mother to his only daughter Mandy. The other three members of The Who also had reasons to grin like Cheshire cats, because only three days earlier they had flown to Manchester to record their debut appearance for Top of the Pops. I Can't Explain was broadcast that night.

The Starlite had begun life in 1935 as one of the capital's Odeon cinemas, but was converted to a ballroom to facilitate dances in 1955. Throughout the sixties, acts like Ben E King, Geno Washington, The Kinks, The Yardbirds and The Hollies all performed at the Starlite. The Who also played again at the Starlite on 13th March and 15th May in 1966 (they were due to play on 16th October 1966 but this was cancelled) and on 12th February 1967.

GOING MOBILE TEN
THE RAILWAY HOTEL,
HARROW AND WEALDSTONE

Other than the Marquee, the Railway Hotel is possibly the most significant venue in the story of the early Who years. An important club night was held at the Railway Hotel in Harrow and Wealdstone by Richard Barnes and Lionel Gibbins. The first club night was held on the 30th June 1964. The BluesdayR&B club nights were held each Tuesday and The Who (the High Numbers) would play two sets during the night, which earned them £20 at first (a few pounds more than what they got working under Bob Druce). And because of the type of music being played, groups of Mods made the club night their own. And what they were to witness excited them.

QUADROPHENIA LONDON TOUR.

For many people, The Who's film *Quadrophenia* is the best youth culture film ever made. In 2013 Simon Wells dedicated an entire book to the making of the film and it's the most detailed book on the subject, including both interviews with the makers of the film and the cast, and several unseen photographs taken during the making of the film.

Quadrophenia is packed full of memorable quotes that many fans of the film are extremely fond of: 'I don't think they make Levis in your size', 'I am one of the faces', 'Get in there my son' all effortlessly roll off the tongue and transport the fan to that particular scene in the film. Much of the film takes place in London, but some iconic scenes in Brighton too, the seafront scene where Jimmy and a large swell of Mods being chanting 'We are the Mods' has since gone down into youth culture history, as has the infamous Jimmy and Steph intimate moment in the alleyway just off East Street. Then there's the Florida ballroom that The Who themselves performed several gigs in during the time when the Mods were descending on Brighton on bank holidays and spending the weekend dancing, meeting like-minded people and in some cases having battles with their rivals - the rockers.

Quadrophenia was also the film that helped the second wave of Mod launch off. By the time Quadrophenia had been released bands such as The Jam were already recognised as a Mod band, and they helped pave the way for others like Secret Affair, the Lambrettas and The Chords. And, for a second time in its history, Carnaby Street became the Mod Mecca, as shops like Melanddis and Shelleys supplied the 'gear' that this new Mod movement opted for.

The cast included original characters; the majority being Mods and friends of the lead character Jimmy Cooper who was played by Phil Daniels. Steph was played by Leslie Ash, Chalky played by Phillip Davis, Dave played by Mark Wingett, Ace Face played by Sting, Kevin Herriot played by Ray Winstone, Spider played by Gary Shail, Monkey played by Toyah Wilcox, Peter Fenton played by Garry Cooper, Ferdy played by Trevor Laird, Mr Cooper played by Michael Elphick, Mrs Cooper played by Kate Williams and Harry played by Timothy Spall.

The film was Released on 14th September 1979. It was directed by Franc Roddam, Produced by Roy Baird and Bill Curbishley. Writing credits to Pete Townshend, Dave Humphries, Franc Roddam, Martin Stellman.

The Quadrophenia London locations in order as they appear in the film:

The sea, the pebble beach, a lonesome young Mod called Jimmy, snippets of songs from the Quadrophenia album float in and out before the film cuts to a happy, free, cocky looking Jimmy riding his Lambretta down the Goldhawk Road. Jimmy is next seen surrounded by a gang of rockers on their heavy bikes, there are some verbal exchanges 'fuck off, bollocks' before the rockers on their much faster bikes overtake his lighter, more stylish Lambretta. The tone of the film has been set, the opening scenes are instantly engaging and offer a hint of what is to come.

The next scene shows Jimmy pull up outside what is meant to represent the Goldhawk Club in Shepherds Bush. He calls over Ferdy, a guy who pushed pills around; Jimmy buys a bag for 'one quid'; a price he moans over. Jimmy then enters the club.

GOING MOBILE ONE
LEICESTER SQUARE TUBE STATION.

The Goldhawk Club actual location 29 Shelton Street, Covent Garden, was the site of the club where Jimmy and the Mods go and band called Cross Section (a band from the Medway towns) who are playing a version of High Heel Sneakers, a song covered by so many artists like Jimmy Smith and Stevie Wonder. The venue in which the scene was filmed wasn't actually a dedicated music venue at the time when Quadrophenia was being made; it was actually called The Basement Youth Club. After a night spent in the 'Goldhawk' club, Jimmy goes home.

GOING MOBILE TWO
WILLESDEN JUNCTION TUBE STATION

A few minutes' walk from Willesden Junction tube station is where Jimmy's family home was located-115 Wells House Road. He wanders into his sister's bedroom looking for some scissors, but in the process of trying to find them in a dark room, he knocks over a pot of nail varnish. His sister complains and squeals 'you're so bloody clumsy'. Jimmy jokes back before retreating to his own bedroom where he uses the scissors to cut out an article from a newspaper. He sticks it to the wall; it's a piece about the residents and authorities of Brighton preparing themselves for the forthcoming bank holiday - RIOT POLICE FLY TO SEASIDE reads the article, which Jimmy positions beside another cut out RUN RUN RUN. The Who released a song of their own called Run Run Run on their A Quick One album. This scene finishes with Jimmy slumping down onto his leopard skin patterned bed sheets. Alongside the other cut-outs and posters of tits and arse is an image of Pete Townshend.

Next up is the comical scene set in a public baths (which was filmed at the public baths that have since been replaced by Porchester Hall, Porchester Centre, Queensway). The person in the baths beside Jimmy's starts to sing Gene Vincents Be Bop A Lula, to which Jimmy takes offence and starts singing The Kinks You Really Got Me back. Before long both are in a 'sing off' and slinging remarks at each other 'why don't you just turn over and do a few underwater farts'.

Jimmy and the other guy then realise that they know each other; it turns out Jimmy used to go to school with Kevin Herriot. They are next seen in a café where Jimmy has already purchased some pie, mash and liquor and plonked himself down on a vacant table. Kevin joins him, dressed like a rocker. Jimmy is both shocked and surprised 'that gear you've got on; its leather.' Kevin is invited to sit down but they only manage a brief chat before Jimmy makes his excuses, saying he has to leave. It turns out some of Jimmy's Mod friends have arrived. They make a point 'what's this fucking rocker doing here then?' they ask, but Jimmy has already bolted, he cannot afford to be seen fraternising with the enemy.

GOING MOBILE THREE
SHEPHERDS BUSH MARKET TUBE STATION

This scene was filmed in A COOKES, 48 Goldhawk Road. Written in red on the white brick wall on the two-story building was 'A. Cookes, Traditional Pie, Mash, Liquor and Eels'. The premises had been used as a pie and mash shop since 1891 but Cookes only took it over in 1934.

Following the café scene, Jimmy visits his tailors where he needs to pay off some of the Hire Purchase on his new suit, one of his friends is having a fitting 'fuckin' rent a tent'.

Jimmy is next seen visiting Steph at her place of work.

GOING MOBILE FOUR
SHEPHERDS BUSH MARKET TUBE STATION

Askens Supermarket on Goldhawk Road was where Steph worked. 'Pow', in the film Jimmy visits her and tells her about his intentions of going to Brighton, and to impress her with the details of the new suit he is having made at the tailors. He exits the supermarket with the wishful words 'I am one of the faces'. Askens is now gone but was situated stood between Barnborough Gardens and Woodger Road.

That evening, Jimmy and his Mod mates meet in a pub. They learn there is going to be a party and decide to go.

GOING MOBILE FIVE
WEMBLEY CENTRAL or
WEMBLEY NORTH TUBE STATION

The infamous party that Jimmy and his mates gatecrash, pushing past the boyfriend of the host, turning off the lights and turning up the volume on My Generation for another iconic scene which depicts the bonding and the like-minded gang mentality of a bunch of young Mods from the mid-60s. Jimmy's facial expression as he dances to My Generation is priceless. It's one the film's best-loved scenes.

And then getting a shag in the host's parents' bedroom and bathroom 'get in there my son', cries Jimmy once he sees what his best friend Dave is doing to some girl lying half naked on the bed. The Kitchener Road party address was actually at 63 Clarenden Gardens, Wembley. Jimmy signs of this scene by riding his scooter across the garden, demolishing the flowers and the fence before making his exit.

The following day, Jimmy is at work and evidently feeling the worse from having popped a few pills. He falls asleep on the train on the journey home 'I wound up in bleeding Neasden' to find his dinner in the oven and a questioning mother who also scolds him about his lifestyle 'it's not normal' to which Jimmy returns 'oh yeah what's normal then?'

Jimmy is next seen in the garden shed, he is trying to fix something on his scooter. Kevin Herriot arrives on his bike. They discuss their differences and Jimmy defends his Mod connection and lifestyle 'it isn't the bikes is it? It's the people' and 'I don't want to be the same as everybody else... that's why I'm a Mod'. Such was the Mod attitude and way of thinking at that time.

The next few scenes follow Jimmy at work and playing cards whilst there's a private screening that's advertising some cigarette brand. The scene offers another of the film's most memorable lines 'I don't think they make Levi's in your size.'

Jimmy is also seen taking a detour to a record store, where he sits in one of the listening booths. Whilst he drools over some photographs of a pretty girl in a bikini The Who's Anyway, Anyhow, Anywhere gets some airplay.

That evening Jimmy joins his friends in another of their hang-outs.

GOING MOBILE SIX
ANGEL TUBE STATION

Alfredo's Snack Bar (restaurant/cafeteria) at 4-6 Essex Road, Islington. The art-deco designed building has been a café since the 1920s and is a Grade Listed 11 building. The premises are now owned by the Meat People. The first time that Jimmy and his mates are in Alfredo's, Night Train by James Brown is playing on the juke box. Some play-fighting occurs and the owner turfs the Mods out onto the street. It's all done in good humour and the owner knows he'll be allowing them all back in soon enough. However, later on in the film Alfredo's is also the scene where Jimmy and Dave have their fight.

It's after the first Alfredo scene that one of Jimmy's mates Spider's scooter breaks down.

GOING MOBILE SEVEN
LATIMER ROAD TUBE STATION.
BRAMLEY ARMS PUB in BRAMLEY ROAD

In Quadrophenia, it is outside the Bramley Arms that Spider and his girlfriend get attacked by rockers after his scooter breaks down - 'has your mothers hairdryer broken down' says one of the rockers. And not far from the Bramley Arms is the scrap yard where another of Jimmy's associates Pete Fenton works 'and I like money'. The pub was also used in the making of the 1951 film the Lavender Hill Mob, starring Alec Guinness and Stanley Holloway.

News of Spider's unfortunate run-in with the rockers reaches Jimmy and his friends. They are seen exiting a club whose doorway advertises posters of the Marquee Club and the Yardbirds. They rush off on the scooters, intent on seeking revenge. They spot some rockers, Kevin Herriot is amongst them.

GOING MOBILE EIGHT
SHEPHERDS BUSH MARKET TUBE STATION

The alley that runs alongside the railway line between Goldhawk Road Station and Shepherds Bush Station is where Kevin gets chased and beaten up by Jimmy and his mates.

Events are now gradually building up to Jimmy and the Mod gang getting ready to go to Brighton. Over the course of the next few scenes, Jimmy argues with his dad 'dressing up like a bloody freak', they go to Ferdy's house because they need to score pills for Brighton and they break into a chemist's after getting 'stitched up' for a bag of pills that turn out to be only paraffin, although at the time of scoring they thought they had '250 leapers to see us through to Christmas'. While in the chemist, Chalky puts some rubber Johnnies over his fingers to prevent leaving any finger prints behind. They do manage to find some French blues before they make a hasty exit and go to finish off their evening in Alfredo's. It's at this point that Jimmy and Steph's relationship takes a turn, for the better in Jimmy's opinion, and they leave the café to go and have a kiss and cuddle.

One of the last scenes before Jimmy heads off to Brighton shows him back at home wearing sopping wet Levis. 54321 by Manfred Mann, one of Ready Steady Go's theme tunes, is heard playing and then The Caesar's (Who's) Anyway, Anyhow, Anywhere to which Jimmy plonks himself down onto the sofa and air drums his way through the song while his father mocks him 'that'll make you deaf you know.'

Brighton is the setting of several of Quadrophenia's greatest scenes. There is dancing in the ballroom, Green Onions by Booker T and the MGs sounds great. It's in the ballroom where Jimmy also dives off of the balcony into the crowd before getting thrown out by the bouncers. And it's in Brighton where the Mods chant 'we are the Mods, we are the Mods, we are we are we are the Mods'. It has become such a well-known chant; and the fighting also breaks out. Jimmy has a special moment with Steph up an alleyway, but he also gets arrested and finds himself standing shoulder to shoulder with the Ace Face (played by Sting) and the other 'sawdust.'

Jimmy has to return home battered and bruised and few quid down. On entering his home, he is confronted by a very angry and disappointed mother who has found some of his pills. They fight and she throws Jimmy out. He then loses his job as well as any chance of developing any relationship with Steph.

GOING MOBILE NINE
SHEPHERDS BUSH MARKET TUBE STATION

The corner of Galloway Road and Sawley Road, which is north of the Uxbridge Road in the Shepherds Bush area, is where the GP van collides with Jimmy's scooter. 'Look what you've done, you've killed me scooter.' Not far away is Orchid Street (just off Yew Tree Road) the scene of the argument between Jimmy and Steph following the unfortunate U turn in their relationship that stemmed from events during their Brighton weekend shared together.

Jimmy has now lost his scooter. He decides to buy a bottle of whiskey and return to Brighton - 'nothing seems right apart for Brighton' he had told Steph during their argument.

GOING MOBILE TEN
PADDINGTON STATION

Jimmy leaves for Brighton. 5.15 is the Who song played during these scenes. It's also the scene where Jimmy is found applying eye-liner, the expression on his face is intimidating and menacing to say the very least. Additionally, there is the scene where Jimmy plonks himself down in between two gentlemen, the look of disgust and defiance on Jimmy's face is brilliant. 'Out of my brain on the train' says it all.

Quadrophenia finishes up in Brighton. The final scene shows the GS Vespa that belonged to the Ace Face being launched off of a cliff top (actually Beachy Head not in Brighton) and crashing onto the rocks below. There is no sight of Jimmy. Roger Daltrey's final words are moving - 'you stopped dancing' and then the credits begin to roll and the greatest youth culture film ever made is complete.

PART 2: CENTRAL LONDON TOUR
GOING MOBILE START

Bar Italia has made Frith Street its home since 1949, but actually it has an intriguing previous history. It was on this location, that on the 26th January 1926 John Logie Baird provided the first public demonstration of the television. Nowadays, there is a blue plaque reminding the world of this great achievement and there is a television nailed to the wall at the back of the long narrow bar that repeatedly shows all manner of Italian related sports and news channels.

However, it was in 1949 that Lou and Caterina Polledri opened their coffee bar at 22 Frith Street. They already owned a café in Covent Garden but saw an opportunity to open a second in Soho which was growing increasingly popular with Italians. The Polledris installed a Gaggia machine and nearly sixty years later it's still there supplying the likes of Paul Weller and Dave Stewart and is often a meeting point of writers and musicians.

Little has changed regards the interior of the bar. The original tiles on the floors and walls still remain; there are stools and mirrors that run along the length of the bar and on any day it will be full of people sipping away at their coffees. The bar Italia has been a popular meeting place since the day of the coffee bar culture modernists of the 50s, the mods of the 60s and the rock n rollers of the 70s, 80s and 90s; Pulp even wrote a song about the bar which is included on their 1995 album Different Class.

Today the Bar Italia remains 'the place' to be seen and have a meeting, and it even has its own scooter club: the Bar Italia Scooter Club, who meet frequently and park their impressive Vespas and Lambrettas outside of the bar; it's a wonderful sight that evokes fond memories of 50s and 60s mod scene.

Jazz musician Ronnie Scott had been one of the faces in the ranks of the first wave of the Soho Modernists. He was included in the line-up that formed the Club Eleven (41 Great Windmill Street), along with other London jazz big-hitters John Dankworth and Tony Crombie. Following Club Eleven, Scott opened another club in Gerrard Street but then moved that to the Frith Street address in December 1965. By 1968 he had converted the upstairs space into an area that could also cater for live music and this area attracted such rock bands as the Who in 1969 and the Jam nearly a decade later.

The upstairs area was also where Jimi Hendrix joined Eric Burdon on stage for a jam. This was the last time that Hendrix performed live to an audience. Two days later the world was informed that Jimi Hendrix was dead.

On 1st May, a few days before the Who set off for another American tour, they performed Tommy upstairs at Ronnie Scott's (which is opposite the Bar Italia) to a crowd mainly made up of the press. At first there was some jeering from some 'drunken' members of the press and a heavy sense of being judged. By the end of the night the Who had won the press over.

Frith Street also plays another part in the history of The Who. It was in one of the restaurants in the street, where Pete Meaden, who had once worked in the kitchens, was offered £500 by Chris Stamp to hand over the managerial rights of The Who. Meaden accepted the money (he later learned that he could have been paid £5000).

THE WHO • 97 • IN THE CITY

GOING MOBILE TWO

Walking a few paces down Frith Street you'll find yourself joining Old Compton Street, now you're really going mobile, cross over to the other side, face right and continue to walk in that direction until you reach the site of the infamous 2i's Coffee Bar at number 59. During the days when the Beatles were free to wander the streets of London they would also pass the infamous home of skiffle music that was the 2i's coffee bar. The club no longer remains, but there is a green plaque on the wall to remind us where the coffee bar once was. Seeing the 2i's coffee bar would have surely evoked memories in the members of the Beatles, especially when they looked back on their days when they were called the Quarrymen. The 'world famous 2i's coffee bar-home of the stars' first fired up its coffee machine in 1956; while it hissed away and churned out mouth-watering aromas, the basement area below hosted such greats like Marty Wilde, Adam Faith and Cliff Richard. It was also in the basement of the 2i's that record producer Shel Talmy auditioned the Who before taking them into the studio to record a demo of I Can't Explain.

At the end of the road and almost opposite the 2i's at number 70 was where the offices of Track Records were located. The doorway has since been boarded up.

Facing opposite Old Compton Street is Brewer Street. Pete Townshend lived in one of the fifth-floor flats on the corner (87 Wardour Street). It was in that flat where he built an area that included a record player and would host all-night parties.

GOING MOBILE THREE

Leaving Old Compton Street and turning right into Wardour Street, it's only a short walk to the premises where the Marquee Club were once situated. 'Keith Moon (1946-1978) Legendary Rock Drummer With The Who Performed Here At The Site Of The Marquee Club In The 1960's', are the words written on the Heritage Foundation blue plaque that Roger Daltrey helped to unveil at number 90 Wardour Street on Sunday 8th March 2009. Also present at the unveiling was Keith's mother Kit, who, like Daltrey, also said a few words thanking people for the gesture and recognition.

The Marquee Club was opened in Wardour Street in March 1964 by Harold Pendleton following the closure of the club's Oxford Street venue. The Yardbirds, Long John Baldry and Sonny Boy Williamson performed on the opening night. A week later the Yardbirds returned to record their Five Live Yardbirds album. The Who played their first gig at the Marquee to approximately only thirty paying customers. However, Pendleton allowed them to return and before long their Tuesday nights residency had become a huge success,which truly helped the band gain popularity amongst a much wider audience and attract further attention from the London Mod scene.

The iconic slogan 'Maximum Rhythm and Blues' with the image of Pete Townshend demonstrating his windmill arm motion, while clutching his Rickenbacker was soon installed. The brilliant Anyway, Anyhow, Anywhere was written in the Marquee. The song was also used as one of the Ready Steady Go theme tunes. In the film Quadrophenia, The Who are featured playing on RSG whilst Jimmy, the films main character (played by Phil Daniels) enthusiastically watches on bare chested and wearing soaking wet Levis, as he also tries to ignore the mocking words from his father (played by Michael Elphick).The Who's first appearance at the Marquee was on 24th November 1964.

Not too far from the Marquee was another popular drinking hole amongst many music fans before going to the Marquee. The Ship at 116 Wardour Street was often frequented, amongst many other rock musicians, by Keith Moon. It was also in the Ship that George Harrison invited Peter Frampton to play on his debut solo album All Things Must Pass. The Ship has also been a convenient meeting point before heading off to any number of the nearby clubs that have existed in Soho throughout the decades.

Soho has always been an attractive gathering place for people looking for an exciting night out. Just around the corner from the Ship, in Broadwick Street, there is another pub, the Bricklayers Arms, which served a similar function to the Ship in the 50s and 60s (it closed as a pub in 1964), and it was in the room above this pub that Brian Jones formed the Rolling Stones in 1962.

GOING MOBILE FOUR

Just a short walk from the Ship was the old Roundhouse pub at 83-85 Wardour Street. It was at these premises that the London Skiffle Club was opened by Cyril Davies in 1952. Soon Davies teamed up with Alexis Korner to form the London Blues and Barrell House Club which helped create a British buzz around such blues artists as Muddy Waters. The music introduced and enjoyed at the London Skiffle Club would go on to have a huge influence on all the members of the Who and contribute to their own unique playing styles. Pete Townshend had a flat on the fifth floor in Wardour Street (and on the corner of Brewer Street). Townshend employed a carpenter to build areas that would house his growing record collection and musical recording equipment and the flat soon turned into a den that Townshend would often invite friends back to, to smoke some grass and play some records.

When Townshend wasn't entertaining at his flat he would sometimes frequent the Colony Club located on the first floor at 41 Dean Street. The club had been run by Muriel Belcher since the late forties and had a reputation for attracting the 'creative types'. Francis Bacon was amongst the regulars.

Turning back to retrace your steps down Wardour Street, within a few minutes you can be standing outside the building that once accommodated both the Flamingo and Whisky A Go Go clubs. The Flamingo attracted popularity due it to being an all-nighter (on Fridays), which suited the nocturnal pill-popping habits of Londoners searching for a good night out. The club was owned by the brothers Rik and John Gunnell, two well-known names from the 50s Soho set. Modernist jazz was the music on offer at the beginning but by the early 60s this had been overtaken by cooler mod sounds that included soul, R&B and Jamaican ska. The club was recognised as a place to keep your wits about yourself due to it being frequented by some of the seedier side of Soho's finest, and for a while the club was popular with black US soldiers, they loved the music policy and they loved their blues and greens and sometimes a good old fashioned punch-up, but in 1963 the US army forbid them from going, so they had to find new places to wind down.

Georgie Fame famously debuted at the Flamingo and in 1963 recorded the brilliant live album titled Rhythm and Blues at the Flamingo. It was a popular venture for jazz and R&B musicians to record live albums in and around London's famous and respected clubs during the 50s and 60s.

GOING MOBILE FIVE

Advertised as the 'Notre Dame De Danse' the Detours' first appearance at the Club Durane, Notre Dame Church Hall, 5 Leicester Place, Leicester Square was on Friday 26th July 1963. The original building had been bombed in World War Two but a new building was erected and opened as a club in 1953. In 1965 the Cavern in the Town opened on the Notre Dame premises. The Who returned to playon10th April and 19th June 1965 and returned on11th March 1966.

The club didn't survive long but it was the place where another young mod band called the Small Faces would attract the attention of London's Mods. Kenney Jones was the Small Faces drummer and would take over drumming duties for The Who after Keith Moon's death. The Small Faces made their debut at the venue on 29th May 1965, performing just five songs. Throughout the remainder of the sixties and the seventies, the premises continued to serve as a popular music venue, and was especially prominent during the first Punk wave of 1977. Nowadays the building is the home of the Leicester Square Theatre.

Exactly next door was another important 60s club; the Ad lib. To access the club, the punter would have to enter an elevator, via some double glass doors and be transported skywards. The Ad lib was owned by Bob and Al Burnett, but run by Bob Morris, and became a haunt for many of the 'faces' of the day; the club was especially favoured by the Beatles. From the venue's large windows those 'faces' could look out across London whilst they freely smoked a joint away from the interfering eyes of the local Police or journalists. Due to a fire incident in 1966 the club was forced to close down.

GOING MOBILE SIX

On the 29th January 1967 the Who played two shows (6.00 and 8.30) at the Saville Theatre, Shaftsbury Avenue. (they also returned later that year on 22nd Oct). The Who were joined by the Jimi Hendrix Experience, the Thoughts and the Koobas.

The Beatles' manager Brian Epstein had been the theatre's leaseholder since 1965 and he merged with Robert Stigwood to put on a series of Sunday night concerts in the theatre. On the night that the Who played in January they gave a debut performance of A Quick One (While He's Away), which was witnessed by Paul McCartney and John Lennon.

The Saville Theatre at 135 Shaftsbury Avenue had opened in 1931 with the play For the Love of Mike. The 1400 capacity venue suffered bomb damage in the Second World War and in 1955 had a complete refurbishment. By the sixties, bands were appearing in the theatre and the Beatles even shot their promotional film for Hello Goodbye in it. The Rolling Stones played in December 1969-that same month the Saville Theatre closed. It reopened the following year as an ABC Cinema and has remained a cinema (now an Odeon) ever since.

GOING MOBILE SEVEN

On Friday 18th October the Who were booked to perform at the Brunel University Students Union 'Midnite Rave' event held in the Lyceum. The magnificent Rococo style building with its tall pillars on Wellington Street, just off of the Strand, had been a theatre since 1756. Built and re-built several times since then, it has hosted the English Opera House, the first exhibition of waxworks from Madame Tussauds, and many of the world's biggest and favourite bands like Queen, Led Zeppelin, Genesis and The Clash. The Lyceum had become a Mecca Ballroom 1951 and during the early sixties was another Mod stronghold. This was partially due to the music that got played but the beautiful wooden dance floor was also a massive pull. On 15th December 1969 Keith Moon found himself playing drums alongside Eric Clapton, George Harrison, Yoko Ono and John Lennon in the Plastic Ono Band on the Lyceum's stage.

GOING MOBILE EIGHT

The Who then spent the majority of November back in the USA before returning home to play on the 14th December at The Coliseum, St Martins Lane. The Coliseum was the home of the English National Opera and on the night the Who performed, the 2500 capacity venue was a sell-out. This was to be the Who's last performance in London of the decade. They had been playing in their own back garden of London relentlessly since they were the Detours, bashing out their set back in the Paradise Club in Peckham in July 62, they had released four albums My Generation, A Quick One, The Who Sell Out and Tommy and although the number one spot had eluded them they had also released Zoot Suit, I Can't Explain, Anyway, Anyhow, Anywhere, My Generation, Substitute, A Legal Matter, The Kids Are Alright, I'm A Boy, La LaLa Lies, Happy Jack, Pictures of Lily, Whisky Man, The Last Time, I Can See For Miles, I Can't Reach You, Call Me Lightning, Dogs, Magic Bus, Pinball Wizard and I'm Free.

GOING MOBILE NINE

Another Mod stronghold and without doubt one of the most important Mod clubs running in the centre of London throughout the 'peak' Mod years was the Scene Club in Ham Yard, 41 Great Windmill Street, Soho. Like so many clubs in London and indeed Britain at the time, the Scene also operated from a basement. By the time the High Numbers were playing at the Scene they had they first single Zoot Suit/I'm the Face to promote. The band's Mod manager Pete Meaden had had 1000 copies of the record pressed and was busily running around London trying to boost sales and generate interest in 'his' Mod creation. In 2015, one copy of the original record fetched over fifteen hundred pounds on Ebay.

The Scene club had originally been the site of a jazz club called the Piccadilly. The Piccadilly was run by Giorgio Gomelsky. Gomelsky left in early 1962 to open a new club in Richmond called The Crawdaddy. The High Numbers first played at the Scene Club on 22nd July 1964.

GOING MOBILE TEN

The first club that opened in Carnaby Street was the Florence Mills Social Club; this was in 1934 and catered for the early lovers of jazz. It would be a further twenty years before the Roaring Twenties opened its doors and the sounds of Jamaican ska and calypso burst out. Pete Townshend visited the club on several occasions.

But it's not the club that have made Carnaby Street famous, it's the fashions - and spearheading this was a certain John Stephen (who said 'Carnaby is my creation' in 1967) who opened his boutique 'His Clothes' in the street in 1957, only after his other shop in Beak Street was burnt down. Stephens was from Glasgow but had moved to London in 1952. He found employment working in Vince Man's shop in Newburgh Street. It was with his partner and boyfriend Bill Franks that the Carnaby Street venture was initially shared with. Other shops were created with names like Mod Male and Domino Male-they catered for the London mod scene. And it was in the Carnaby Cavern that Pete Townshend walked in one day and informed the shopkeeper that he'd like a jacket made from a Union Jack flag. The Carnaby Cavern agreed; unlike the tailors in Savile Row, that had refused a few weeks earlier.

GOING MOBILE ELEVEN

Just around the corner from Carnaby Street, in Kingsley Street is the Bag O Nails Club. All of the members of The Who frequented the club from 1966 onwards. There are countless stories of events and incidents that occurred in the club; Moon for example would take pleasure in walking across the tables, and the people's meals that were upon them.

GOING MOBILE TWELVE

One of the most popular clubs that opened in London in 1966 was The Speakeasy at 48-50 Margaret Street (just off of Regent Street). The club had a coffin as the counter where the guest paid their few pennies before stepping down into the main area. The club opened in December 1966 and was popular amongst local and touring musicians. During its life the Speakeasy hosted many an impromptu jam session and on occasion these included Jimi Hendrix. It was also the venue where Track Records launched themselves as a record label with ambition.

Kinks drummer Mick Avory points out 'I saw Keith do some stupid things in the Speakeasy, but the management never threw him out; if anything they expected those behaviours.' It was in the 'Speak' that in 1969 Deep Purple made their debut. It was also in the club that Pete Townshend befriended Paul Cook and Steve Jones of the Sex Pistols. That night he was attending a John Otway gig in the club.

Additionally another club in London that The Who liked to hang out in from 1965 onwards was the Scotch of Saint James. It was in the 'Scotch' that Moon asked Paul McCartney if he could join the Beatles. McCartney replied telling him to ask Ringo. It was also in the Scotch of Saint James that in February 1966 Townshend watched a young Stevie Wonder perform a blistering soul set that simply blew him away.

GOING MOBILE THIRTEEN

Then, on 8th February, they played at the Regent Polytechnic, Portland Hall, Little Titchfield Street. The venue had been hosting bands since the student union had formed in 1965. It was in this venue that Jimi Hendrix made his debut UK appearance when he joined Cream live on the stage. Other acts like Pink Floyd, Fleetwood Mac and blues man Howlin' Wolf also played at the Regent Polytechnic. The Who's support on the night they played were Family. Family were a band formed from the ashes of an R&B outfit called the Roaring Sixties. By 1969 they were playing a mixture and fusion of rock, folk, psychedelia and jazz. Jenny Fabian, author of the novel Groupie drew inspiration from Family only in her book, also published in 1969, she called the band Relation.

GOING MOBILE FOURTEEN

Between the 12th and 14th April the Who camped out in the IBC (International Broadcasting Company) Studios to record a number of tracks with ShelTalmy. Recorded amongst tracks from Bo Diddley, James Brown and Martha Reeves and the Vandellas, the Who also recorded Anyway, Anyhow, Anywhere; which would be released at the end of the following month on 21st May.

The IBC had been formed by radio enthusiast Leonard Plugge in the early 1930s (Plugge's home in Lowndes Square was where the film Performance, starring Mick Jagger, was filmed) and the studios at 35 Portland Place were used extensively in the 60s to record many of the brilliant acts of the period-the Kinks, Jimi Hendrix, Rolling Stones, Small Faces and even the Beatles. Ex-Animal turned artiste manager Chas Chandler bough the studios in the early 70s and re-named them Portland Place Studios.

GOING MOBILE FIFTEEN

Tiles was a basement club in Oxford Street located opposite the 100 Club on the corner of Chapel Street and that's where the entrance was. The club opened its doors as Tiles in March 1966 after a stint under the ownership of Alexis Korner, who had had it since 1964 when it was called the Beat City Club. Jeff Dexter was one of the house DJs who presented his popular 'Jeff Dexter record and light show'. Other DJs that served up their sounds were Clem Dalton and Mick Quinn from the Juke Box Jury show. John Peel also ran his Perfumed Garden show from the club just before it closed in September 1967. Other bands that performed at the venue other than The Who include The Eyes, Manfred Mann, David Bowie, Otis Redding, Pink Floyd and Sugar Pie Desanto.

On the 29th April, the first night that the Who performed, such was the interest that the venue quickly reached its full capacity and hundreds of fans were left milling around Oxford Street considering an alternative option. Meanwhile, in the club below, fans surged towards the stage, interrupting the Who's performance and leaving the band no option other than to cut their set short and abandon the gig. The Who returned for a second time on 29th July.

Within sight on the other side of Oxford Street is the famous 100 Club-The first of the Detours' appearances at the legendary Club was on 13th April 1964 (they returned on 27th April) was also to be the last time that their drummer Dougie Sandom was to play with them. On this particular night the Detours provided support for the Mike Cotton Sound. Cotton was a jazzman and his band had formerly been known as the Mike Cotton Jazzmen. They had been a familiar outfit from the London jazz scene since the mid-50s.

Before the 100 Club was called the 100 Club, it was a restaurant called Mack's. This was in 1942 in the middle of WW2 and it was on occasion used as an air raid shelter due to the club being deep under Oxford Street. Jazz drummer Victor Feldman's father hired the venue on Sundays to give jazz bands the opportunity to play. The opening night was on 24th October 1942. The club speedily gained the attraction of American service men and local jazz fans. The club was advertised using the slogan 'Forget the doodle bug-come and jitter-bug at the Feldman Club'. In 1948 the club had a name change and was called the London Jazz Club. By now Bebop was swinging. The ownership of the club transferred to the Wilcox Brothers and then onto Lyn Dutton. Dutton was an agent and one of his main clients was Humphry Lyttelton. In 1956 the club became known as the Humphry Lyttelton Club

GOING MOBILE SIXTEEN

It wasn't far from the Tottenham Court Road tube station that a subscriber to London's psychedelic scene would have got off in December 1966 to attend the opening night of the UFO Club, held in the Irish Club called the

Blarney, which was located in the basement of 31 Tottenham Court Road, below the Gala Berkeley Cinema. The club was run by Joe Boyd and John Hopkins; and was originally going to be called either UFO or Nite Tripper, they settled on UFO and the club went down in history as the capital's, if not the nation's, first psychedelic club.

Within weeks, the club had its regulars, these included such 'happening' kids as Jenny Fabian; who, before the 60s had extinguished itself, wrote her book called Groupie, which although fictional, was a book very much based on her own experiences as a groupie for the scene and its band members. During the UFO (and then the Middle Earth Club) days, Fabian courted Jimi Hendrix, Andy Summers and Syd Barrett. In fact Pink Floyd became the UFO Club's house band in its very early days and the club and its scene very much helped to put Pink Floyd on the map.

Once Pink Floyd outgrew the UFO, other bands such as Tomorrow, Procol Harum and Soft Machine replaced them. Sitting comfortably inside this new psychedelic scene, that was flourishing on its LSD consumption and enjoying its colourful paisley and polka dot wafty clothing, an underground magazine called International Times was born. The International Times, known as IT, was an out of this mundane world creative collaboration between John 'Hoppy' Hopkins, Barry Miles, Jim Haynes, David Mairowitz, Peter Stansil and Tom McGrath, and produced on a fortnightly basis.

The newspaper attracted the attention of the Metropolitan Police and the IT offices were raided several times. There was a deep, suspicious attitude from the authorities and they seemed intent on shutting the IT down. In response, on 29th April 1967 at the Alexandra Palace, a benefit concert titled the 14 Hour Technicolor Dream was held and included performances from Pink Floyd, the Pretty Things, The Move and the Crazy World of Arthur Brown. This event cemented itself firmly in the international world of psychedelia history.

GOING MOBILE EXTRAS

The below locations are best reached by tube and well worth a visit for any Who fans.

Keith Moon died at his flat at **12 CURZON PLACE** (NEAR GREEN PARK TUBE) on 7th September 1978 and was buried at the **GOLDERS GREEN CREMATORIUM**. The practice of cremation wasn't made legal in Britain until 1885. The Golders Green Crematorium in Hoop Lane was the first of its kind to be built in London. It opened in 1902. The crematorium was built by Ernest George and Alfred Yeates and the famous Victorian gardener and journalist William Robinson designed the gardens that surround the main building and mausoleums. The Golders Green Crematorium is only a few minutes' walk from Golders Green Tube Station and faces the Golders Green Jewish Cemetery. Keith Moon shares the crematorium with fellow friends and musicians like Phil Seamen, Ronnie Scott, Tubby Hayes and Marc Bolan, and one of his old managers Kit Lambert isn't far away either.

Keith Moon (23.08.1946 - 07.09.1978) 'There is no substitute' (the words on Keith's plaque at the Golders Green Crematorium. His ashes were scattered on the garden of remembrance. Shortly after Moons death The Jam recorded a version of the Who song So Sad About Us and this was included as the B-side to their single Down in the Tube Station at Midnight.

113 IVOR COURT, GLOUCESTER PLACE (BAKER STREET). This was Kit Lambert's and Chris Stamp's home and the early headquarters for the High Numbers/Who. Andrew Loog Oldman had offices in the building too at numbers 138 and 147.

8 CHESHAM PLACE (Townshend's home after Eaton Place and before Old Church St, Chelsea (1966))

35 SUNNYSIDE ROAD, EALING, where Pete and Richard took over the flat from Tom Wright. It was in the flat that the name the Who was considered and then decided on.

EMI STUDIOS, located on Abbey Road was made famous because of The Beatles. And so was the nearby zebra crossing - not a day passes when dozens of Beatles fans and tourists are photographed walking across the crossing, just like the fab four had done been photographed doing, back in 1969. It was also in the Abbey Road studios that The Beatles recorded All You Need Is Love. A host of people joined them for the occasion and these included some of their friends and fellow musicians Mike Jagger, Keith Richards and Keith Moon, who all helped out with backing vocals. The High Numbers auditioned for EMI in the studios in September 1964.

ROYAL ALBERT HALL AND TCT. It wasn't until the 5th July that the Who were back playing in London and when they did it was at the Pop Proms at the Royal Albert Hall. Chuck Berry was also on the bill and both bands wanted to headline. The matter was eventually resolved by both acts closing one of the two shows on the day. There were many Rolling Stones fans sitting beside the Who fans on the occasion because the Who's concert had been held on the same day as the Stones' Hyde Park concert; their first performance without Brian Jones.

84 EATON PLACE. This was where Kit Lambert and Chris Stamp lived. In January 1965 they held the launch party to mark the release of I Can't Explain.

THE WHO — 101 — IN THE CITY

THE ROUNDHOUSE in Chalk Farm, Camden would have been the place to go on a hot summer's night in London's psychedelic sixties. The Middle Earth Club began its life at the venue and was a natural continuation from the UFO club, which had existed for a short period in Covent Garden. The crowd was pretty much made of the same smiling faces.

The Who played alongside the Move and the darlings of the London psychedelic scene Pink Floyd on New Year's Eve in1966, which was promoted as the Giant New Year's Eve Freak Out All Night Rave. There were equipment difficulties on the night, but it didn't prevent the 'psychedelic ravers' achieving their hazy dreams. However, Townshend was observed putting some extra zest into his smashing up his guitar performance at the end of their set.

After the Middle Earth Club ceased, the Roundhouse was taken over by the Implosion Club. This was a psychedelic rock step up from the sounds of the previous two years. The Implosion Club nights ran on Sundays and during the club's life such big hitters as Deep Purple and Frank Zappa performed. The Roundhouse continued to host live music for many years to come and the list of rock legends is endless. For a period the venue closed, but it has since been refurbished and now a much plusher Roundhouse exists and once again hosts live music, although it looks nothing like it did at the time of the Implosion Club. Pete Townshend only took LSD on four occasions, and one of those was at the Roundhouse on that New Year's Eve 1966. The Who played the same night, albeit about 3am. LSD was a very new drug to many people in 1966, there was still very little known about the effects and it certainly wasn't everyone's choice of drug, but it was a huge factor and influencer in much of the music that was churned out during this period and this included the Who. Six days after the Roundhouse trip, Townshend went to the UFO Club to see Pink Floyd, who really were the darlings of, and at the epicentre of, the emerging London acid scene.

WHO'S LONDON MAP OF LOCATIONS

SEE FOLLOWING PAGES FOR LARGER MAPS FOR EACH SECTION OF THE BOOK

Complete Key to Locations mentioned in the book

GOING MOBILE PART 1

1. Acton Town Hall-High St Acton, W3 6NE
2. White Hart-Hugh St Acton, W3 9DE
3. Goldhawk Club, Goldhawk Rd, Shepherds Bush, W12
4. Feathers Hotel, Ealing Broadway, Ealing, W5 2NT
5. Ealing Blues Club, 42a Ealing Broadway, Ealing, W5 2NP
6. Fox and Goose, Hanger Lane, Ealing, W5 1DP
7. The Myllet Arms, Western Ave, Perivale, UB6 1DM
8. Oldfield Hotel, Greenford, UB6 0AP
9. Starlite Ballroom, Allendale Rd, Greenford, UB6 0RA
10. Railway Hotel, Station Rd, Harrow and Wealdstone, HA3 7AB

QUADROPHENIA TOUR

11. (PRETEND GOLDHAWK CLUB) 29 Shelton St, Covent Garden, WC2H 9JQ
12. Jimmy's Home, 115 Well House Rd, NW10
13. A. Cookes, 48 Goldhawk Rd, Shepherds Bush, W12 8DH
14. Askens Supermarket, Goldhawk Rd, Shepherds Bush, W12 8DH
15. PARTY HOUSE AT KITCHENER RD, IS 63 Clarenden Gardens, Wembley, HA9 7LE
16. Alfredo's café, Essex Rd, Islington, N1 3PD
17. Bramley Arms, Bramley Rd, North Kensington, W10
18. Shepherds Bush Market, Goldhawk Rd, Shepherds Bush, W12 8LH
19. SCOOTER CRASH SITE, CORNER OF Galloway Rd and Sawley Rd, W12 0PJ
20. Paddington Train Station, W2 1NY

PART 2 CENTRAL LONDON

21. Bar Italia, Frith St, Soho, W1D 4RF
22. 2I's Coffee Bar, Old Compton St, Soho, W1D 6HR
23. Marquee Club, Wardour St, W1D 5PA
24. Old Roundhouse, 83 Wardour Street, W1D 6QD
25. Club Durane, 5 Leicester Place, WC2H 7BX
26. Saville Theatre, Shaftsbury Ave, WC2H 8DP
27. The Lyceum, Wellington St, WC2E 7RQ
28. The Coliseum, St Martin's Lane, WC2N 4ES
29. The Scene Club, 41 Great Windmill St, Ham Yard, W1D 7LU
30. Carnaby Street, Soho, W1F 7DA
31. Bag O Nails Club, Kinglsey St, Soho, W1S 1PH
32. The Speakeasy, 48-50 Margaret St, W1W 8SE
33. Regent Polytechnic, Little Tichfield St, W1W 7BY
34. IBC Studios, 35 Portland Place, W1B 1QG
35. 100 Club, 100 Oxford St, W1D 1LL
36. UFO Club, 31 Tottenham Court Rd, W1T 1AL

EXTRAS

37. 12 Curzon Place, W1J
38. 113 Ivor Court, Gloucester Place, NW1 6BL
39. 8 Chesham Place, SW1X 8HN
40. 35 Sunnyside Rd, Ealing, W5 5HU
41. EMI Studios, Abbey Rd, NW8 0AH
42. Royal Albert Hall, SW7 2AP
43. 84 Eaton Place, SW1X 8LN
44. The Roundhouse, Camden, NW1 8EH

GOING MOBILE PART 1

1. Acton Town Hall-High St Acton, W3 6NE
2. White Hart-Hugh St Acton, W3 9DE
3. Goldhawk Club, Goldhawk Rd, Shepherds Bush, W12
4. Feathers Hotel, Ealing Broadway, Ealing, W5 2NT
5. Ealing Blues Club, 42a Ealing Broadway, Ealing, W5 2NP
6. Fox and Goose, Hanger Lane, Ealing, W5 1DP
7. The Myllet Arms, Western Ave, Perivale, UB6 1DM
8. Oldfield Hotel, Greenford, UB6 0AP
9. Starlite Ballroom, Allendale Rd, Greenford, UB6 0RA
10. Railway Hotel, Station Rd, Harrow and Wealdstone, HA3 7AB

QUADROPHENIA TOUR

- ⑪ (PRETEND GOLDHAWK CLUB) 29 Shelton St, Covent Garden, WC2H 9JQ
- ⑫ Jimmy's Home, 115 Well House Rd, NW10
- ⑬ A. Cookes, 48 Goldhawk Rd, Shepherds Bush, W12 8DH
- ⑭ Askens Supermarket, Goldhawk Rd, Shepherds Bush, W12 8DH
- ⑮ PARTY HOUSE AT KITCHENER RD, IS 63 Clarenden Gardens, Wembley, HA9 7LE
- ⑯ Alfredo's café, Essex Rd, Islington, N1 3PD
- ⑰ Bramley Arms, Bramley Rd, North Kensington, W10
- ⑱ Shepherds Bush Market, Goldhawk Rd, Shepherds Bush, W12 8LH
- ⑲ SCOOTER CRASH SITE, CORNER OF Galloway Rd and Sawley Rd, W12 0PJ
- ⑳ Paddington Train Station, W2 1NY

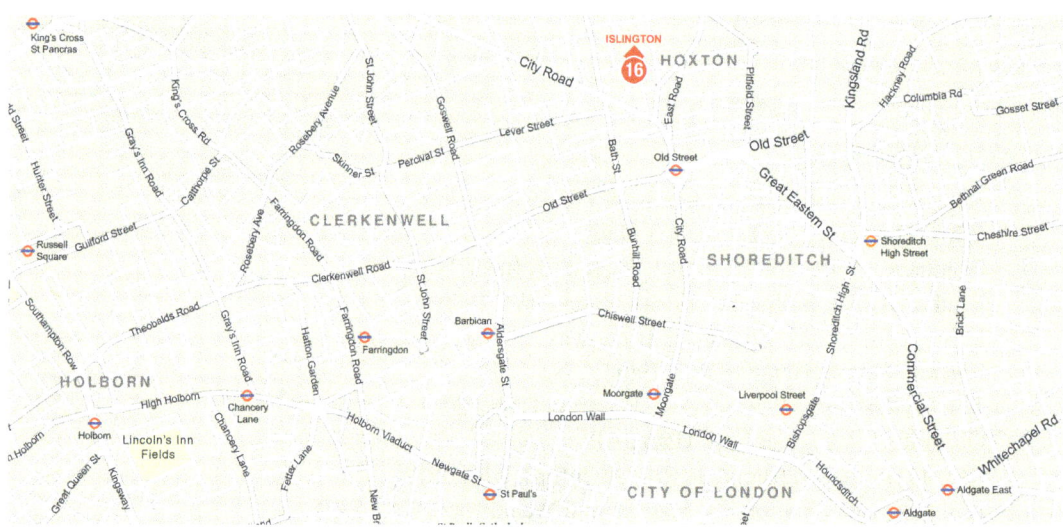

THE WHO 106 IN THE CITY

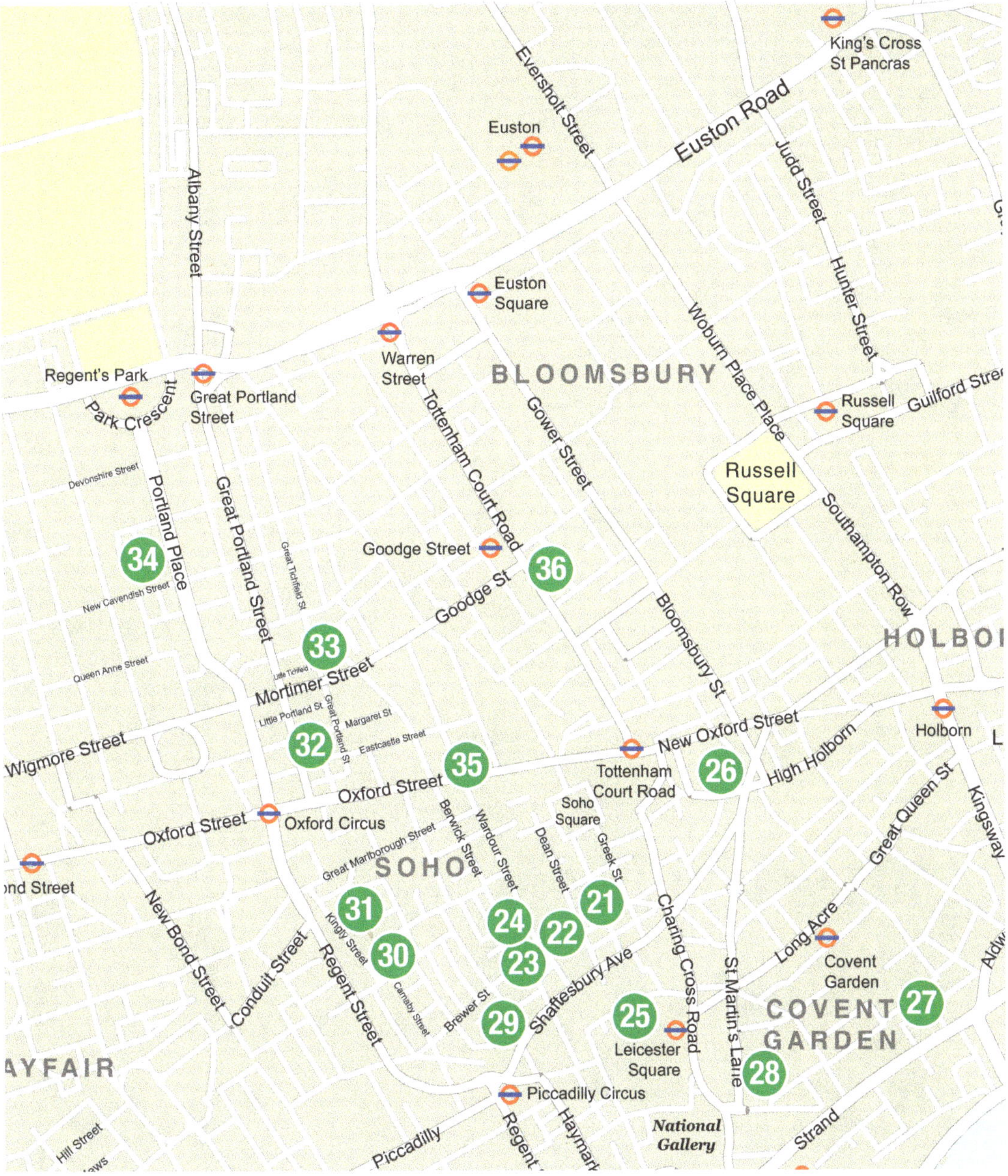

PART 2 CENTRAL LONDON

- ㉑ Bar Italia, Frith St, Soho, W1D 4RF
- ㉒ 2I's Coffee Bar, Old Compton St, Soho, W1D 6HR
- ㉓ Marquee Club, Wardour St, W1D 5PA
- ㉔ Old Roundhouse, 83 Wardour Street, W1D 6QD
- ㉕ Club Durane, 5 Leicester Place, WC2H 7BX
- ㉖ Saville Theatre, Shaftsbury Ave, WC2H 8DP
- ㉗ The Lyceum, Wellington St, WC2E 7RQ
- ㉘ The Coliseum, St Martin's Lane, WC2N 4ES
- ㉙ The Scene Club, 41 Great Windmill St, Ham Yard, W1D 7LU
- ㉚ Carnaby Street, Soho, W1F 7DA
- ㉛ Bag O Nails Club, Kinglsey St, Soho, W1S 1PH
- ㉜ The Speakeasy, 48-50 Margaret St, W1W 8SE
- ㉝ Regent Polytechnic, Little Tichfield St, W1W 7BY
- ㉞ IBC Studios, 35 Portland Place, W1B 1QG
- ㉟ 100 Club, 100 Oxford St, W1D 1LL
- ㊱ UFO Club, 31 Tottenham Court Rd, W1T 1AL

EXTRAS

- ㊲ 12 Curzon Place, W1 J
- ㊳ 113 Ivor Court, Gloucester Place, NW1 6BL
- ㊴ 8 Chesham Place, SW1X 8HN
- ㊵ 35 Sunnyside Rd, Ealing, W5 5HU
- ㊶ EMI Studios, Abbey Rd, NW8 0AH
- ㊷ Royal Albert Hall, SW7 2AP
- ㊸ 84 Eaton Place, SW1X 8LN
- ㊹ The Roundhouse, Camden, NW1 8EH

www.ingramcontent.com/pod-product-compliance
Lightning Source LLC
Chambersburg PA
CBHW080600090426
42735CB00016B/3296